The Court of France
1789–1830

The Court of France 1789–1830

Philip Mansel

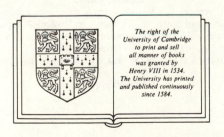

The right of the
University of Cambridge
to print and sell
all manner of books
was granted by
Henry VIII in 1534.
The University has printed
and published continuously
since 1584.

Cambridge University Press

Cambridge
New York   New Rochelle
Melbourne   Sydney

Published by the Press Syndicate of the University of Cambridge
The Pitt Building, Trumpington Street, Cambridge CB2 1RP
32 East 57th Street, New York, NY 10022, USA
10 Stamford Road, Oakleigh, Melbourne 3166, Australia

First published 1988

Printed in Great Britain at The Bath Press, Avon

British Library cataloguing in publication data

Mansel, Philip, 1961–
The court of France, 1789–1830.
1. France. Royal courts, 1789–1830
1. Title
944.04

Library of Congress cataloguing in publication data

Mansel, Philip.
The court of France, 1789–1830.
Bibliography.
Includes index.
1. France – Civilization – 1789–1830. 2. France –
Court and courtiers – History. 3. France – Kings and
rulers – History. 4. France – History – Revolution,
1789–1799 – Influence. 1. Title.
DC33.5.M34 1988 944.05'0880621 88–5010

ISBN 0 521 30995 6

Jamais peuple n'a été plus fait pour la Cour

Prince de Ligne, 1787

Contents

Plates

Figures

Acknowledgements

The author would like to express his deep gratitude to all those who have helped him with hospitality or advice since he began research on the court of France in 1974. In particular he would like to thank those who permitted access to archives or pictures, or read the manuscript or the thesis in which it originated: Messrs. Christies and Co. Ltd, Henri Curial, Comte A. de Dreux-Brézé, René and Béatrice de Gaillande, P. Girault de Coursac, the Duc de Gramont, Georges de Grandmaison, Alain de Grolée-Virville, Dr David Higgs, Professor Douglas Johnson, Comte F. de La Bouillerie, Nicholas McClintock, Dr Roger Mettam, Comte G. de Montesquiou, the Duc de Mouchy, the late Comte François de Nadaillac, Comte Charles de Nicolay, Dr Curtis Noel, Mgr le Comte de Paris, Jean-Michel Pianelli, the late Count L. Lucchese-Palli, Sothebys and Co. Ltd, Baron Louis Thierry de Ville d'Avray, Emmanuel de Waresquiel and Michael Weinstein.

Footnotes

To help avoid confusion for the reader in the footnotes between the many titles beginning or consisting solely of the words *Journal*, *Mémoires* or *Souvenirs*, after the first mention such titles are subsequently referred to by author's surname in italic (for example, Duc de Lévis, *Souvenirs et Portraits*, 1882, becomes *Lévis*).

Introduction 5 May 1789

It was a fine day and the hall, despite its size, soon filled up. The deputies of the clergy, the nobility and the Third Estate sat in the middle, spectators from Paris in boxes round the sides. The King arrived at one o'clock. He sat facing the deputies 'in all the pomp of Majesty', on a golden throne covered in fleurs de lys. The Queen, dressed in violet and silver and covered in diamonds, was one step lower. Beside and in front of them were the royal family, the court, guards and members of the government. It was the opening of the States General at Versailles on 5 May 1789. France was in ecstasy, convinced it was about to enter a new age of liberty and prosperity. Louis XVI's speech was interrupted with repeated cheers of *Vive le Roi!* Even the long analysis of the budgetary deficit by his minister Necker met with applause.[1]

The principal figures at the opening of the States General, Louis XVI, Necker, Mirabeau, the deputies of the three estates, have often been described. However, one group has been ignored. The court officials who escorted the King and surrounded his throne, people such as the *premiers gentilshommes* and *capitaines des gardes*, the *grand écuyer* and the *grand maître des cérémonies* have not found a historian. The court was one of the largest institutions in France, the States General met in rooms belonging to one department (the *menus-plaisirs du Roi*) and organised by another (the *cérémonies*), yet the court remains an enigma. A recent work, *La Cour de France*, by M. Solnon, stops in

---

[1] Gouverneur Morris, *A Diary of the French Revolution*, 2 vols., 1939, I, 68–9 and n., entry for 5 May 1789, letter to Mrs Robert Morris; Marquis de Ferrières, *Correspondance inédite*, 1932, p. 45, letter to Madame de Ferrières, 6 May 1789; Madame de Laage, *Souvenirs*, Evreux, 1869, p. lxxxvii, letter of 13 May 1789.

1789. To explore the court of France in the years after 1789, when it had to face new challenges and learn to play a new role, is the purpose of this book.

Language is one reason why the court remains a mystery. The word court has never been precisely defined. It could mean the royal households, the people who had been presented at court or simply the act of paying court. It was also used, often in a pejorative sense, for the government or the king. Politicians like Barnave were eager to deny their 'liaisons with the court' during the revolution. In this book, however, 'the court' will be taken to mean the personal households of the monarch and his family, and the palaces and what happened in them. To explore this magnetic field, which attracted some of the most important events and people in France, will shed light on the fate of the crown of France and the nature of the revolution.

Even the smallest detail about the court can be revealing. Every schoolchild knows that Louis XVI wrote *rien* in his agenda for 14 July 1789. It is less well known that in the private language of the court, as Madame de Staël explained to Gustavus III of Sweden, the word *rien* simply meant that the King was staying in his own apartments, reading or working with his ministers, rather than going out.[2] It did not mean that he did 'nothing'.

[2] Madame de Staël, *Lettres*, 1962– , I, i, 139, letter of 11 November 1786 to Gustavus III.

CHAPTER I

❧ ❦

Revolutions

Tout se tient dans une monarchie; la cour, naturellement composée de ce qu'il y a de plus considérable dans la nation, est le lien nécessaire entre le peuple et le trône ... Enfin un tyran a des enemis, mais il ne manque pas de partisans, au lieu qu'un monarque sans cour est un grand arbre déraciné que le moindre coup de vent renverse.

Duc de Lévis, *Souvenirs et Portraits*, 1882

For centuries the court of France had been one of the most important institutions in Europe. It was the centre of power in France when France was the leading power in Europe. It was also the largest single influence on the manners and customs, the decorative arts, fashions and pleasures of the European elites. The court was to France what the army was to Prussia: the supreme source of national pride and a vital element in national identity. The court was so impressive that even the king's own cousins, the princes de Condé, were proud to serve there, as hereditary *grands maîtres de la maison du Roi*.

The accession of Louis XVI in 1774 introduced a new phase in its history. Like many monarchs of the day, for example his cousin Charles III of Spain and George III of Great Britain, Louis XVI disliked magnificence. Contemporaries praised 'that noble simplicity of tastes which characterises him and which he prefers to the vain adornments of splendour'. In contrast to Louis XIV and Louis XV, he expressly desired service at his court to be 'reduced to what was absolutely necessary'.[1] There was no obligation to attend the court and there were frequent economy drives. Positions were abolished in 1774, 1780 and above all 1787 and 1789. In all, perhaps one-third of those existing in 1750 disappeared during his reign.

[1] M. Genty, *Discours sur le Luxe*, 1783, p. 57; Duc de Lévis, *Souvenirs et portraits*, 1882, p. 266.

3

The cost of the court fell from 37,650,000 *livres* in 1786 to 31,650,000 in 1788. The King himself checked the smallest details of the expenditure of the *petits appartements*, the department which was responsible for his private apartments and suppers. The stables, responsible for all forms of transport, were traditionally one of the most extravagant departments of the court. The number of horses in the King's stables fell from the stupendous total of 2,215 in 1784 to 1,195 in 1787.[2]

Social life at court was also becoming simpler, as it was in aristocratic society in Paris. There was a general relaxation in deference and display: the open house, the formal circle and the elaborate silk or satin *habit habillé* for men were going out of fashion. At the same time fewer people went regularly to pay their respects to the King at Versailles. They felt it was a waste of effort, since the royal family rarely talked to people paying court.[3] Louis XVI was a silent monarch, with few friends or favourites. In 1783, when he created the Duc de Croÿ Marshal of France, he did not say a word, 'as ceremonies bore the King'.[4] Courtiers were reduced to analysing the expression on his face or the duration of his silences: it was all they had to go on.

Marie-Antoinette could be charming when she wanted. But she also enjoyed making fun of people going to court, particularly the elderly. She preferred life among a group of friends, the *société de la Reine* which aroused so much envy, to holding court in her state apartments. At the Petit Trianon they enjoyed a more informal and more exclusive existence than was possible in the palace of Versailles. Amateur theatricals were among their favourite amusements. In August 1785, for example, the Queen played Rosine, the King's brother the Comte d'Artois Figaro and the Comte de Vaudreuil, *Grand Fauconnier de France*, Almaviva in Beaumarchais's *The Barber of Seville*: the King with a few courtiers and servants provided the audience.

---

[2] René-Marie Rampelberg, *Le Ministre de la maison du Roi Baron de Breteuil*, 1976, p. 49; Archives Nationales (AN) C (Papers of the Liste Civile) 222, *Dépenses des Petits Appartments depuis le 1er de juillet 1774 jusqu'au 1er de janvier 1776 du temps de Guimard*, with corrections by Louis XVI; Henri Lemoine, 'La Fin des écuries royales', *Revue de l'histoire de Versailles*, December 1933, pp. 182, 205.
[3] Duc de Croÿ, *Journal inédit*, 4 vols., 1906–7, III, 294, entry for 1776/7; M. A. de Lescure, *Correspondance secrète inédite sur Louis XVI, Marie-Antoinette, la cour et la ville*, 2 vols., 1866, II, 85, entry for 5 December 1786; Marquis de Bombelles, *Journal*, Geneva, 1977– , I, 138, entry for 13 August 1782.
[4] *Croy*, IV, 285, entry for 17 June 1783.

The *société de la Reine* also met in the salon of the Duchesse de Polignac, the Queen's favourite and *gouvernante des enfants de France*: the Duc de Lévis, one of the most acute observers of the court, remembered enjoying 'a real country-house life' there in the years before 1789. People played cards, billiards or music, gossipped and criticised the Queen behind her back. The Duchesse de Polignac, frivolous, informal and kind, was one of the few court officials whom the King liked. She was a niece of the Comte de Maurepas, the most important minister at the beginning of his reign, and the King used her to keep the Queen amused and, as far as possible, out of mischief.[5]

However, the court remained a centre of hospitality and splendour for people outside the *société de la Reine*. On the King's instructions the Duchesse de Polignac entertained visitors to the court as well as her own friends. The Queen gave balls in the winter in wooden rooms erected in a palace courtyard. They could be very enjoyable. In January 1786, for example, there was a scare when a few hundred unemployed workers marched on Versailles. The palace railings were closed and the number of guards on duty doubled. But the King made a joke of the precautions and the Marquis de Bombelles wrote in his diary: 'This evening's ball at the palace was not at all affected by this ridiculous revolt; people danced with the greatest gaiety.' Nobody felt they were dancing on the edge of a precipice.

Indeed after the triumphant peace in 1783 at the end of the War of American Independence, the French monarchy seemed both strong and successful. Louis XVI was more popular than any king of France since Henri IV; and on special occasions his court was a very impressive sight. On New Year's Eve 1784 more people came to pay their respects to the royal family than anyone could remember. Whereas 177 women had gone to court in 1757 to congratulate Louis XV on surviving Damiens's assassination attempt, 241 went in 1785 to congratulate Louis XVI on the birth of his second son the Duc de Normandie (the future Louis XVII).[6]

---

[5] Philippe Huisman and Marguerite Jallut, *Marie-Antoinette*, 1971, p. 129; *Lévis*, p. 330; *Bombelles*, II, 105, 235, entries for 19 January 1786, 15 September 1788.
[6] *Bombelles*, II, 16, 77, 104 entries for 31 December 1784, 15 November 1785, 11 January 1786; Lescure, *Correspondance*, I, 553, letter of 27 April 1785; J. N. Moreau, *Mes Souvenirs*, 2 vols., 1901, I, 601, diary for 11 January 1757.

These men and women all came from what was known as the *noblesse présentée* (it was also called the *noblesse de cour*, or *la cour* for short). For, although the court had been simplified, it had not changed its nature. Its formal social life was still confined to that section of the nobility sufficiently ancient or well connected (that is to say relations of ministers, marshals and *chevaliers* of the order of the Saint-Esprit) to have gone through the gruelling and expensive process of being presented at court. Rules for presentation had been tightened in 1732, when it had been decided that the applicant had to prove noble birth since 1400. On his accession Louis XVI had affirmed that he wanted to admit only 'the most distinguished nobility', with exceptions for those who had performed 'outstanding exploits'. New families did gain access: 30 per cent of the 558 individuals presented at court between 1783 and 1788 came from families which had not gone before. However, the *noblesse de robe* or legal nobility, and nearly all families whose nobility was recently acquired, continued to be excluded from formal receptions and entertainments at court; the bourgeoisie was not even considered.[7]

Chateaubriand could be presented, and was impressed by the pomp of Versailles and the grace of the Queen. But his brother, who was an officer of a *parlement* or law-court, was barred; others excluded were the future zealot of the counter-revolution the Comte d'Antraigues and the family of Alexandre de Beauharnais, the first husband of the future Empress Josephine.[8]

No other court possessed such an extensive and exclusive caste around the throne. Comte Alexandre de Tilly, a provincial noble who served as a page at Versailles, called the rules for presentation 'preliminaries which the other sovereigns of Europe would not have imagined in their wildest dreams'. When he went to the court of St James's, he noted that it was 'larger than at Versailles because it is easier to go there'. Moreover George III and Queen Charlotte *talked*. One Englishman, who had not received 'one single word from one of the Royal Family' in France, remarked in fury: 'our own King ... would speak civilly

---

[7] AN c 220, Louis XVI to Duc d'Aumont, 9 July 1774; François Bluche, *Les Honneurs de la cour*, 2 vols., 1957, *passim*.

[8] Chateaubriand, *Mémoires d'outre-tombe*, 3 vols., Librairie Générale Française, 1973, I, 167, 174; Jacques Godechot, *Le Comte d'Antraigues*, 1986, p. 15; Jean Hanoteau, *Le Ménage Beauharnais*, 1935, p. 84.

to even a French *captain*'. All nobles and all officials of the rank of councillor, and their wives, could be presented at the court of Sweden after Gustavus III reorganised it in 1778.[9] Official rank in the service of the monarch was beginning to replace birth as a condition of admission to the courts of Vienna and St Petersburg.

People who had not been presented at court were not completely excluded. The palace of Versailles was more open under Louis XVI than it is today. Anyone well dresssed had access to the state apartments. Members of the public could present petitions to the King on his way to mass or to the hunt. People of the rank of lieutenant-general, bishop and *premier président* and above could attend the King's *lever* and *coucher*. The King granted audiences freely.

However, formal presentation at court was a gratifying distinction in an age which regarded social life as both admirable and obligatory. Presentation was also a help to a career in the army, which is one reason why the rules were so resented. The famous military reformer the Comte de Guibert, who served on the Conseil de la guerre in 1787–9, attributed to the 'disastrous regulation of presentations' the fact that so many senior military commands went to members of the *noblesse présentée*. Because they had been presented to the King, which was a guarantee that they belonged to the traditional military nobility, they were considered eligible for military commands. The court of Louis XVI was a combination of contrasts, a bewildering mixture of exclusiveness and domesticity, military service and frivolity. In the spring of 1782 the return of colonels and *jeunes gens présentés* to their regiments from a winter of pleasure in Paris and Versailles was delayed. The reason was to provide the Queen with enough men of suitable rank to dance at the ball she gave in honour of the future Paul I of Russia.[10]

[9] Comte Alexandre de Tilly, *Mémoires*, 1965, p. 314; Sir Robert Murray Keith, *Memoirs and correspondence*, 2 vols., 1849, II, 30, Henry S. Conway to Keith, 19 November 1774; Karl Lofstrom, 'Le Costume national de Gustave III, le costume de cour et la présentation à la cour', *Livrustkammaren*, IX, July–August 1972, p. 143.

[10] Comte de Guibert, *Oeuvres militaires*, 5 vols., 1803, V, 209, *Mémoire adressé au public et à l'armée sur les opérations du conseil de la guerre*, 1789. For hostility to the rules for presentation from the *noblesse de robe* see for example AN 291 AP (Papers of the Président d'Aire) Barentin (a former *garde des sceaux*) to d'Aire, 28 July 1793; F. Barrière, *Tableaux de genre et d'histoire*, 1828, p. 267, Chevalier de Lille to Prince de Ligne, 26 April 1782, cf. *La France et la Russie au siècle des lumières*, Grand Palais, 1986, p. 117, Duc de Villequier to Vergennes, 20 February 1782.

The court of Louis XVI was extravagant as well. It was larger than the central government. There were in all about 2,500 people in the King's household in 1789: in comparison there were approximately 660 officials in the government ministries (war, foreign affairs, finance, marine, justice and the *maison du Roi*), whose staff was divided between Paris and Versailles. The minister of the *maison du Roi* had supreme authority over the court (and waged an unending war with the heads of court departments to cut costs) and was in effect minister of the interior as well.

In addition, since the royal family in 1789 was exceptionally large, there were 12 other independent royal households: for the Queen; the King's aunts Madame Adélaïde and Madame Victoire; his sister Madame Elizabeth; his children the Dauphin, the Duc de Normandie and Madame Royale; his brothers the Comte de Provence (known as Monsieur) and the Comte d'Artois; their wives; and the children of the Comte d'Artois, the Ducs d'Angoulême and de Berri (like the King's two younger children they shared the same household). One tradition of the court of France was that every member of the royal family had an enormous household of his or her own, in order to emphasise their rank and grandeur. When the households of the Comtes de Provence and d'Artois were set up by Louis XV, the Duc de Croÿ rightly called them 'ruinous and larger than those of other sovereigns'. The total number of officials and servants in the court of France in 1789 was probably over 6,000.

The palaces also increased in number and luxury in the 1780s. Louis XVI had inherited the time-honoured trinity of Versailles, Fontainebleau and Compiègne, to which the entire court and much of the government moved for certain periods of the year. The court's annual visit to Fontainebleau during the autumn hunting season was particularly agreeable: it was said that if two friends had quarrelled they were bound to be reconciled at Fontainebleau. The ministers and the chief court officials entertained lavishly. Madame de Staël described the exaggerated laughter and craning necks of the courtiers straining to attract the Queen's attention at supper in the apartment of the Duchesse de Polignac or of the Princesse de Lamballe (plate 3). For the Queen had some of the influence once exercised by Madame de Maintenon or Madame de Pompadour.

Partly because a precedent was set if the King granted a request, she was used by the government as a channel for promotions and favours at court, in the army and even in diplomacy. She was thought to be so powerful that she had her own party, nobles favourable to the Austrian alliance and supporters of its architect the former foreign minister, the Duc de Choiseul. The Polignac family and their friends obtained innumerable favours, including large sums of money, inevitably exaggerated by rumours: the Duc de Polignac became *surintendant des postes de France*. The King, however, rarely joined in the social life of his court: he spent the day hunting, reading, practising metalwork on his private forge and working with his ministers.[11]

The King also possessed smaller residences such as Marly, Choisy and La Muette. Nevertheless he bought the palace of Saint-Cloud between Paris and Versailles from the Duc d'Orléans in 1784 and Rambouillet from another cousin, his *grand veneur* the Duc de Penthièvre, in 1785. The first he gave to the Queen – the first time a queen consort of France had her own palace – the second was used as a sheep-breeding station and hunting-lodge. The King's brothers acquired estates in the Ile de France, Monsieur at Brunoy, Grosbois and L'Isle Adam, the Comte d'Artois at Saint-Germain, Maisons and Bagatelle, in addition to their palaces in Paris, the Luxembourg and the Temple. By 1789 the countryside around Paris resembled a vast park, dominated by the palaces, *châteaux* and pavilions of the House of Bourbon. Those that remain are still one of the glories of France, the equivalent in celebrity and popularity of the country houses of England.

All were refurnished in the style now known as Louis XVI. The King's simplicity of taste did not extend to his own furniture: it is among the most elaborate ever made, just as the service he ordered from the royal porcelain factory at Sèvres in 1784 is one of the finest and largest ever created. After 1784 the royal *garde-meuble* spent about 1,600,000 *livres* a year on furniture. There had been an economy drive and the court only represented about 6 per cent of government expenditure in 1789 (33,240,000 *livres* of 531,444,000, according to Necker). Nevertheless it remained the most luxurious in Europe.

---

[11] Clive H. Church, *Revolution and Red Tape*, 1982, p. 333; *Croÿ*, III, 51, diary for March 1773; Staël, *Lettres*, I, i, 139, letter to Gustavus III, November 1786.

Its chief rival, the court of the Holy Roman Emperor in Vienna, did not have the same all-pervading luxury. Its furniture and china, and all its residences except Schönbrunn, were second-rate. However the court of Vienna was in some ways more monarchical and elitist. The court of France was relatively domestic and informal. Its routine still revolved round the King's person. The *lever*, the ceremony when the King rose and dressed, and the *coucher*, when he undressed and went to bed, were the most important moments of the court's day. They were also the only opportunities to see the King apart from the Sunday receptions or, for a few favoured members of the *noblesse présentée*, his supper parties in his private apartments, where the food was said to be the best in France.

The *lever* and the *coucher* took place in the King's bedroom. Rank was shown by time not space, by when an individual was admitted to the bedroom (even the ordinary public was admitted when the King was not there), rather than by where he could go in the palace. The *entrées de la garde-robe, du cabinet* and *de la chambre* gave their holders varying times of access to the King's bedroom. The recipients show the relaxed character of the court. They included an astonishing mixture of princes, court officials, doctors, servants, colonels who had been presented and even women: wives of the most senior court officials and senior ladies-in-waiting. There was no system. Admission was decided by favour and domestic service rather than official rank. As the great Austrian diplomat Kaunitz noted with surprise, at the court of France there was no 'grading by antechamber, designed to give a high idea of the honour of approaching the person of the sovereign', such as could be found at his own court. Referring to this absence of distinctions of rank, Louis XVI when young had written 'everything is better regulated in the other courts of Europe'; but he made little change to the etiquette of his court after he ascended the throne.[12]

A further sign of the domestic nature of the court of France was the structure of the King's household. Some of its largest departments

[12] Papiers de la Famille de Thierry de Ville d'Avray (henceforward referred to as TVA), *Entrées chez le Roi 1756–1815*; Prince de Kaunitz, 'Mémoire sur la cour de France', 1752, *Revue de Paris*, August 1904, p. 844; Comte de Waroquier, *Etat de la France*, 2 vols., 1789, I, 94–5; Louis XVI, *Réflexions sur mes entretiens avec M. le Duc de La Vauguyon*, 1851, p. 179.

were devoted to his physical needs – the *garde-robe* to his clothes, the *bouche* to his food, the *menus-plaisirs* to his amusements and so on. Louis XVI's great-grandfather King Stanislas Leczynski of Poland thought that the court of Versailles was distinguished above all by its *luxe de domestiques*. There were armies of servants, some of whom held very important positions.

The court officials who ran the King's daily life were the *premier gentilhomme de la chambre*, who controlled his social relations with individuals (institutions were the responsibility of the *grand maître des cérémonies*); the *capitaine des gardes*, who was responsible for security once the King left his apartments; and the *premier valet de chambre*, who was in charge of his private apartments, his secret relations with individuals and his private money. These positions were so important that each was divided among four people, who served every three months or every four years. Other leading court positions, such as the *grand aumônier* (Monseigneur de Montmorency-Laval), the *grand écuyer* (the Prince de Lambesc), the *grand maître de la garde-robe* (the Duc de Liancourt) and the *premier maître d'hôtel* (the Baron d'Escars) who were in charge of the King's chapel, stables, clothes and food respectively, were left in the hands of one person. These only controlled large court departments, not access to the King.

The *premiers gentilshommes* and *capitaines des gardes* , the Ducs de Richelieu, de Duras, de Villequier and de Fleury, and the Duc de Guiche, the Comte de Luxembourg (a Montmorency), the Duc d'Ayen and the Prince de Poix (both Noailles) came from some of the grandest families of the *noblesse présentée*. Their families had served at court for generations and they felt almost as much part of it as the King himself.

The *premiers valets de chambre* were members of the upper bourgeoisie or lesser nobility. Yet because they were more trusted, they were in some ways more important. A contemporary wrote of their 'service which is so intimate and so noble because it is entirely confidential'. They were near the King for most of the day and involved in his most private affairs. They had been able to influence Louis XV's choice of mistresses and had acted as intermediaries in the conduct of his secret foreign policy. Holding a huge candelabra, they escorted Louis XVI to the Queen's bedroom, when he went there. Thierry de Ville d'Avray, a favourite of Louis XVI (he was head of the *petits appartements* and *intendant du garde-meuble* as well), was the intermediary through whom the Girondins made their last approach to the King in July 1792.[13] Most positions at court, as in other areas of French life, could be bought and were known as *charges*. The importance of the premiers valets de chambre is shown by the price of their *charges*. The *capitaines des gardes* paid 500,000 *livres* for theirs, the *premiers valets de chambre* 200,000. Below them were many other menial positions, such as *huissier* or *garçon de la chambre*, which were occupied by men of wealth and education who had paid up to 100,000 *livres* for their *charges*. They included future Senators of the Empire, such as Davous, Guéheuneuc and Clément de Ris.

Because the court was essentially social and domestic in character, it lacked positions of honour without domestic duties, which could be given to members of the elite, in order to 'acquire supporters', or reward 'officers who had served well', in the words of two plans of 1790. This was a further difference from other courts, which swarmed with chamberlains or *gentilshommes de la chambre*. Such positions were particularly appropriate as a means of winning support or adding lustre to the court, since they required no practical qualifications beyond good manners. In 1780 the Emperor Joseph II inherited 1,500 noble chamberlains from his mother. Although he did not make much use of them, they were at last a means of attaching nobles to the personal service of his dynasty. Louis XVI's Bourbon cousin, King Charles III of Spain, had 60 *gentilhombres de cámara*, who included some of the richest grandees, such as the Dukes of Alba, Ossuna and Medina Celi as well as prominent provincial nobles. Since the reign of Louis XIV, who stopped creating *gentilshommes de la chambre*, the king of France had had no equivalent.[14]

By the end of the eighteenth century such a gap was an anachronism.

[13] Abbé Proyart, *Oeuvres complètes*, 17 vols., 1819, XI, 93; AN c 183, *Reflexions*, 15 June 1790; Rohan Butler, *Choiseul*, Oxford, 1980, p. 531; TVA, *Premiers valets de chambre*, f. 25; Paul et Pierrette Girault de Coursac, *Enquête sur le procès du Roi Louis XVI*, 1982, p. 530; cf. BM Mss 41170 f. 127, Monsieur to Gustavus III, July 1791, where he assumes that a *premier valet de chambre* or his apartment are the safest means to communicate with the King.

[14] AN c 183, *Reflexions*, 15 June 1790; AW 03 (Papers of the Maison du Roi 1814–30), 529, *Mémoire 1790*; *Österreich unter Joseph II*, Melk, 1980, p. 97; Archives of the Royal Palace, Madrid, leg 210 Camara 1762 (I am grateful for this reference to Dr Curtis Noel); Bibliothèque Nationale (BN) Mss Français 32773 f. 30, J. F. d'Hozier *Liste des gentilshommes de la chambre du Roi*, 1786.

For the tide was turning against monarchy. Every monarch in Europe was experiencing what Madame de Boufflers described to Gustavus III of Sweden as 'the shock of the aristocracy with the monarchy': Gustavus III himself was to feel it in a particularly disagreeable form when he was murdered by aristocrats at a masked ball in 1792. Respect for monarchy was diminishing, because of an increase in the pretensions of the nobility rather than of the failings of the monarchs. Some nobles now wanted to exercise their domination of society through institutions rather than royal favour.

The 'shock of the aristocracy with the monarchy' was particularly severe in France. There was an enormous nobility – it probably included 150,000 people – which, unlike for example the Austrian, was eager to serve the King. Comte de Liederkerke-Beaufort, a Belgian who served as a page of Monsieur in the 1780s, noted with surprise that in 'the nobility of France ... the eldest sons, like the younger ones, have to serve for fear of being despised'. The natural outlet for this desire to serve was the army. However, even in the eighteenth century when the officer corps was almost a noble preserve, not all French nobles could serve in it in peacetime. Ministers were aware, as Louis XVI's leading minister, Maurepas, said in 1777, that 'there are too many nobles to place, and not enough places for them'.[15] There was no alternative structure of court or administrative service with positions prestigious enough for nobles. The creation of chamberlains or *gentilshommes de la chambre* could have satisfied French nobles' desire to serve, and to demonstrate their attachment to the King.

Such a change had already taken place in the households of the King's brothers. After 1771, unlike previous cadets of the House of France, each prince had *gentilshommes d'honneur*, 'people of quality ... to accompany him everywhere'. As their name implied these positions were in no way demeaning. As a result Louis XVI's brothers had almost as many members of the *noblesse présentée* in their households, 24 compared to 27, as he did. The court, *ce pays-ci* as it was still called,

---

[15] A. Geffroy, *Gustave III et la cour de France*, 2 vols., 1867, I, 266, Madame de Boufflers to Gustavus III, 25 October 1772; Comte de Liederkerke-Beaufort, 'Souvenirs d'un page du Comte de Provence', *Revue de Paris*, May 1952, p. 59; Croÿ, III, 25; for the Austrian nobility's unwillingness to serve, which was the despair of Metternich, see N. Lemontey, *Essai sur l'établissement monarchique de Louis XIV*, 1818, p. 343n.; Comte de Montbel, *Souvenirs*, 1913, p. 353.

with its strange domestic routine, its ludicrous rules for presentation, and anachronistic household structure, was isolating the King from the ruling classes. It was a barrier rather than a link. At the same time the abolition by 1787 of the *maison militaire*, the *mousquetaires*, *chevau-légers* and *gendarmes de la garde* for reasons of economy removed 800 positions dedicated to the personal service of the King. They had been open to the rich as well as the well born, and had been one of the most reliable repressive forces in Paris.

The Affair of the Diamond Necklace in 1785 revealed and widened the gulf between the monarchy and the ruling classes. The Rohan were one of the leading families of the court (the others were the Lorraine and the Noailles): their rank of *prince étranger*, which had annoyed Saint-Simon so much, gave them precedence over dukes. One Rohan, Madame de Marsan, had brought up Louis XVI and his brothers and sisters, and was almost part of the family: Monsieur called her *ma chère petite chère amie*. Another Rohan, the Prince de Soubise, a friend of Louis XV and Madame de Pompadour, was captain of the *gendarmes de la garde*. A third, the Cardinal de Rohan, was *grand aumônier de France*. He had also been ambassador in Vienna, where his extravagance and scepticism had angered the Empress Maria Theresa.

Marie-Antoinette followed her mother's line and never spoke to the cardinal. Desperate to regain her favour, he was tricked by his fortune-hunting mistress, Madame de Lamotte, into buying a diamond necklace for over a million *livres* in the belief that it was for the Queen. One of Madame de Lamotte's stratagems was to hire an actress to impersonate the Queen at a meeting with the cardinal by night in the park at Versailles. Another was to forge a letter signed 'Marie-Antoinette de France', although such a senior court official as the Cardinal de Rohan should have remembered that members of the royal family signed 'Louis' or 'Marie-Antoinette', without qualifications.

When the scandal broke, the King was horrified: he called it 'the saddest and most terrible business that I have yet seen'.[16] The cardinal was arrested by his orders in front of the court, as he was about to

---

[16] AN R 5 (Papers of the Maison of the Comte de Provence, 1771–91) 56, *Règlement pour le service honorifique de Monseigneur le Comte de Provence*, 1 April 1771; AN 286 Mi 2 (Rohan papers), Louis XVIII to Madame de Marsan, 2 September 1801; Louis XVI to Vergennes, 16 August 1785 (letter displayed at the Vergennes exhibition, Galerie de la Seita, Paris 1987).

accompany the King to mass. The Queen's name was dragged through mud in public at his trial: but it did not prevent her from performing in *The Barber of Seville* at her private theatre beside the Petit Trianon four days after his condemnation. She was already unpopular, both at court and in Paris, for her rudeness, extravagance and loyalty to Austria. Now she was detested. When she went to Paris, she was greeted by silence in the streets and hisses at the opera. That year the most fashionable colours, red and yellow, represented the cardinal's robes on the straw of his prison cell. The arrest of the Cardinal de Rohan, his ignorance of royal traditions and popularity at his trial, showed that the machinery of the court was breaking down. Courtiers began to worry. The Duchesse de Polignac told her friend the Marquis de Bombelles that she had said to the Queen that 'it was time that she took up her role again, that of holding court with dignity and that she should not come every afternoon to mingle in a salon where the habit of seeing her familiarly lessened the respect she should inspire'.

In 1787 and 1788 an aristocratic revolt against the financial and political reforms of Louis XVI demonstrated the isolation of the monarchy and almost paralysed the government. Although most court officials remained loyal, Louis XVI dismissed two, the Marquis de Bois-gelin a *maître de la garde-robe*, and the Duchesse de Praslin one of the Queen's *dames du palais*, for their opposition. Hostility to the government could turn to contempt for the King as well as the Queen. As Thierry de Ville d'Avray informed him, Louis XVI was, on occasion, laughed at by his own courtiers at the *coucher*. The Comtesse de Brionne, born a Rohan, married to a Lorraine and mother of the *grand écuyer*, the Prince de Lambesc, was one of the most prominent ladies of the court (and one of Talleyrand's first mistresses). At a party she gave in January 1789 'all the most elegant people in Paris' laughed at a song mocking Madame's weakness for the bottle, the Comtesse d'Artois's fondness for *gardes du corps*, the King's love of hunting and drinking and the illegitimacy of his second son: apparently it was accepted as a subject for jokes.[17] The monarchy had lost the respect of the ruling classes.

With the opening of the States-General the pleasure-loving court of

[17] *Découverte*, XXIV, 48, memoirs of Thierry de Ville d'Avray; *Bombelles*, II, 213, 247, 276, diary for 18 July, 10 October, 1788, 23 January 1789.

France entered a harsher world. Hitherto the letters of Monsieur to his *capitaine des gardes*, the Duc de Lévis, whom he loved as a son, dealt with love affairs and the theatre, the poems of Horace and the best time to see magnolias in flower. Like courtiers' conversation, they were frivolous and occasionally highly obscene. Towards the end of 1788 there was a change of tone. Politics now dominated the world of the court, as they would until 1830. They had less time to meet, since either Monsieur was presiding over a bureau of the Assembly of Notables or Lévis was sitting in the National Assembly. The prince instructed him how to behave there: Lévis should defend the prerogatives, but not the financial privileges, of the nobility. Above all he must defend the rights of 'monarchy pure and simple': the King should retain control of legislative and executive power, law and order and finance, and the right to make war and peace.[18]

Before the opening of the States-General the Third Estate deputies, especially Mirabeau, a member of the provincial nobility who had been elected a deputy of the Third Estate, had been infuriated by the decision of the young *grand maître des cérémonies*, the Marquis de Dreux-Brézé (whose family had held the office since 1701), that they should wear the black costume that 'the legal nobility is in the habit of wearing at court': the nobility wore cloth of gold. However this rule was followed in the end and the Third Estate deputies found themselves well treated at court. They received the *entrée* to the King's *lever* and *coucher* and were given free tickets to the court theatre. Ladies of the court such as the Duchesse de Polignac and the Maréchale de Duras invited them to supper. The Queen opened the Petit Trianon, her private retreat, for them.

The court was not a crucial issue in 1789. Dreux-Brézé's attitude when telling the Third Estate to withdraw from the *salle des menus-plaisirs* after the *séance royale* of 23 June provoked the famous outburst from Mirabeau: 'Go and tell your master that we are here by the will of the people and can only be removed by the force of bayonets' (see plate 1). But events like the union of the nobility and the clergy with the Third Estate in the National Assembly, the storming of the Bastille, the farmers' revolts in the countryside, the renunciation of privileges

---

[18] Letters of Monsieur to the Duc de Lévis, 1787–9, consulted by kind permission of M. Alain de Grolée-Virville.

on the night of 4 August, and the decision to buy out all owners of *charges* with money raised by confiscating church property were far more important.

The court was as divided in its attitude to the revolutions sweeping France as the rest of the nobility. The Duchesse de Polignac, who called her salon *l'hôtel de la liberté*, had entertained and encouraged noble deputies opposed to joining the Third Estate in the National Assembly.[19] The Prince de Lambesc commanded a regiment which charged a crowd in Paris. Both became so unpopular that they had to leave the country (at the same time as the Comte d'Artois), after the fall of the Bastille.

But many other court officials, like most of France, believed that they had entered a new era of liberty, equality and fraternity. Among them were the Duc de Liancourt, *grand maître de la garde-robe*, the Marquis de Chauvelin, *maître de la garde-robe* and the Noailles family, who were related to one of the heroes of the revolution in 1789, the Marquis de La Fayette. One Noailles, the Prince de Poix, governor of the château of Versailles and one of the *capitaines des gardes*, declared in July that his *gardes du corps* would never obey orders against the National Assembly. His brother, the Vicomte de Noailles, a friend of Mirabeau, led the Assembly's renunciation of privileges. Most of the servants in the royal households (for example Cléry, who later served Louis XVI in his prison of the Temple), like the citizens of Versailles, were enthusiastic supporters of the revolution which would deprive them of their livelihood. The attitude of the court shows that the revolution was a product of, not a break with, the *ancien régime*.

The King contemplated resistance. On 15 July, after the fall of the Bastille, Thierry de Ville d'Avray was sent to Compiègne to prepare it for the court.[20] But Louis XVI was tied to Versailles by the lack of reliable troops, the power of the National Assembly and his own sense of duty. He did not stay there long. The main force guarding the court, the Gardes françaises, hitherto a model to the rest of the army, had deserted and led the attack on the Bastille. This regiment provided the nucleus of the Garde nationale de Paris, under the command of La

[19] Georges Lefebvre (ed.), *Recueil de documents relatifs aux séances des Etats Généraux*, 4 vols., 1953–70, I, 78; *Bombelles*, II, 317, diary for 22 May 1789; Marquis de Ferrières, *Correspondance inédite*, 1932, p. 58, letter to Madame de Medel, 4/5 June 1789.
[20] *Journal des amis de la constitution*, 1 July 1789 (reference kindly communicated by P. Girault de Coursac); TVA, Thierry de Ville d'Avray, *Portrait d'un bon Roi*, 1790, f. 12vo.

Fayette, which assumed responsibility for law and order in Paris and the defence of the revolution.

The King's refusal to sanction some of the National Assembly's decrees in September heightened popular discontent. Abandoned by those guards he had not disbanded, he was now in direct personal danger and summoned the régiment de Flandre to Versailles to protect the court. On 1 October the Gardes du corps gave a banquet in its honour in the theatre at Versailles which had been built for the celebrations for the King's marriage 19 years before. Many toasts were drunk, and the song O *Richard O mon Roi, l'univers t'abandonne* from an opera by the Queen's favourite composer, Grétry, brought tears to loyal eyes. When the royal family appeared at the end of the evening, it was greeted with rapture.

The court's last evening of frivolity at Versailles had terrible consequences. For it was enough to provide the revolutionaries in Paris with a pretext for action. On 5 October a hungry Parisian mob arrived at Versailles, followed by the Garde nationale under La Fayette, demanding that the King should sanction the Assembly's latest decrees. The King was hunting near Meudon; the Queen was in the garden of the Petit Trianon. Both hurried back to the palace. That evening there were plans for the court to retreat to Rambouillet (as most *gardes du corps* did during the night); but they were not put into effect. La Fayette guaranteed the safety of the royal family and then left to sleep in the town at the Hôtel de Noailles.

The palace railings were opened at about five next morning as usual by the Garde nationale de Paris. Its soldiers had been eager to resume service at court and occupied the posts they had once held as *gardes français*. Soon after a few hundred people, mainly women, swept towards the palace. They were screaming that they wanted to cut off the Queen's head, eat her heart, and stew her liver; and they would not stop there. Two *gardes du corps* died defending the Queen's apartments. As the mob hammered at her door, she fled by a secret corridor to the King's bedroom. The Garde nationale under La Fayette arrived and replaced the Gardes du corps in control of the palace. The King no longer commanded his own guard.

Hitherto the court had absorbed the National Assembly and the revolution into its routine. There had been few fundamental changes, as is shown by the fact that on 5 October the King was hunting, the Queen was in her garden and Versailles was still the royal residence. Now the court entered a new world of yelling mobs, splintering doors and blood. Weakness and fear replaced power and pleasure in the palaces of the King of France. He was a prisoner of the revolution and agreed to move to Paris. He had to beg the mob to spare the lives of the remaining Gardes du corps; and the Queen had to appear alone on the palace balcony to acknowledge its triumph. The procession of carriages taking the royal family from Paris to Versailles was escorted by a screaming mob brandishing the heads of the murdered Gardes du corps.

The King and the royal family were followed in the next few weeks by their households, the ministries and the National Assembly: only a few sections of the court, such as the riding school attached to the stables, stayed behind. Versailles soon regretted its enthusiasm for the revolution: in 1790 the mayor wrote to Louis XVI begging for money to help the thousands who in the past 'existed only through his presence and his charity'.[21]

In Paris the King's residence and the seat of his court was a long brown building in the west of the city, the palace of the Tuileries (see figure 1). Begun by Catherine de' Medici in the second half of the sixteenth century, it had been finished and decorated by Louis XIV a hundred years later. It contained 368 rooms and consisted of three sections: the pavillon de Marsan to the north, the pavillon de l'Horloge in the middle and the pavillon de Flore to the south, which overlooked the Seine and was linked to the Louvre by a long gallery built by Henri IV. After Louis XIV had moved to Versailles, the Tuileries had only been used by the court at the beginning of the reign of Louis XV, from 1715 to 1722. Since then it had been divided into apartments for artists and courtiers, a *pied à terre* for the Queen and a theatre. As Louis XVI later complained, it was uncomfortable and nothing was ready for the royal family.

On 6 October existing tenants were evicted by the *grand maréchal des logis* the Marquis de La Suze, and the King, his aunts, sister, wife

---

[21] *Procédure criminelle instruite au châtelet de Paris*, 3 vols., 1790, I, 26, 39, *dépositions* of Du Repaire and de Miomandre, *gardes du corps*, II, 42, 49, *dépositions* of Duc d'Ayen, *capitaine des gardes*, and Thierry de Ville d'Avray, *premier valet de chambre*; AN C 189, mayor of Versailles to Louis XVI, 14 April 1790.

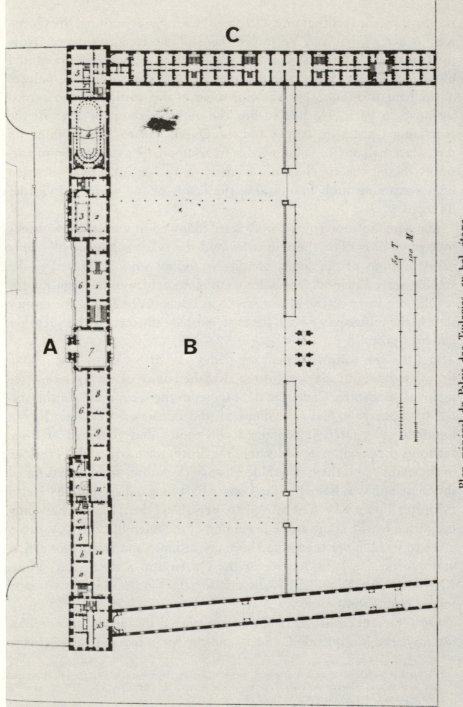

A   B

C

Plan général du Palais des Tuileries au bel étage.

and children and their court officials moved in. In 1787, 200 court officials, 20 members of the *noblesse présentée*, 10 guards officers and 10 ministers and senior officials had apartments in the palace of Versailles. Two years later about half that number were lodged in the Tuileries and its precincts. For the first time in centuries ministers did not have apartments in the King's palace; the court and the government were becoming more distinct.

Magnificent royal furniture was sent from Versailles to the Tuileries by the *garde-meuble*: it took the opportunity of the court's removal to Paris to complete the refurnishing of the other royal palaces, which were never so splendid or well maintained as at the fall of the monarchy.[22]

Overnight Paris became a court city, for the first time since 1722. Its population was swollen by the thousands attached to the royal households and the court continued its social routine in the Tuileries until 9 August 1792 (with an interruption of two months after the return from Varennes in 1791). The horrors of the revolution meant that going to court could be slightly unnerving. On 8 October 1789 Lord Robert Fitzgerald, a British diplomat, reported that 'The King was much dejected and said little. Her Majesty's voice faltered and the tears ran fast down her cheeks as she spoke and all their Attendants seemed impressed with the deepest melancholy and concern.'

1 The palace of the Tuileries (J. C. Legrand, *Description de Paris*, 2 vols., 1818, I, 238–9) The Tuileries was the principal residence of the rulers of France after 1789. Its structure changed less than its inhabitants. The *pavillon de Marsan* accommodated, in succession, Madame Adélaïde and Madame Victoire, revolutionary committees, the Emperor's treasury, the Comte d'Artois and the Duchesse de Berri. Louis XVI, Napoleon I, Louis XVIII, Charles X and Louis-Philippe I in turn lived in the apartments south of the *salle des maréchaux*. The *pavillon de Flore* was occupied by Madame Elizabeth and the Princesse de Lamballe, revolutionary committees, monarchs visiting the Emperor (including the Pope in 1804) and, after 1814, court officials.

LEGEND

1 *salle des Cent-Suisses*	10 *salle du trône*	c *cabinet particulier*
2 *salon de la chapelle*	11 *grand cabinet*	d *cabinet particulier*
3 *chapelle*	12 *galerie de Diane*	e *'chambre' à coucher*
4 *salle de spectacle*	13 *pavillon de Flore*	f *cabinet de toilette*
5 *pavillon de Marsan*		
6 *galerie vitrée*	**The King's apartments**	A *jardin des Tuileries*
7 *salle des maréchaux*	a *salle des gardes*	B *cour du carrousel*
8 *salon bleu*	b *salon de famille*	C *aile neuve*
9 *salle de la paix*	b *salle à manger*	

22 AN 03 132, *Etat des poèles et cheminées existants dans le château des Tuileries*, 1826; KK 540, *Logements au Château de Versailles*, 1787; AN 01 1682, *Logement du roy aux Tuileries du 6 octobre 1789*; Pierre Verlet, *French Royal Furniture*, 1963, p. 53.

However, after the shock of the October days, court life continued. People were presented and the royal family attended mass in public, as before. In the summer of 1790, as in 1788, the court moved to the Queen's palace of Saint-Cloud. Every day the King held his *lever* and *coucher*, which were attended by both supporters and opponents of the revolution. One morning in May 1790 before the *lever*, for example, the Austrian ambassador the Comte de Mercy-Argenteau met the Comte d'Angiviller, *directeur des bâtiments du Roi*, in an ante-chamber in the Tuileries and discussed Mirabeau's offer to sell his services for 5,000 *livres* a month. On 20 June 1791 the royal family had to wait for La Fayette to leave the King's *coucher* before they themselves could leave for Varennes. People also went to court on Sundays to watch the King and the royal family go to mass: it was customary for royalists in Paris to go every two or three weeks. It was a way of showing loyalty to the King, learning the latest news and meeting people. The royal family also dined in public on Sundays and Thursdays, the Queen held a card party on Sundays, Tuesdays and Thursdays and there was a reception for ambassadors on Sundays and Thursdays.[23]

The old exclusiveness persisted at some ceremonies. Access to the King's bedroom continued to be governed by the traditional *entrées*, which continued unchanged until the fall of the monarchy. In April 1792, 108 women (the King counted them himself) were received by the Queen on the occasion of the death of her brother the Emperor Leopold II. This figure, 42 per cent of the figure on her mother's death in 1780, shows that emigration was far from universal among the *noblesse présentée* and that large numbers of them continued to go to court.[24]

However, the rules about going to court were relaxed and there may have been a rise in attendance. While France was being transformed by a series of revolutions, agricultural, ecclesiastical, administrative and

---

[23] J. M. Thompson, *English Witnesses of the French Revolution*, Oxford 1938, p. 71; Girault de Coursac, *Enquête sur le procès du Roi Louis XVI*, p. 192, Mercy-Argenteau to Marie-Antoinette, 7 May 1790; Albert Mousset, *Un Témoin ignoré de la révolution française: le Comte de Fernan-Nunez*, 1921, p. 93, Fernan-Nunez to Florida Blanca, 13 October 1789; Madame Elizabeth, *Correspondance*, 1868, p. 121, letter of 13 October 1789 to Madame de Bombelles.

[24] TVA, *Entrées chez le Roi*; Abbé de Salamon, *Correspondance secrète ... avec le Cardinal de Zelada*, 1898, p. 352, letter of 19 March 1792.

political, there was also a small revolution at court. The registers of the *maître des cérémonies* show that more institutions wanted to go to court and greater honours were paid to them: the Districts of Paris and the *corps de marchands*, for example, went for the first time. Deputies no longer attended in ceremonial dress 'not even the Bishops and *curés*', and the commune of Paris no longer knelt when received by the King. In 1791 the wife of the British ambassador wrote, 'There was a great crowd at court on New Year's Day.' Comte Roger de Damas, whose brother Charles was a devoted courtier of Monsieur, found the apartments of the King and Queen crowded with the kind of people who would not have been allowed access in the old days. One or two politicians and officers of the Garde nationale, such as Bailly, the Mayor of Paris, Pastoret, *procureur-général du départment* and the future Maréchal Berthier received the *entrées de la chambre*, while La Fayette, who already had the *entrées de la chambre*, was given the *entrées du cabinet*.[25]

The old distinctions between the *noblesse de robe*, the *noblesse présentée* and the *noblesse de province* were fading away in face of the threat from the revolution. Moreover, going to court was cheaper than in the past. Although the evidence is contradictory, it is probable that people going to court could wear the simple black or blue *frac* or tail-coat instead of the expensive silk- or satin-embroidered *habit habillé*. It had been *de rigueur* on Sundays before 1789 and the King, to encourage the Lyons silk industry, continued to wear it. Malesherbes, the aged ex-minister who was one of the most prominent *parlementaires* of his day, found the new costume hard to get used to after the black suit he had worn as a *noble de robe*: the sword kept getting between his legs. But he continued to go to court for the sake of seeing the King.[26] Indeed people stopped going to court only when it was physically impossible. Only on 9 August 1792, when Paris was in turmoil and

[25] M. A. de Beauchesne, *Madame Elizabeth*, 2 vols., 1869, I, 554–60; Lord Granville Leveson-Gower, *Private Correspondence*, 2 vols., 1916, I, 29, Lady Sutherland to Lady Stafford, January 1791; Roger de Damas, *Memoirs*, 1907, p. 113; TVA, *Entrées chez le Roi*.

[26] Thompson, *English Witnesses*, p. 96, letter from Lord Mornington, 27 September 1790; M. A. de Beauchesne, *Louis XVII*, 2 vols., 1853, I, 133. On the other hand in early 1790 a deputy was refused entry to the Tuileries because he was wearing a tail-coat and some people assumed they had to wear the *habit habillé* to court: see Philip Mansel, 'Monarchy, Uniform and the Rise of the Frac', *Past and Present*, XCVI, August 1982, p. 129.

an attack on the Tuileries was imminent, was the *coucher du Roi* suspended and royalists told not to come to the palace.[27]

The expansion of court life after 1789 shows that both the idea and the reality of the court were compatible with the revolution. Revolutionaries wanted a splendid and dignified court which would demonstrate the King's acceptance of the revolution and their own political and social triumph. La Fayette attached almost as much importance to the routine of the court as the Marquis de Dreux-Brézé. In November 1789 La Fayette wrote to Mounier that the only signs that the King was not free after the transfer to the Tuileries were the absence of *gardes du corps* and the fact that he no longer went hunting. Nobody thought that the King of France could live like Frederick the Great who, according to Guibert, was 'a King without a court, without guards, without personal splendour'.

The court was so much part of national life, it had such a powerful influence on manners and customs, the decorative arts and food, that its disappearance was unthinkable. Its riding school was one of the best in Europe, at a time when everyone wanted to ride. It was founder and chief patron of the luxury industries making furniture, china, tapestry and carpets which employed so many Parisians, and inspired so many imitators. Sèvres, Gobelins, Aubusson and Beauvais were names which were almost as famous in Europe as those of Versailles, Marly and Fontainebleau. The court's standards of display helped keep the silk looms of Lyons in business, as innumerable petitions to Louis XVI testify. Some of the greatest French writers, Molière, Racine and Voltaire, had been officials of the court, as were famous contemporary writers like Rulhière, Chamfort and Ducis. Among revolutionary figures, Siéyès, Marat and Beaumarchais had held positions at court (but not for long). The court was involved in so much: the founder of the famous chocolate firm of Meunier became *fabricant de chocolat de Madame Victoire* in 1789. The journalist Mercier, while admitting that the court no longer had the same prestige as in the past, wrote in the 1780s of Parisians' contempt for the English court and pride in their own: 'what is your King? He is badly housed, frankly speaking

---

[27] François de La Rochefoucauld, *Souvenirs du 10 aout 1792 et de l'armée de Bourbon*, 1929, p. 7.

it is pitiable. Look at ours ... What grandeur! What splendour! What magnificence!'[28]

Such love of grandeur had been one of the driving forces behind the court of France and was now its guarantee of survival. In 1790, during debates over the civil list in the National Assembly, Lebrun the future Second Consul, in language worthy of Louis XIV, said: 'You desire your King to be the most magnificent of Kings, as you are the greatest of nations. You do not want to destroy a splendour which distinguishes the French court.' French society had been transformed, the feudal system abolished, titles of nobility made illegal (which meant the end of presentation at court in June 1790); but the court must go on.

Other speakers agreed with Lebrun, who also praised Louis XVI's 'severe economy'. To cries of *Vive le Roi!* the King was voted a civil list of 25 million *livres* a year, as he requested. In addition he would have the revenue of the *domaine de la couronne*, the farms and forests around the palaces of Versailles, Saint-Cloud, Fontainebleau, Compiègne, Saint-Germain and Rambouillet (the other royal residences were to be sold). This revenue would have increased, since the land was no longer used for hunting. The King, who had already abolished the *petits appartements*, disbanded his beloved hunt in September 1790; with the weakening of law and order since 1789, much of the game in the royal forests had been slaughtered and devoured, so hunting was no longer a pleasure.[29] Although the Assembly subsequently assigned payment of all military and political pensions and of the guard (previously paid, in part, by the ministry of war) to the civil list, the figure was reasonable: indeed it would be maintained, despite a steep increase in prices, as the basis of subsequent civil lists until 1830 (for a further discussion see chapter 9).

By 1791 the *maison du Roi* was one of the few institutions in France which had not been transformed since the start of the revolution: in December 1790, for example, young Monsieur de Duras succeeded his

[28] Général de La Fayette, *Mémoires, correspondance et manuscrits*, 6 vols., 1837–8, II, 417, La Fayette to Mounier, 23 October 1789; M. de Guibert, *Oeuvres complètes*, 5 vols., 1803, V, 475, 'Eloge du Roi de Prusse'; L. S. Mercier, *Tableau de Paris (nouvelle édition corrigée et augmentée)*, 8 vols., Amsterdam, 1782, IV, 149.
[29] P. Girault de Coursac, 'Affaire de la liquidation des pensions et des charges de la maison du Roi', *Découverte* (Bulletin trimestriel pour l'Etude de Louis XVI et de son Procès, henceforth referred to as *Découverte*), XLVIII, December 1984, *passim*, especially p. 10.

grandfather, the old Maréchal, as one of the four *premiers gentils-hommes*. Inevitably, in a volatile revolutionary society, pressure for change grew stronger. On 28 February 1791, the day known as *la journée des poignards*, a rumour that the King was surrounded by royalist courtiers with daggers in their pockets led to an invasion of the Tuileries by a Paris crowd: the King had to tell his courtiers to leave.

On 17 April the King was prevented from leaving for Saint-Cloud, where he had spent the summer of 1790, by a mob which kept his carriage immobile in a courtyard of the Tuileries for two hours while it screamed abuse. The unpopularity of the clergy in his household was one reason: the *grand aumônier* Monseigneur de Montmorency-Laval had not accepted the civil constitution of the clergy. The King had to lean out of his carriage window and command the *gardes nationaux* to release Duras, whom they had dragged from the carriage steps and were about to attack. The next day the Department of Paris, by no means an extremist body, presented an address attacking the King's household and the people going to court as counter-revolutionary. They feared that the King's politeness to them indicated 'the real leanings of your heart' and asked him to make 'the firmest bulwarks of liberty' court officials. Immediately after, probably on the King's suggestion, some senior court officials, Duras, Montmorency-Laval, d'Angiviller and others resigned their *charges*. A formal proclamation abolishing the *charges* was issued by the King on 18 June 1791, three days before he fled from the Tuileries.[30]

The outrage of 18 April, which proved that he was a prisoner in the Tuileries, finally decided Louis XVI to leave. His escape on the night of 20/21 June emphasised the vulnerability of the court. Whereas in October 1789 the court had been invaded by the revolution, in June 1791 it was abandoned by the King. He kept secret his decision to flee to the fortress town of Montmédy in the east of France, where he believed that loyal troops under General Bouillé awaited him. The journey was organised by an outsider and a foreigner, the Queen's handsome Swedish admirer Count Axel von Fersen, colonel of the regiment of Royal Suédois. The royal family left the Tuileries by a secret door in the middle of the night. They were accompanied only by three *gardes*

[30] *Découverte*, XIX, September 1977, p. 46; *Moniteur*, 20 April 1791, p. 451; AN C, 223, letters of resignation, April 1791; AN O 1 201, Proclamation of 18 June 1791.

du corps, two maids and Madame de Tourzel, who had replaced the Duchesse de Polignac as *governante des enfants de France*. They were followed by the Queen's coiffeur Léonard with Madame Elizabeth's jewels and the King's red and gold military uniform – a sign of the military role he planned to assume once he was surrounded by reliable troops.

During the journey, for the first time in their lives, the royal family left the world of the court and had to behave as private people: the King and Queen played the parts of servants, Madame de Tourzel that of the Baronne de Korff returning to Russia. The ease with which they played their parts (like the flight to the Petit Trianon) may be a sign of the strain imposed on them by their rank. Neither Louis XIV nor Louis XV, nor indeed a modern monarch, would have found the acting so easy.

The incompetence or worse of Bouillé and Choiseul, the officers responsible for the reception of the royal family, rather than the delays in its journey led to its capture at Varennes. The royal family was sub-jected to even more brutal threats and insults than on 18 April during its nightmare journey back to Paris in the middle of a heatwave. A noble was lynched in front of their eyes; people spat in the King's face. Yet they maintained their extraordinary composure.[31]

After the King was taken back to the Tuileries, there was an interrup-tion of two months in court life: the royal family was watched day and night, even in its private apartments, by the soldiers of the Garde nationale de Paris. In September Louis XVI recovered some of his free-dom and approved the new constitution drawn up by the National Assembly. It left him with the right to choose ministers, veto the decisions of the Legislative Assembly and decide war and peace. But it deprived him of real executive power.

France was now a modernised, decentralised, 'egalitarian' society. A transformation in the court to prove the sincerity of the King's accep-tance of the constitution seemed more urgent than ever. Just as, in England, ministers tried (not always successfully under George III) to staff the royal household with their supporters, so in France politicians wanted Louis XVI to fill his household with supporters of the revolution.

---

[31] The best accounts of the flight to Varennes are Eugène Bimbinet, *Fuite de Louis XVI à Varennes*, 1868; and P. Girault de Coursac, *Sur la Route de Varennes*, 1982.

Although many counter-revolutionary court officials had left, criticism of the King's welcome to returning emigrés and of the composition and behaviour of the royal household continued. Without mentioning names, La Fayette complained that people attached to the King attacked the National Assembly in the apartments of the Tuileries. He suggested that the Queen should receive 'the wives of certain officials elected by the people, that these were very trivial matters, very petty measures but their effect would be certain'. Barnave also attacked the composition of the court, writing to the Queen that Brissac and *les gens de la maison du Roi* made counter-revolutionary remarks.[32]

The most thorough onslaught came from someone who knew the court from inside. The Comte de Narbonne had the reputation of being one of the most able and charming nobles of his generation. Born in 1755, he may have been an illegitimate son of Louis XV. Through the influence of his mother, the favourite lady-in-waiting of Madame Adélaïde, he rose to be her *chevalier d'honneur* and colonel of a regiment at the age of 31. Like many nobles bred at and for the court (such as his great friend Talleyrand, son of a *dame du palais*, who had risen as rapidly in the church as Narbonne in the army), he adapted to the revolution with ease. He proclaimed that his attachment to the King did not stop him loving the revolution and he put his words into practice.

With a mixture of tact and determination he ensured the departure of Madame Adélaïde and Madame Victoire from France in February 1791: if he had been at Varennes, the King's journey might have had a different ending. Later that year, with the help of his mistress, Madame de Staël, he became minister of war. He was popular, energetic and determined to make the constitutional monarchy work.

In a *mémoire* he read to the King and the ministers in February 1792 he attacked the welcome given to emigrés at court. The King should choose as court officials 'bourgeois men of property ... people whose choice proves that the King believes in the equality which he has sanctioned' and should maintain 'a suite such as the majesty of the throne requires'. The constellation of palaces around Paris was so much part of French royal life that it influenced the course of the revolution. In

---

[32] AN c 184, Laporte to Louis XVI, 7 January 1791, La Fayette to Louis XVI, 7 September 1791; Alma Söderhjelm (ed.), *Marie-Antoinette et Barnave. Correspondance secrète*, 1934, p. 196, Barnave to Marie-Antoinette, 1 December 1791.

July 1789 Louis XVI nearly left for Compiègne and in October for Rambouillet. In April 1791 his inability to go to Saint-Cloud was proof that he was a prisoner in Paris. In February 1792 Narbonne suggested that the King should make a journey to one of his palaces in the Ile de France to prove that he was free.

At the same time the court was under attack from other quarters. The great Girondin orator Vergniaud denounced it in letters and speeches as a 'continuous centre of intrigues'. A deputation from the Legislative Assembly complained that it had been received by courtiers in the Tuileries with 'the most mocking and insulting smiles', and that only one of the two *battants* (leaves) of the doors had been opened for them. Thus in 1792, in the fourth year of the revolution of liberty and equality, the routine of the King and the composition of the court still mattered.[33]

In fact a court which included Liancourt, Chauvelin, the Prince de Poix and Narbonne himself was not completely reactionary. If it had been its members would already have emigrated to Coblenz, where Monsieur and Artois were organising the forces of counter-revolution. Only 12 of the 28 senior court officials in the King's household emigrated before August 1792. Nor was the behaviour of the court a reliable guide to the feelings of the King. In 1771–4 six of the eight *premiers gentilshommes* and *capitaines des gardes* of Louis XV opposed his reassertion of royal authority and abolition of the *parlements*. Yet they kept their positions and the King pursued his policy. The Bourbons' good manners and self-control meant that they were polite to everyone, emigrés, *constitutionnels* and revolutionaries. They did not base their social life on a political system. They regarded their court as primarily a domestic and social institution, indispensable but not especially important. If possible it should be kept separate from politics.

Nevertheless in the winter of 1792 the government prepared to transform the court. The Legislative Assembly agreed to reimburse the existing court officials and servants for the value of their *charges* which came to about 33 million *livres*. Then Louis XVI would have felt free to appoint a new 'constitutional' household. Its organisation was under discussion in February and March 1792, when the new Garde constitu-

---

[33] Emile Dard, *Le Comte de Narbonne*, 1943, p. 33; AN C 185, *Mémoire lue au Conseil par M de Narbonne le 24 fevrier 1792*; Eugène Lintilhac, *Vergniaud*, 1920, pp. 63, 155; *Archives parlementaires*, XXXVIII, 197–200.

tionelle, commanded by the Duc de Brissac, the lover of Madame du Barry and one of the most faithful courtiers of Louis XVI (he had been *capitaine des cent-suisses de la garde*), came into service. A plan in Louis XVI's handwriting survives. The court would be smaller and simpler, but there were to be 18 chamberlains under a *grand* and a *premier chambellan*. One of his ministers Bertrand de Molleville drew up another plan based on 'the former almanach of Versailles and that of the court of London'. After 1789 the court of France began to lose its distinctive character and to resemble the other courts of Europe.[34]

However these plans were never put into operation, despite the eagerness of Laporte, intendant of the civil list, and the courtiers. Narbonne and his colleagues were dismissed in March. The declaration of war on 20 April against Austria on the advice of the new Girondin ministers ensured that money was no longer available. The war, the King's veto of measures against refractory priests and for an 'armed camp' near Paris, and his dismissal of the Girondin ministers on 13 June heightened tension in Paris. Popular fears mounted as the French army suffered its first defeats – the result of the incompetence of the Girondin ministers and the looting of munitions stores since 1789, rather than of treachery by the King. The Garde constitutionelle had to be disbanded since Brissac was sent for trial by the Legislative Assembly, and other officers were threatened with the same fate.

Throughout the hot threatening summer of 1792, people continued to go to court. Faithful old royalists like Malesherbes, Brissac's father-in-law the Duc de Nivernais, the Duc du Châtelet former colonel of the Gardes françaises and many others, could no more do without the court than an addict without drugs. Royalists still counted the smiles of Madame Elizabeth ('that smile was certainly for me', wrote the Comte de Paroy, remembering one Sunday at the Tuileries) and the nods of the Princesse de Lamballe. They thought it was a duty to show their loyalty by appearing at the Tuileries and regarded emigration as political suicide. A system of entry cards to the state appartments was reorganised in early June and again at the end of July. One list of 207 applicants for cards includes Malesherbes, Chateaubriand, the father of Lamartine

---

[34] Maréchale de Beauvau, *Souvenirs*, 1872, p. 15; AN c 184, plan for a new *maison du Roi*; Bertrand de Molleville to Louis XVI, 13 February 1792; an applicant for a court position in 1820 claimed that 12 chamberlains, *six d'epée et six de robe*, were appointed: AN o3 371, M. d'Osmont to Marquis de Lauriston.

and officers of the disbanded Garde constitutionelle. Their state of mind is indicated by the request of one Breton noble for a card in order to 'make a rampart of my body for the best of kings and his august family'. But most were not noble.[35]

There was no attempt to expand or systematise the entry cards and only a few hundred people, in addition to the royal households, received them (10 years later Bonaparte remembered that, although he was in Paris, he did not have a card). The numbers were too few to form an adequate defence but enough to alienate the Garde nationale to whom the defence of the palace was entrusted.

The first invasion of the Tuileries that year took place on 20 June. Armed crowds yelling for the recall of the Girondin ministers and screaming *A bas monsieur Véto! Au diable le Véto!* and worse invaded the royal apartments. Cannon were dragged up the staircase and the doors of the royal apartments were battered open. Having ordered his courtiers to leave, the King was accompanied only by his ministers, a few gardes nationaux and the devoted old Maréchal de Mouchy (the father of the Prince de Poix and a former governor of the palace of Versailles). The King, who for six hours stood by a window in the *oeil de boeuf*, the room next to his bedroom, disarmed the howling mobs by his good manners, by what revolutionaries called 'the treacherous gentleness of the tyrant'. He drank to the health of the nation and put on the red bonnet of the revolution. The next day his habitual politeness for once deserted him and he said 'Be quiet!' when the Mayor of Paris sought to excuse the invasion as a 'visit' by the people to give advice.[36]

After news of the outrage emerged, public opinion rallied to the King. But in the second half of July his hopes of survival were destroyed by the defeat of the French, the advance of the allies and the publication, on the Queen's advice, of the Brunswick Manifesto which threatened Paris with destruction if harm came to the royal family. Another 'visit' to the Tuileries was inevitable. It came in the morning of 10 August.

[35] Girault de Coursac, *Enquête*, pp. 462–3; Comte de Paroy, *Mémoires*, 1895, p. 254; AN c, 192, *Liste des personnes qui demandent des cartes*; AN c 218, anon., letter of 25 July 1792; cf. Louis Roulleau de La Roussière, *Un Officier de la Garde royale Brissac*, n.d. p. 24.
[36] Comte Remacle, *Relations secrètes des agents de Louis XVIII*, 1899, p. 222, despatch of 11 January 1803; AN c 222, *Déposition* by M. de Bourcet 27 June 1792; Girault de Coursac, *Enquête*, p. 498; Madame Elizabeth, *Correspondance*, p. 418–19, letter to Madame de Bombelles, 3 July 1792.

The regiment of Gardes suisses had been supine throughout the revolution. On 20 June it had retired to its quarters and done nothing. Now its senior officers proposed to defend the Tuileries with the aid of between two and three hundred royalists. Among them were the aged Maréchal de Mailly, the Baron de Vioménil and the Chevalier de Coigny, both of whom had been at Coblenz, former officers of the Garde constitutionelle like d'Hervilly and Pontlabbé who had the *entrées de la chambre*, and army officers such as de Boissieu and d'Attilly.

During the night of 9/10 August the palace was packed with troops and courtiers, but they could not cooperate. The Garde nationale suspected that the courtiers were counter-revolutionary; the courtiers feared that the Garde nationale was disloyal. As in May 1789 clothes heightened conflict: the gardes nationaux were irritated by the black tail-coats of the courtiers which formed such a contrast with their own tricolour uniforms. They had refused entry to some courtiers on the grounds that 'it was not the time to pay court to the King, that no one was admitted except in the uniform of the Garde nationale'.[37]

The cannoniers of the Garde nationale, the people with the biggest guns, deserted in the night. At five o'clock in the morning Louis XVI reviewed the Gardes suisses and what remained of the Garde nationale. The courtiers and the gardes suisses cried *Vive le Roi!* but the response was discouraging. Soon most of the Garde nationale deserted.

Nine hundred gardes suisses and a few hundred courtiers, however brave, were no match for an armed mob and the cannon of the Garde nationale. Louis XVI, who had sent all regiments to the front, felt that a defence of the Tuileries was useless. Having forbidden his forces to fire, he left at ten in the morning. He walked through the Tuileries garden with his family and a few guards and courtiers to the building of the Legislative Assembly. Back in the palace the senior officers of the Gardes suisses, Bachmann and Maillardoz, and the municipal authorities ordered that force should be met with force. Many courtiers, servants and gardes suisses died in the defence of the Tuileries and in the massacres and executions during the following weeks.[38] Particu-

---

[37] Girault de Coursac, *Enquête*, p. 515; AN c 192, *Dépositions* of Toupet and Frenot, 16 August 1792. This refusal by the Garde nationale may be the origin of constitutional royalists' allegations that they were expelled as 'counter-revolutionary' courtiers.

[38] Girault de Coursac, *Enquête*, pp. 558–9; AN w 249, *Déposition* of Jean Pierre Thierard; A. Lhôte de Selancey, *Des Charges de la maison civile des Rois de France*, 1847, p. 81.

larly horrible fates were reserved for Brissac and the Princesse de Lamballe. Brissac was murdered as he was being taken through the town of Versailles: his head was thrown through the window of Madame du Barry's house at Louveciennes. In Paris the Princesse de Lamballe was literally ripped to shreds; her heart was eaten by one of her murderers once he had found a restaurateur willing to cook it. Being a courtier was as dangerous as being a member of the royal family during the revolution.

The King and his family remained in the Legislative Assembly for three days, with a few devoted courtiers and servants such as the Prince de Poix and the *premier écuyer*, the Comte de Briges. On 13 August they were taken away to the Comte d'Artois's town residence the Temple, and lodged in a medieval tower in the garden. The Commune of Paris had decreed that 'all the people formerly in the service of the King and his family will be dismissed and that family will be surrounded only by people chosen by the mayor and the procurator of the commune'.[39] The revolution had imprisoned the King and appeared to have destroyed the court.

The court was not a major factor in the fall of the monarchy: the war, the emigration and the violence of the revolutionaries were more important. However, the court reveals much about the character and policies of the King. When the independent civil list replaced the old *ministère de la maison du Roi* in 1790, he had been advised to use it as a political weapon to strengthen the monarchy. He now had his own income free of ministerial control, and the opportunity to win 'people who were his and only his'. Many people believed that 'it is your ministers who have ruined everything', since they had kept the credit for government decisions for themselves.

Louis XVI chose as intendant of the civil list Arnaud de Laporte, a former intendant-general of the navy – Louis XVI's favourite government department. Born in 1737, like Brissac educated at the lycée Louis-le-Grand, he was honest, moderate and devoted to the King. Laporte acted as the King's agent, within the context of the constitution, trying to direct public opinion and strengthen the monarchy. He put the King in touch with Mirabeau whom he described, in March 1791, as 'the only man who, in the present circumstances, which are most critical,

[39] Beauchesne, *Louis XVII*, I, 219, 169n.

can really serve Your Majesty'.[40] Mirabeau had previously been working for the Queen (through Mercy-Argenteau) and Monsieur (through Lévis), not the King.

The role of Laporte and the civil list show that the policies of the King and the rest of the royal family were independent and conflicting. Someone like d'Angiviller was constantly begging the King to have 'perfect union' with the Queen. But this had not existed since the day of their marriage. The Queen had been used as a channel for favours and promotions, but had not been consulted over government policy. She distrusted Laporte, as she had previous favourite ministers of her husband like Maurepas and Vergennes. In 1791 she told Fersen to communicate with her by a different channel, since 'M. de La Porte, who takes everything to the King, had given him your parcel' – a parcel containing newspapers with messages written by Fersen in invisible ink.[41]

Whereas the Queen wanted foreign intervention and sent money and jewels abroad for safe-keeping, there was no connection between the civil list and the plans of the emigration and the foreign powers. Louis XVI gave no money to his brothers, only small sums towards the education of his nephews, the Ducs d'Angoulême and de Berri in Turin. The *gardes du corps* were paid only if they produced certificates of residence in France. The sole link between the civil list and the emigration was the payment made by the treasurer Septeuil, one of the four *premiers valets de chambre*, for the journey of the Queen's secretary Goguelat to Vienna in February 1792. But this was also the only occasion when it was the Queen, not the King, who gave Septeuil an order. Laporte was sufficiently sure that he had acted in accordance with the constitution to take the registers of the civil list to the Legislative Assembly on 10 August: they have since disappeared, and he was guillotined on 24 August.[42]

Laporte was more important to the King than his courtiers. As a child Louis XVI had written that courtiers were driven by 'sordid self-interest, base flattery, furious jealousy, a perpetual intrigue of cunning

---

[40] AN c 185, d'Angiviller to Louis XVI, 25 April 1790; AN c 183, *Reflexions*, 15 June 1790; AN c 187, Laporte to Louis XVI, 2 March 1791.

[41] AN c 185, d'Angiviller to Louis XVI, 2 March 1790, cf. his letter of 5 March 1790, where he writes *la reine, qui ne fait qu'un avec Votre Majesté*; letter of Marie-Antoinette to Fersen, 7 December 1791, sold at Christies, 5 May 1982.

[42] P. Girault de Coursac, 'Fausse lettre et fausse témoignage', *Découverte*, xxv, March 1979, p. 9; *idem*, *Enquête*, pp. 36, 162.

and lies'. His experiences as King had not caused him to change his mind. An example of his contempt and distrust for his own courtiers was his fierce rebuke to the Prince de Poix who was trying to persuade him to wear military uniform to review the Garde nationale: 'You are not at all in my confidence ... you are often mistaken about people and things.'[43] He never adopted military uniform, not even that of the Garde nationale, as he was urged to after 20 June 1792. He ordered courtiers who had come to defend him to leave the Tuileries, both in February 1791 and June 1792, although they begged to stay.[44] He preferred to be surrounded by the established authorities, the ministers and the Garde nationale, rather than by his court.

The most important people in the King's life were his ministers. They saw the King for longer, and more privately, than anyone except his family. The *ministre de la maison* was more powerful than the grandest court official. Court officials lived in the same buildings, the palaces of Versailles, Fontainebleau and Compiègne, as ministers and saw them constantly. But it was courtiers who waited in ministers' antechambers, not the other way around. Even the most powerful families at court, the Rohan or the Noailles, had little influence on the nomination of ministers. The only court officials who became ministers, the Prince de Montbarey *capitaine des suisses de la garde de Monsieur*, the Maréchal de Beauvau, a *capitaine des gardes* and friend of Necker who was briefly a *ministre d'état* in 1789 and Narbonne did not owe their ministerial to their court office. The names of some of the senior court officials, Richelieu, Fleury, Chamillart de La Suze show that ministers' families infiltrated the court rather than the other way around. The longest serving minister of Louis XVI, Vergennes, foreign minister from 1774 until his death in 1787, was the minister with least contact with the court – although he did obtain the office of *capitaine des gardes de la porte* for one of his sons.

A court is an institution which lives on emotions. Its purpose is to raise the prestige of the monarch and to satisfy feelings such as ambition, vanity and love of splendour. These emotions remained important

[43] Louis XVI, *Réflexions*, p. 167; 'Un Conseiller mal écouté', *Découverte*, XVIII, June 1977, p. 43.
[44] Duc de Lévis-Mirepoix, *Aventures d'une famille française*, 1949, p. 279, Duc to Duchesse de Lévis, 21(?) June 1791.

during the revolution, as the King knew. In 1791 he wrote to his brothers to explain his acceptance of the constitution that: 'The bourgeois sees nothing above him; vanity is satisfied, this new pleasure eliminates everything else.' But Louis XVI did not use vanity as a weapon. In 1792 he wrote to the infuriated Legislative Assembly, about the ceremonial for its reception in the Tuileries, that 'attaching no importance to a matter of this nature', he left its regulation to the Assembly itself.[45] He was more interested in the great issues of war, religion and the fate of the poor than in what went on in his own palace. His court helped to alienate both the old and the new ruling classes from the monarchy.

Louis XVI was a practising Christian for whom the poor were as important as the rich and servants as real as court officials. His hunting diary, which gives detailed descriptions of six or seven hunts a month, is exceptionally egalitarian: servants such as Pierre Flocard and Parago are mentioned as often as the huntsman Monsieur de Caqueray. His last thought before he was executed was for his servants who had lost their livelihoods. Years later his surviving family still called bad weather *le temps de la mort de Motte*, after one of his personal servants, who had died during a storm in 1769 when he was a boy.[46]

The King's indifference to his court, and failure to use vanity as a weapon, were luxuries which no monarch at the end of the eighteenth century could afford. In an age of political uncertainty a court could be used to emphasise the King's commitment to a policy, to win or reward supporters and to increase the prestige of the monarchy. In the middle of the revolution La Fayette, Barnave and many other politicians showed intense interest in the organisation and etiquette of the court, and many people still wanted to go there. Far from being incompatible with the revolution, the court was particularly important because of it. This would be understood by a monarch who would pay minute attention to every aspect of his court, namely Napoleon I.

[45] Musée de l'Histoire de France, Louis XVI to Comtes de Provence and d'Artois, September 1791; *Archives parlementaires*, xxxviii, 199, Louis XVI to Legislative Assembly, 6 February 1792.
[46] Louis XVI, *Chasses du Cerf Années 1789 et 1790*, sold at Sothebys Monte Carlo, 28 February 1987; Girault de Coursac, *Enquête*, p. 609; Louis XVIII, *Correspondance privée*, 1836, pp. 30–41, Louis XVIII to d'Avaray, 2 December 1810.

CHAPTER 2

Crossing the desert

Je recommande à la bienfaisance de la nation toutes les personnes qui m'étaient attachées.

Louis XVI to the Convention, 20 January 1793

The royal family reacted to life in prison with the same astonishing self-possession it had shown throughout the revolution. Madame Elizabeth mended the King's clothes. The King and Queen gave their children lessons and played skittles. The proclamation of a republic on 22 September 1792 and the execution of the King in front of silent crowds on 21 January 1793 appeared to seal the fate of the monarchy and the court. The Queen and Madame Elizabeth were guillotined 10 and 15 months later respectively. Louis XVII died in 1795, still a prisoner in the Temple: his sole acts as King had been to take precedence of his mother and to sign a secret letter to his uncle 'Louis', like his predecessors, rather than 'Louis-Charles', as he was baptised. Only his sister Madame Royale survived.

The material possessions of the court suffered almost as much as the royal family. Within a few days of the fall of the monarchy the crown jewels were stolen from the *garde-meuble* on the place de la Révolution (now Concorde). The last horses in the royal stables were given to the first generals of the Republic. The palaces were used as schools or museums or left derelict: Marly was pulled down to be sold as building materials. Between 1793 and 1795 a series of sensational sales (which for once justify the phrase 'sale of the century') disposed of most of the royal furniture at ludicrous prices. So many fleurs-de-lis were chipped off the fronts of buildings in Paris that it looked like a city 'besieged and battered'.[1]

---

[1] Henri Lemoine, 'La Fin des écuries royales', *Revue de l'histoire de Versailles*, December 1933,

However, a few years of republican rule were not enough to destroy the court of France. Moreover there was no wholesale onslaught on the personnel of the royal households or their property (perhaps because so many had supported the revolution). Many continued to live in Paris after the fall of the monarchy. In the prison of the Temple, the royal family was supplied with food cooked by former employees of the royal kitchens and of the Comte d'Artois. Their last letter to Monsieur and Artois in Hamm was smuggled out and taken abroad by Monsieur de Jarjayes, a colonel on the general staff and former director of Louis XVI's military office, who was also husband of one of Marie-Antoinette's *premières femmes de chambre* and her intermediary with Barnave.[2] Senior servants such as Silvestre, *premier valet de garde-robe* and librarian of Monsieur, or Rabel, *garçon de la chambre du Roi*, went straight into government ministries in 1792. Many of the court craftsmen bought back the furniture they had made, just as footmen hung on to their liveries, in the hope of better times to come.

Thierry de Ville d'Avray had died in the September massacres. However, using the bureaucracy of the first republic to mitigate its brutality, his enterprising widow obtained a formal certificate from his murderers that they had killed him; and this document, proving that he had not emigrated, enabled her to keep some of her fortune. She and her son led a quiet, prosperous existence in Paris once the terror was over. They still possessed relics and documents from the court, locks of the royal family's hair or the list of *entrées chez le Roi*. This extraordinary document stops in 1792 but starts again in 1814, as if nothing had happened in the intervening 22 years.[3] Other servants were supported by the republic, as Louis XVI had hoped. Because the *charges* of the *maison du Roi* had never been repaid, a law was passed by the Convention in August 1793 giving pensions to former employees of the civil

---

p. 206; Verlet, *French Royal Furniture*, p. 55; Henry Swinburne, *The Courts of Europe at the close of the Last Century*, 2 vols., 1895, II, 183.

[2] Beauchesne, *Louis XVII*, I, 260 n.; AN C 183, *Brevet* of 1 April 1792 appointing Jarjayes, *colonel d'état-major* and *directeur adjoint du dépôt général de la guerre, directeur* of the *cartes, plans et mémoires militaires destinés au travail habituel du Roi.*

[3] AN o3 353, *Etat des anciens services des divers officiers de la Chambre du Roi*, 1818; AN o3 355 doss. Silvestre, *État des services*, 1815; TVA, *Entrées chez le Roi* and death certificate.

list if their revenues from their *charges* had been less than 1,000 *livres* a year. These pensions were still being paid in the next century.

The officials of the court also survived, although they did not receive pensions from the republic. The fates of Brissac and the Princesse de Lamballe were exceptional. Relatively few other senior court officials, such as the Maréchal de Mouchy (plate 6) and the Comtesse d'Ossun, *dame d'atours de la Reine*, lost their lives. The others emigrated or lay low.

For example the Prince de Poix, the Marquis de Dreux-Brézé and the Baron de Septeuil managed to escape from France after the fall of the monarchy and reach England. Despite the collapse of their world, and of their standard of living, they were astonishingly cheerful. 'Pillaged, my dear, devastated, in one word sacked from top to bottom', was the news Dreux-Brézé brought Septeuil of his château in France in September 1792. They competed as to who had lost more, and concluded: 'Really France is no longer habitable.' The triumph of the republican armies and the reign of terror confirmed their opinion.

However, even after the fall of the monarchy the frontier between the worlds of the revolution and of royalism was not as impassable as people pretended. In fact Dreux-Brézé returned to France before emigrating again. Thanks to the skill of his faithful agent Monsieur Badelier at arranging false certificates of residence, he lost relatively little property: his estates in Anjou still belong to his descendants. Dreux-Brézé's experience was more typical than that of the Ducs de Guiche and de Richelieu, who lost almost everything: the figure of the faithful agent who saved the family fortunes was surprisingly common. Like most court officials, Dreux-Brézé remained loyal to the Bourbons. He corresponded with Monsieur, and went to see him in Verona in 1795 after he had assumed the title Louis XVIII on his nephew's death. He then retired to his estates. The world of the republic was not wholly alien to him. When his brother-in-law the republican general Custine was guillotined, he expressed more regret than hostility.[4]

Once the reign of terror was over many other court officials, for example the Prince de Poix and the Duc de Liancourt, also returned

---

[4] Alphonse Gautier, *Etudes sur la liste civile en France*, 1883, p. 18; Baron Portalis, *Le Peintre Danloux*, 1909, p. 68; letters of Dreux-Brézé kindly communicated by Comte A. de Dreux-Brézé, especially those of 2 December 1793 and 4 January 1794 to his sister.

to France and tried to lead a normal life. They now spent more time in the country running their estates, but many recovered *hôtels* in Paris: the most hospitable house in Paris for nobles in the early years of the century was the Hôtel de Luynes in the Faubourg Saint-Germain, home of the Duc de Luynes (a Senator) and his wife, a former *dame du palais* of Marie-Antoinette who had supported the first stages of the revolution. One visitor thought it was like the court of France under the old regime.[5] The Maréchale de Beauvau and her daughter the Princesse de Poix also reopened their salons in the Faubourg Saint-Honoré.

A few former court officials decided to forget their family traditions. Liancourt devoted himself to agricultural and industrial experiments. Chauvelin, a *maître de la garde-robe* of Louis XVI, transformed himself into an ambassador of the republic and enemy of the Bourbons. The son of Septeuil became a *chevalier* of the Empire. The two grandest families of the old court, the Rohan (who for most of the eighteenth century had held the posts of *grand aumônier* and *capitaine-lieutenant des gendarmes de la garde*) and the Lorraine, went to live in Austria. The last of the Lorraine, the Prince de Lambesc, *grand écuyer* of Louis XVI, simply swapped courts and became captain of the archer guard of the Emperor Francis II. The Duc de Richelieu avoided the court of Louis XVIII in exile. He entered Russian service and became Governor of Odessa. Including those families which failed through natural extinction, perhaps one-fifth of the old officials broke their ties with the court.

For others, however, the bond of court service was so strong that it survived political hostility. When Monsieur fled to Coblenz in 1791, he hid his plans from Lévis who was in waiting, as Lévis still supported the revolution. He resigned soon after and was replaced by d'Avoray, Monsieur's new favourite. But they exchanged New Year greetings across the political divide in 1792 and Lévis remained a royalist. He was in the Tuileries on 20 June 1792, and emigrated soon after. He was wounded fighting against the revolution with the emigrés and did not return to France until early the next century.

Other supporters of the constitutional monarchy of 1791–2 avoided the emigrés. Narbonne continued to support the principles of the revolution even though he avoided the guillotine only by being smuggled out of France by Madame de Staël. However, court service remained a real

<hr>

[5] *La Rue Saint-Dominique*, Musée Rodin, 1984, p. 32.

force for him. Despite their political differences, he was with his wife and mother at the death-bed of his exiled mistress Madame Adélaïde, in Trieste in 1800.

Since courtiers were primarily personal servants, and every person with money had them, even the republic acknowledged the bond linking them to the Bourbons. In 1795 Madame Royale was released from the prison of the Temple and allowed to leave for Vienna in the company of Hue, an *huissier de la chambre* who had attended Louis XVI in the Temple and her intriguing former *sous-gouvernante* Madame de Soucy. On the journey Madame Royale may have said something indiscreet about divisions within the royal family or events in their prison, since Madame de Soucy was still asking her for large sums of money, and receiving them, in the 1830s.[6]

The tie of personal service was even stronger for those court officials who had emigrated and fought in the Armée des princes. The horrors of the revolution transformed their loyalty to the Bourbons into a passion. At Coblenz in 1791–2 many more people had come into direct contact with Monsieur and the Comte d'Artois than before, through their households, their receptions, above all their shared political commitment. New courtiers were appointed to replace those who stayed in France and for the first time in their lives the princes had aides-de-camp.

After the defeat of the allies and the emigrés in 1792, the princes could no longer afford large households. In 1795 Monsieur had a household of 26 at Verona, including d'Avaray, the faithful *maître de la garde-robe* who had organised his escape from Paris, and four personal servants, Peronnet, Coutent, Guignet and Dubreuil, who remained with him for the rest of his life. His wife, brother, sister-in-law and nephews also maintained households in exile, whose size was limited by lack of money rather than of potential courtiers. Wherever they were, in England, Russia or the Holy Roman Empire, none of the royal family had cause to feel deserted. The monarchy was still alive.

When Monsieur became King in 1795, in accordance with tradition his personal household was dissolved and he inherited the *maison du*

---

[6] Louis XVIII, *Relation d'un voyage de Paris à Coblentz*, 1823, p. 42; Monsieur to Lévis, 19 January 1792 (kindly communicated by M. Alain de Grolée-Virville); Emile Dard, *Le Comte de Narbonne*, 1943, p. 142; Andre Castelot, *Le Secret de Madame Royale*, 1949, p. 314.

Roi. Its senior officials were remarkably faithful. The Cardinal de Mont-morency-Laval, *grand aumônier*, the Ducs de Duras, de Villequier and de Fleury, *premiers gentilshommes*, spent long periods at his court in exile and sometimes acted as his political agents. The Duc de Guiche (who inherited the title Duc de Gramont in 1804), *capitaine des gardes* in waiting on 6 October 1789, and son-in-law of the Duchesse de Polignac, rarely left the King. Hue served as a *premier valet de chambre* and later *trésorier-général* of Louis XVIII. Excluding courtiers' servants, and the households of other members of the royal family, there were 108 people in the *maison du Roi* at Mittau in Courland in 1799–1801, and 45 at Hartwell in England in 1809. There were so many people at Hartwell that the attics had to be subdivided and huts built in the stable courtyards to lodge them all. Even in the poverty of exile constant attention was necessary to stop courtiers abusing their right to free food and lighting as they had at Versailles.[7]

The marriage of Madame Royale, daughter of Louis XVI, and her first cousin the Duc d'Angoulême, son of the Comte d'Artois, at Mittau in 1799 shows the exiled court in action. It was a relatively propitious moment, since Tsar Paul I of Russia was, temporarily, paying Louis XVIII a generous subsidy. The selection of the princess's household revealed her uncles' opposing characters. Artois wanted to appoint a large household, including friends and relations of his old friend the Duchesse de Polignac, who had died in exile. Louis XVIII, always more realistic and sensitive to public opinion, warned him, in a letter which cannot have been agreeable for Artois to read, that such names would have a bad effect. They would convince people that the restoration 'would bring back the old abuses and that there would still be the same people receiving all the favours etc., etc., even at a time when we are almost incapable of bestowing them on anyone'. He pointed out that the public felt that the Duchesse de Polignac was 'one of the causes of the revolution by the immense number of favours accumulated by her family and her friends and by the influence exerted on government policy, at a period so close to that of our disasters'.

---

[7] AN 03 2652, 3, *Aides de Camp de Monsieur*, 1792; Archives du Ministère des Affaires Etrangères, Quai d'Orsay (henceforward referred to as AAE) 630 f. 136, note by d'Avaray 1795; AN 03 2681, *Etats de la Maison du Roi*, 1801, 1809; Baron Hue, *Souvenirs*, 1903, pp. 242–5, 263.

In the end, in accordance with Bourbon tradition, the princess's *dame d'honneur* was the Duchesse de Serent, wife of her husband's former governor. Forceful, pious and a former lady-in-waiting of Madame Elizabeth, she had come especially from Paris with her daughters and remained *dame d'honneur* until her death in 1823. One of her daughters became a lady-in-waiting of the Duchesse d'Angoulême, the other served the Queen, Louis XVIII's difficult drunken wife Marie-Joséphine de Savoie.

The princess finally arrived from Vienna with Hue. They were met at the frontier by the Duc de Villequier, the *premier gentilhomme* in waiting. The marriage was a court ceremony, performed in the palace of the Dukes of Courland by the Cardinal de Montmorency-Laval. The marriage contract was drawn up by the Comte de Saint-Priest, *ministre de la maison* of Louis XVIII, as he had been of Louis XVI. A thousand miles from France, 10 years after the beginning of the revolution, the machinery of the court was still working; and since this was the court of France, there was also a scandal. Marie-Joséphine was passionately, perhaps physically attached to her *lectrice* Madame de Gourbillon. Despite the King's orders she brought Madame de Gourbillon with her to Mittau. Louis XVIII persuaded the Russian governor of Mittau to expel Madame de Gourbillon before she reached the palace. Marie-Joséphine raged and sulked but could do nothing. Madame de Gourbillon had her revenge by helping to persuade Paul I to expel Louis XVIII two years later.[8]

The court was a living mechanism to such an extent that Louis XVIII made several appointments in exile. In 1795 he sacked as *capitaines des gardes* two Noailles famous for their liberal opinions, the Duc d'Ayen and the Prince de Poix (d'Avaray was appointed in their place). It was a time when he was committed to the most extreme emigré views and this move horrified moderate royalists. One journalist, Mallet du Pan, wrote: 'Of all the policies which have been suggested to the King since the death of his nephew, the one which has most alienated opinion is the disgrace of the Prince de Poix, *capitaine des gardes* of Louis XVI.' In 1808 Monseigneur de Talleyrand-Périgord, Archbishop of Reims and Talleyrand's uncle, became *grand aumônier* on the death

---

[8] Ernest Daudet, *Madame Royale*, 1912, pp. 238–40; Comte de Saint-Priest, *Mémoires*, 2 vols., 1929, II, 193; Philip Mansel, *Louis XVIII*, 1981, pp. 87–8, 106–7.

of the Cardinal de Montmorency-Laval. The next year the Comte de Blacas, a loyal and intelligent noble from Provence, became *grand maître de la garde-robe* despite Liancourt's refusal to resign. Blacas soon replaced d'Avaray as the King's confidant, friend and political adviser.[9]

The *maison du Roi* gave the King a semi-royal existence and a reservoir of loyal agents and intermediaries. D'Avaray was the King's most important political adviser throughout the emigration. The Abbé Fleuriel, a chaplain, acted as his secretary. The Duc de Fleury tried to win over the Director Barras for the King. The Duc d'Havré, *chevalier d'honneur* of Marie-Joséphine, dealt, not always wisely, with the double agents swarming around the court like Madame de Bonneuil, Fauche-Borel and Perlet.

The court also survived as a social institution. Coblenz, like the court of Louis XVI in the Tuileries, had witnessed a lowering of barriers within the elite of birth and wealth. At dinner with the princes, it was noted with amazement, 'epaulettes decide who is invited'. As in the great military monarchies of the East like Austria and Russia, service was beginning to replace birth as the principle deciding admission to the court. At Coblenz, and throughout the emigration, the *habit habillé* was abandoned for military uniform. This was a practical decision – there was a war on – with important social consequences. Uniform was cheap and united its wearers in the service of the King: the *habit habillé* had emphasised the difference between the *noblesse présentée*, the *noblesse de robe* and those too poor to afford it.

After Louis XVIII arrived in England in 1807 there was a revival of court life: for the first time since 1792 he was in a country with a large number of French people. He dined in public on certain days at Hartwell House in Buckinghamshire, and his brother and the Duc de Berri, although they lived in London, kept apartments there as if it was a royal palace. In 1809 a reception was held near London for all men 'indistinctly'. However, if rules for men were abolished they were maintained for women; only those presented at court before 1790 were admitted.[10]

[9] A. Michel, *Correspondance de Mallet du Pan avec la Cour de Vienne*, 2 vols., 1884, I, 309, letter of 13 September 1795; F. G. de La Rochefoucauld, *Vie du Duc de Liancourt*, 1827, pp. 46, 59.
[10] P. de Vaissière, *Lettres d'Aristocrates*, 1923, p. 367, Bengy de Puyvallée to M. d'Abzac, 23 November 1791; Mansel, *Louis XVIII*, p. 148.

The survival of the court in exile was helped by the self-confidence and optimism of the royal family and its officials. The traumas of the revolutions and the emigration had strengthened their belief in the monarchy. If its abolition led to terror, war, atheism, inflation and the loss of property, then clearly the monarchy had to be restored. Until the Declaration of Brunswick Louis XVI had shared this optimism. In 1790 he suspended his hunt but continued to pay the huntsmen, in the hope that they would soon be hunting again. The irrepressible lavishness of the court of France, as well as his own optimism, are shown by his remark in 1790: 'When I shall give Elizabeth a household.' (Madame Elizabeth had 17 ladies-in-waiting and 19 *femmes de chambre*. But she was still considered not to have her own household, since she did not have a separate kitchen staff and stables, but used the King's.) In 1792 Brissac was cheerful; he was rich, Madame du Barry was his mistress and, as commander of the Garde constitutionelle, he hoped to restore Paris to Louis XVI as his ancestor had 300 years earlier to Henri IV.[11] On 9/10 August the royalists in the Tuileries were keener to defend the palace than the King himself.

The death of Louis XVI had been in a way a relief. His simplicity, love of the poor and commitment to the constitution of 1791 had aroused little sympathy among his own courtiers. They used his death as a political weapon. La Fare, an emigré bishop, helped his servant Cléry write *Journal de ce qui s'est passé à la Tour du Temple* (1798), which was one of the best-sellers of the day. It helped create the legend of Louis XVI the Martyr King, which resanctified and repopularised the French monarchy. Awkward questions about the vicious conflict between Louis XVI and his brothers in 1791–2 were ignored. Monsieur, now regarded by the emigrés as Louis XVIII, had many of the trump cards in his household: Hue, the Abbé Edgeworth, Louis XVI's confessor who became his own and, after her marriage to the Duc d'Angoulême in 1799, Louis XVI's daughter as well.

After the death of Louis XVI the revolution could be attributed to his weakness and the wickedness of his subjects. Dreux-Brézé thought the revolution was basically a question of ambition: 'It is always the same thing, *Otez-vous de là que je m'y mette*', he wrote in 1795. Lévis

[11] AN o 1 201, *Décisions du Roi*, 23 August, 18 September 1790; Portalis, *Le Peintre Danloux*, p. 185.

attributed the success of the revolution to the fatal combination of a weak king and a factious assembly. It in no way shook his confidence in his own class or in the necessity of a court. He attributed the failure of the King's flight to Varennes to the absence of a *grand seigneur* 'accustomed to speak to him freely'. He believed that the court was the natural support of the throne, that to maintain respect for royalty and the rules of etiquette was the first duty of a monarch, and that the reasons for the revolutions were the policies of the ministers and the desertion of the Gardes françaises, not any fundamental weakness in the monarchy. Even on 10 August in the Tuileries the monarchy might have been saved but for Louis XVI's 'misconceived humanity'.[12] The role of *grands seigneurs* like Choiseul and Bouillé in the failure of the flight to Varennes, the courtiers' lack of respect for the monarchy, the sabotage of Louis XVI's efforts to reform by members of the clergy and the nobility, the impossibility of armed resistance on 10 August, and the political conflicts within the royal family, were conveniently forgotten.

Lévis was so self-confident that in about 1807, although basically royalist and aloof from the Empire, he submitted a programme for a new nobility to the Emperor. The Senate should be hereditary and the new nobility 'accessible to all forms of merit' particularly to the old nobility and members of the Légion d'honneur. Financiers and *les gens à paroles* (in other words lawyers) should be excluded. He said that France now had 'a great monarch but no monarchy': the powers of the Legislative Body should be extended. Like many pre-1789 nobles he wanted a powerful monarchy maintaining class distinctions, but he was also a liberal.

Royalists' conviction that the revolution was simply a passing phase received confirmation by the end of the reign of terror in 1794 and the establishment of a more moderate government, the Directory, in 1795. The Directors began to surround themselves with the shadow of a court. Their official residence was the Luxembourg palace, which was renamed the Palais Directorial. It was restored, and a splendid new staircase constructed by Chalgrin, the architect of its former owner Monsieur. In December 1795 it was refurnished with some of the unsold

---

[12] Letter of Dreux-Brézé to his sister, 26 July 1795; *Lévis*, pp. 328, 334–7, 369, 442–4.

royal furniture.[13] The Directors began to hold receptions for government officials and officers, who wore the official costumes created for them in 1795. The most important of the Directors, Barras, also entertained and hunted on a princely scale in another former property of Monsieur, Grosbois, south-east of Paris. Splendour was returning to France.

Thus by the end of the century the world of the court survived in three forms. In Paris the Directors lived in a palace and held receptions. The royal family in exile maintained households which were direct continuations of those existing before they left France. In France most of the former officials and servants of the court survived with their traditions, ambitions and, in some cases, fortunes intact.

Meanwhile in the rest of Europe monarchy was recovering its strength and confidence. Whereas in the second half of the eighteenth century in almost every country in Europe aristocrats had attacked the monarchy, they were now drawing closer together in face of the common peril of revolution. In Lévis's words, monarchy was beginning to be seen as an indispensable necessity rather than a matter of choice.

[13] AN AF IV (Papers of the Secrétairerie d'Etat) 1311, *Note pour S. M. l'Empereur seul*; Verlet, *French Royal Furniture*, p. 62.

CHAPTER 3

❧ ❧

Napoleon I

Chaque jour Bonaparte ajoute à l'étiquette de sa maison et de sa représentation.
Report to Louis XVIII from his agents in Paris, 1 October 1802

Parisians said that there was nothing but Bonaparte in the constitution proclaimed after he seized power from the descredited Directors in November 1799. Nevertheless his government was at first relatively moderate. It was not certain that the First Consul was aiming for the throne when he moved into the Tuileries on 18 February 1800.*

The palace had suffered since the departure of the King on the morning of 10 August. It had been partially pillaged and a guillotine had been erected on the cour du Carrousel. The Convention had sat in the old royal theatre and the Committee of Public Safety in what had been the Queen's apartments facing the garden (it soon had so much work that it took over the King's rooms on the floor above).[1] It was again attacked in May 1793, when the Girondin deputies were expelled and in 1795, when a royalist mob was defeated by troops under the command of Barras and Bonaparte.

In 1795 one of the Directory's two legislatures, the Council of Ancients had replaced the Convention in the former theatre. It was there that, on the eve of his coup d'état, Bonaparte had made a speech denouncing the Directors and promising 'a republic founded on real liberty'. In 1800 the Tuileries's extraordinary history as a seat of governments and a spectator of their overthrow made Madame Campan call it 'the most famous palace in the universe'. Bonaparte would add to its celebrity.

---

* For a fuller account of the Napoleonic court, see the author's *The Eagle in Splendour: Napoleon I and his Court*, 1987.
[1] G. Lenôtre, *The Tuileries*, 1934, pp. 148, 151, 153.

He possessed a taste for splendour and luxury, and thought of these as useful political weapons. Pierre Fontaine, who had studied in Rome in the 1780s, was his official architect, as he later was of Louis XVIII, Charles X and Louis-Philippe. His diary is a unique record of the process of giving architectural expression to political power. He records in October 1801 that 'The First Consul is very interested in the decoration of the apartments of the château of the Tuileries.' He wants to enjoy 'the pleasures of his taste and the magnificence due to his rank'.[2] Bonaparte had the Tuileries cleared of institutions and individuals not connected to his personal service and it soon looked like a palace again. By 1802 an English visitor was 'much struck with its splendour and magnificence'. Furniture which had belonged to Louis XVI and Marie-Antoinette was installed in the private apartments of Bonaparte and his wife. He also ordered new furniture from Jacob-Desmalter, the great cabinet-maker of the early nineteenth century. Madame Bonaparte's apartments were superb, upholstered in purple and yellow silk, with gold fringes. The outer walls, however, still bore the scars left by the bullets and cannon-balls of 10 August.

He soon acquired another element of a court, a personal household staffed by members of the elite of birth or wealth. In November 1801 four prefects of the palace, Didelot, de Luçay, de Rémusat and Salmatoris-Roussillon were appointed to run the palace. They had no direct experience of the court of Versailles, but came from the recently ennobled (Didelot and de Luçay), the *noblesse de robe* (Rémusat) and – a sign of the growth of foreign influence on the French court – from the court of Piedmont, where Salmatoris-Roussillon had been a *maître des cérémonies*.

By the end of 1801 Bonaparte was also holding regular receptions for the elite of the republic and foreign ambassadors in the Tuileries, on the days he reviewed his guard in the courtyard outside. His receptions were completely different from those of Louis XVI. All distinctions were based on the official hierarchy of the state, rather than proofs of noble lineage. Rank was revealed by space rather than time, by which room a courtier could enter in the state apartments rather than when

---

[2] Madame Campan, *Correspondance ... avec la Reine Hortense*, 2 vols., 1835, I, 28, letter of 29 January 1800; P. L. F. Fontaine, *Journal*, 2 vols., 1987, I, 35, entry for 4 October 1801.

he was admitted into the king's bedroom. There was now a system behind the *entrées*. Officers down to the rank of captain were admitted into the fourth room preceding the *salle des consuls* (formerly the king's *grand cabinet*), field officers into the third, generals into the second, councillors of state and ambassadors into the first. Such receptions were more satisfying to human vanity than those of Louis XVI. Admission was now a right rather than a favour, and provided visible evidence of official success. The First Consul's position at the head of the hierarchy of the state was plain for all to see.

Although he was still only First Consul of the Republic, with two colleagues, Cambacérès and Lebrun, Bonaparte's receptions were very royal. An Irish visitor wrote in April 1802 that 'The etiquette of a court and court dress are strictly observed; and everyone agrees that the splendour of the court of the Tuileries is much greater than ever was the old court of France.' He noted that the First Consul tried to talk to everyone in the *salle des généraux*, and found that he 'has more unaffected Dignity than I could conceive in Man. His address is the gentlest and most prepossessing you can conceive, which is seconded by the greatest fund of Levée conversation that I suppose any Person ever possessed.'[3] Unlike Louis XVI, he talked to people coming to court, and used such conversations as a source of information and a means of proclaiming his policies.

The First Consul's dinners were also very grand. Another Irish visitor reported after a dinner for 200: 'There never was a court more manacled by the observances of Etiquette than the Tuileries.' Count Armfelt, the former favourite of Gustavus III, who had known Versailles under Louis XVI, was amazed by the 'grandiose public splendour, far greater than what you see in our time in most courts ... I find it extraordinary that the first official of the Republic inspires so much respect and behaves with such pride, pomp and ceremony.'[4]

But Bonaparte had a sequence of military, political and administrative triumphs to his credit. France was at his feet and he could do what he liked. In 1802 Bonaparte became First Consul for life and began

[3] Anon., *A Tour in France*, 1802, p. 33; J. G. Lemaistre, *A Rough Sketch of Modern Paris*, 2nd edn, 1803, pp. 159–61; McClintock Papers, John Leslie Foster to Harriet Countess de Salis, 6 April 1802.
[4] Catherine Wilmot, *An Irish Peer on the Continent*, 1920, p. 72, letter of 19 June 1802; Ernest Daudet, *Un Drame d'amour à la cour de Suède*, 1913, p. 257, diary for June 1801.

to use the former royal palace of Saint-Cloud rather than his wife's house at Malmaison as a country residence. She was given four ladies-in-waiting, Mesdames de Talhouët, de Luçay, de Rémusat and de Lauriston. Some of the basic elements of a court, outward splendour, formal receptions and personal households for the ruler and his family had returned to Paris. Bonaparte was clearly aiming for the throne.

Public opinion seems to have welcomed the return of a court. Few people now cared about the republic and its ideals. They had suffered so much, only to produce the result that, as Madame de Staël wrote to Necker, 'the people are more oppressed than ever'. A court in Paris meant jobs in the new households for Parisians and a revival of what the *Gazette de France* called 'a number of branches of industry fallen with the monarchy'.[5] The furniture, embroidery, china, and tapestry trades had struggled to survive since 1792, helped by foreign customers who still regarded Paris as the capital of luxury in Europe: the old royal factories of Sèvres, Aubusson, Gobelins and Beauvais still existed. But no private patrons could take the place of a French court. Moreover a court, with its standards of luxury and display, would encourage the people going to it to spend more on clothes and carriages.

The return of conspicuous consumption was greeted with joy. A Russian visitor Countess Golovine, whose livery resembled the former *petite livrée* of the King, claims that when Parisians saw it in the streets they shouted 'Ah! The good old days are coming back!' Certainly in 1800, when King Charles IV of Spain sent 20 of the best horses in his stables as a present for the First Consul, escorted by servants in his livery of blue, silver and red, the same as the *grande livrée* of his cousin the King of France, the French government was alarmed about possible public excitement.

Bonaparte soon adopted a livery of his own. When he went in state to Notre-Dame on Easter Day 1802 to celebrate the signing of the Concordat, he appeared as a monarch. The Regent diamond, which Louis XVI had worn at the opening of the States-General, gleamed in his sword hilt. Parisians were overjoyed by their first sight of his footmen in a splendid new livery of green and gold. According to an English

---

[5] Comte d'Haussonville, *Madame de Staël et Monsieur Necker d'après leur correspondance inédite*, 2 vols., 1925, II, 280, Madame de Staël to Necker, 1 October 1803; Jean Tulard, 'La Cour de Napoléon', in Karl Werner (ed.), *Hof, Kultur und Politik im 19. Jahrhundert*, Bonn, 1985, p. 57.

visitor ordinary people in the streets cried 'Ah! There is the bag and
livery again ... it is like the old days – at last we can recognise our
country.' They did not mind that there was a far greater display of
military might, by the Garde consulaire, than the royal guards had ever
shown at ceremonies under Louis XVI.[6]

Despite such popular enthusiasm, the return of a court in France
was not inevitable. One current of opinion preferred simplicity to splendour. General Moreau, the victor of Hohenlinden, was the most popular
and effective general in the French army after Bonaparte and the hero
of those soldiers who were still republicans. He preferred not to go
to receptions at the Tuileries, saying that he was too old to stoop. When
he did go, he wore a plain dark coat rather than one of the splendid
uniforms which were already a characteristic of the French army. He
was becoming the rallying point for royalist as well as republican opposition to the First Consul. In rivalry with the court of the Tuileries
he began to entertain at his elegant *hôtel* in Paris and at Grosbois in
the country, which he had bought from Barras.[7]

Other European courts, as Armfelt noted, continued to follow the
late eighteenth-century fashion for simplicity. In England there was,
in the words of one prime minister's daughter, 'a woeful deficiency
of royal splendour'. The King lived in the Queen's House and receptions
at court were becoming less frequent. An English visitor to Vienna,
once the residence of the most formal court in Europe, wrote, 'Admirable
indeed is the simplicity which reigns at court.' The Emperor Francis
I held few receptions and walked or drove through the streets of his
capital without guards or courtiers. In Berlin, according to another trav-
eller, 'The house in which the Royal Family lives is quite like a private
gentleman's ... the King walks about and rides without attendants.'
Bonaparte himself enjoyed the informality of life at Malmaison.

However, he did not feel that he could permit himself the simple
life of a Habsburg or Hohenzollern. In France a ruler, particularly one
as insecure as the First Consul, who was under attack from both royalists
and republicans, needed the respect provided by the splendour and formality of a court. A court was popular and part of French traditions,

---

[6] Comtesse Golovine, *Souvenirs*, 1910, p. 295; Michel Poniatowski, *Talleyrand et le consulat*,
1986, p. 584; Anne Plumptre, *A Narrative of a Three Years' Residence in France*, 3 vols.,
1810, I, 1245.
[7] Ernest Picard, *Bonaparte et Moreau*, 1905, pp. 358, 373.

as is shown by the fact that it was revived in 1804, four years before an aristocracy. As Stendhal wrote, 'if [Napoleon] wanted to be king a court was necessary to seduce the feeble French people over whom the word court is all-powerful'.[8]

Moreover, many of Bonaparte's supporters wanted a court. For many of the elite of the republic the destruction of the monarchy and the proscription of the nobility after 1789 had been accidents. Underneath their surface enthusiasm for 'liberty, equality and fraternity' many of them were as greedy for titles, favours and rewards as the courtiers of Versailles had been: indeed, since they were less blasé, their appetite was greater. Generals and ministers of the First Consul, such as Talleyrand, Duroc, Berthier and Bessières, were in reality no less monarchical or elitist than the royalists: they had all served Louis XVI. If they later served the republic, it was out of desire to join the winning side rather than blind enthusiasm. Their commitment to the ideals of the revolution would be exposed in the searing light of the Napoleonic court, where they acted as the personal servants of one of the most autocratic monarchs of the day.

By 1800 the crushing of popular disturbances, and the elimination or emigration of many of the old elite, left the field free for Bonaparte and the elite of the republic to show themselves as they really were. A court would be proof of their success, and a means of satisfying their ambitions and strengthening the regime. There was already a military equivalent of a court in the Garde consulaire, an elite unit which guarded the First Consul and his palaces. Its soldiers had better pay, more glamorous uniforms and higher rank than the line army: yet it aroused little resentment. Another form of court also existed since the antechambers of the Tuileries were fuller than under Louis XVI.

From the point of view of the court the revolution simply meant the replacement of one set of courtiers by another in the antechambers of the Tuileries. It did not result in a shift of power from palace antechambers to legislative chambers. The revolution had cleared the air. It removed some of the surplus nobility which had clogged Versailles and had provided too much competition for too few places. The French elite was so large and eager to serve that it could supply enough material

[8] Lady Louisa Stuart, *Selections*, 1899, p. 122; J. G. Lemaistre, *Travels ... through parts of France, Switzerland and Germany*, 3 vols., 1806, II, 343; Wilmot, *Irish Peer*, p. 216, diary for 23 August 1803; Stendhal, *Napoléon*, 2 vols., 1929, I, 208.

for several courts, as indeed it did after 1800. In France a new court was created out of the post-revolutionary elite; and the same elite later secured positions in the courts created by the Emperor's family outside the Empire. Meanwhile the old court officials survived in exile and inside France, while many emigrés won office in other European courts.

As the First Consul acquired more self-confidence, his court became more elaborate. In September 1803 Caulaincourt, one of his aides-de-camp, a member of an ancient family of the *noblesse présentée* whose mother had been a lady-in-waiting of the Comtesse d'Artois, became inspector-general of the First Consul's stables. Salmatoris-Roussillon was made head of buildings and furniture, Rémusat of parks and gardens. The First Consul's best friend and most trusted aide-de-camp, Duroc, like him a member of the provincial nobility, was put in charge of the household and the hunt.

In 1804 the regime, and Bonaparte's life, were threatened by royalist conspiracies inspired by Artois. Some of his most determined agents were Armand and Jules de Polignac, sons of the favourite of Marie-Antoinette. They owed their lives to the intercession of Josephine and her daughter, Hortense – one of the many examples of links between royalism and its enemies. Josephine and Hortense were often helpful to well-connected royalist conspirators. Moreau, who had been involved in the conspiracy, became a popular hero during his trial, but was sent into exile. Bonaparte reacted to the challenge first by having the grandson of the Prince de Condé, the Duc d'Enghien, kidnapped and executed and then by taking the throne. In May he was proclaimed Emperor of the French by the Senate.

In July, five months before his coronation, the official *maison de Sa Majesté l'Empereur* came into existence. It was a simplification and redefinition of the old *maison du Roi* rather than a new departure. Indeed the civil list, 25 million francs a year, and the palaces (although they were in a very different state), were exactly the same as those granted to Louis XVI in 1791.

The Emperor's household consisted of six departments under the *grand aumônier* his uncle Cardinal Fesch, the *grand chambellan* Talleyrand, the *grand maréchal du palais* Duroc, the *grand écuyer* Caulaincourt, the *grand veneur* Maréchal Berthier and the *grand maître des cérémonies* Ségur. The *intendant-général de la maison*, Monsieur de Fleurieu, was in charge of the finance of the court. For the first time in the history of the court of France, and before other European courts, officials were given special uniforms. There was a different colour for each department: scarlet for the *chambre*, red for the *palais*, blue for the *écuries*, green for the *vénerie* and violet for the *cérémonies*.

Many different plans for the new court had been drawn up, some of which were based on those of 1791–2. However, little is known about the process of organisation beyond the following letter, the first to be entered in the letter-book of the *grand maître des cérémonies*. On 22 Messidor An XII of the French republic Duroc wrote 'I beg M. de Ségur to come tomorrow to Saint-Cloud towards half past twelve with the draft of his attributions. The Emperor wants to finish the organisation of his household tomorrow, and we are meeting for that. I also beg M. de Ségur to bring a plan for Sunday's ceremonial.'[9]

Apart from the Emperor and Duroc, Ségur was probably the chief influence on the new court. The son of the minister of war who had introduced the law of 1781 restricting officer's rank to the old nobility, he had been ambassador to Catherine II from 1784 to 1789. Like Fleurieu, who had been one of the last ministers of marine of Louis XVI, and governor of his son in 1792, Ségur had been a loyal servant of Louis XVI in 1789–92. As ambassador to Prussia in 1792, he had tried to stop foreign powers supporting Provence, Artois and the emigrés. He spent the reign of terror in the village of Châtenay outside Paris, and then lived by his pen, publishing poems, history books and the plays he had written for Catherine II's theatre in the Hermitage. He was a witty, cosmopolitan man of the world, a member of the Académie française who knew the courts of Versailles and St Petersburg as well as the France of the revolution. He had a taste for court life. He had applied for a position at court in 1791, and believed in etiquette. He wrote in 1801 that it is as necessary to monarchs as costumes are to actors. He also needed money.

Ségur was an ideal choice as *grand maître des cérémonies*. He worshipped the Emperor, played cards with the Empress, and corresponded

[9] Bibliothèque de l'Ecole des Beaux-Arts, manuscrits, Pierre Fontaine, *Notes relatives aux fonctions que j'ai remplies depuis le 3 novembre 1799* (henceforward cited as Fontaine), entry for 24 September 1803; Bibliothèque Thiers, Fonds Frédéric Masson (henceforward referred to as FM), 116 Duroc to Ségur, 22 Messidor An XII; various plans for the household are in FM 107 ff. 300–7.

with Princesses Caroline and Elisa. He was almost part of the family and his own family was equally devoted to the Emperor. His son Philippe became governor of the school of pages; the wife of his second son Octave was a lady-in-waiting of the Empress.

Ségur drew up successive editions of the *Etiquette du palais impérial*, the volume defining court officials' attributions which Madame de Stael called 'the most revealing document of the degradation to which one can reduce the human race'. He was proud of his job. When the King of Saxony visited Paris in December 1809, Ségur told the Saxon ambassador Monsieur de Senfft that 'they were concerned with a completely new theory, that of a meeting of crowned heads in the capital of one of the two states without incognito'.[10]

Ségur's knowledge of foreign courts, as well as the wishes of the Emperor, may have ensured that the character of the Napoleonic court was European as well as French. It was not casual, social and domestic like Versailles but institutional, international, military and elitist. The court was no longer a haphazard accumulation of households and traditions. It resembled a government institution. Official position in the service of the Emperor, rather than birth, was the main factor determining access to its receptions and entertainments (see chapter 4). The Emperor retained greater control over the subordinate households than Louis XVI: the head of each department in the Empress's household was under the authority of the equivalent official in the Emperor's. An important part of the household was the secretariat of state. It consisted (in 1813) of seventy officials under a former revolutionary politician, Maret Duc de Bassano, who had transformed himself into a devoted courtier of Napoleon. The Emperor used it as an instrument of centralisation and control over the government. He boasted that with the officials and files of the secretariat of state he could govern his empire wherever he was.[11]

The court was also more international than that of Versailles. Indeed it was probably the most international court since that of the Emperor Charles V. The titles of chamberlain and *grand maréchal du palais*

[10] AN c 184 46 Ségur to Louis XVI, 7 May 1791; Ségur, *Tableau historique et politique de l'Europe*, 3 vols., 1801, II, 71; Madame de Staël, *Considérations sur la révolution française*, 3 vols., London, 1818, II, 334–5; Comte de Senfft, *Mémoires*, Leipzig 1863, p. 87.
[11] AN 02 200, *Règlement* of 28 Thermidor An XII; FM 106 Maison de S. M. l'Empereur et Roi, 1813; Baron Fain, *Souvenirs*, 1909, pp. 166–84.

and indeed Emperor were foreign and, according to one of the Emperor's secretaries Méneval, the court's organisation was based on 'the imperial monarchy of Germany' as well as on the French monarchy.[12] Etiquette was now as formal as in the courts of Russia and Austria and, in contrast to Versailles, was based on grading by antechamber. From the start many courtiers, such as Salmatoris-Roussillon or the Belgian chamberlain Mercy-Argenteau, were from the elites of the countries recently annexed to the French Empire, Belgium, Piedmont and later Tuscany, Rome and Holland. The Emperor used court office to attach the aristocrats of Europe to his regime. Among his chamberlains were Prince Sapieha from Poland, Count van Bylandt from Holland and Prince Corsini from Rome. Among the Empress's *dames du palais* were the Duchesse de Dalberg from Baden, Madame Vilain XIIII from Belgium and Madame de Brignole from Genoa. By 1814 26 per cent of the senior officials in the households of the Emperor and Empress were foreign. Napoleon also had a separate Italian household as King of Italy, which served him when he visited Italy in 1805 and 1807 and sent a delegation to his wedding in 1810.

The military character of the court is shown by the fact that, unlike Louis XVI, the Emperor had aides-de-camp and *officiers d'ordonnance*. Moreover, from Generals Duroc and Caulaincourt down, most of his court officials were serving officers rewarded with court positions rather than, as at Versailles, courtiers who had acquired military rank. The *grand veneur*, Maréchal Berthier, was Napoleon's indispensable chief of staff, and later became Vice-Constable, Prince of Neufchâtel and Wagram and the richest man in the Empire. Like the Emperor himself, who wore the uniform of the *chasseurs* or *grenadiers* of the guard, they usually wore military uniform at court. Paris was now the seat of an autocratic military court like St Petersburg and Berlin and the Garde impériale was the principal armed force in the city.

The court was less domestic than before. There was no *luxe de domestiques*, or army of subordinate positions like *premiers valets de chambre* and *garçons de la chambre* open to the upper bourgeoisie or lesser nobility, as there had been at Versailles. Nor were there departments devoted to the monarch's physical needs. The *garde-robe* was absorbed

---

[12] Baron de Méneval, *Mémoires pour servir à l'histoire de Napoléon Premier*, 3 vols., 1894, I, 335.

into the *chambre*. The *bouche* was part of the *service du palais* under Duroc, and the *mobilier de la couronne* performed the functions of the *menus-plaisirs*.

Whereas the *grand aumônier, grand écuyer, grand veneur* and *grand maître des cérémonies* performed approximately the same functions as those of Louis XVI, the roles of the *grand maréchal du palais* and *grand chambellan* were different. Duroc, *grand maréchal du palais*, was the head of the court. He was in charge of the palaces, their defence and the distribution of lodgings, and always had the largest apartment in a palace (after the imperial family), where he entertained for the Emperor. He performed the duties of the *grand maître, gouverneur du château, grand maréchal des logis* and *premier maître d'hôtel* before 1789. He organised the Emperor's life, and was one of the most important people in it.

Serious, devoted and discreet, Duroc was said to be the conscience of the Emperor. De Bausset, a *préfet du palais*, adds: 'No one knew better than him the tastes and character of this prince nor exercised on him a more marked and persistent influence: what was remarkable is that the Emperor himself recognised this influence and did not try to avoid it ... he wanted to make the Emperor loved and to force public opinion.' Duroc was polite, in a cold and distant way, and relatively popular at court: however, Castellane, an officer whose diary is one of the best sources for this period, says that the only person he cared about was Mlle Bigotini of the opera.[13]

The *grand chambellan* replaced the four *premiers gentilshommes* of Louis XVI as the organiser of the social life of the court. Talleyrand was a suitable choice for the position, since he loved luxury and had been one of the first people to entertain on a lavish scale during the Consulate. He was also foreign minister and one of the Emperor's most important advisers. Like Berthier he was a natural monarchist who had known the court of Louis XVI at first hand. His mother had been the senior *dame du palais* of Marie-Antoinette and he had been one of the officials of the department of the Seine who had asked for a 'constitutional' court in 1791. Although he later deplored the Napoleonic court's vulgarity and lack of dignity, he was partly responsible for

[13] L. F. J. de Bausset, *Mémoires anecdotiques sur l'intérieur du palais*, 2 vols., Brussels, 1827, II, 136; Maréchal de Castellane, *Journal*, 5 vols., 1895–6, I, 85, diary for December 1811.

it. He encouraged Napoleon's taste for pomp and etiquette, and may have helped to organise the court. His friend Madame de Rémusat wrote: 'Monsieur de Talleyrand was consulted on everything.'[14]

Under the *grand chambellan* there were 18 chamberlains in 1804 and 105 in 1814. In all the number of positions of sufficient status to be acceptable to members of the elite of power, birth and wealth in the households of the Emperor, the Empress and (in 1814) the King of Rome (Napoleon's son) rose from 83 in 1804 to 217 in 1814. There had been 52 in those of the King, the Queen and the Dauphin in 1789. This is one of the great differences between the old court and the new. In size the *maison du Roi* under Louis XVI was just as large – about 2,500 compared to 2,752 in the *maison de S.M. l'Empereur et Roi* in France in 1813 (and the latter figure is inflated by the staff of the crown factories and domains, see appendixes, pp. 197 and 199). However, the *maison de S.M. l'Empereur et Roi* had more positions for members of the elite than the *maison du Roi*; and it was open to the 'bourgeois men of property' whose admission had been urged by Narbonne in 1792.

The greatest difference between the courts of Louis XVI and Napoleon I was that, whereas all senior positions in the court of Louis XVI had been reserved for the *noblesse présentée*, the court of Napoleon I was open to non-nobles and members of the *noblesse non-présentée* as well. The appendix on p. 198 shows the composition of the court and its evolution.

The Napoleonic court was the first in Europe where so many senior positions were filled by non-nobles. Curial, for example, the son of a Chambéry lawyer who was an officer in the Garde impériale, and Germain, son of a regent of the Banque de France, became chamberlains. Many non-noble court officials came from the fringes or the lower ranks of the court of Versailles. Berthier's father had been an official in the ministry of war next to the palace of Versailles, and his mother a nurse of Louis XVI and his brothers. Bessières, the most active commander of the Garde impériale, whose wife was a *dame du palais*, had been a soldier in the Garde constitutionelle. Maréchale Ney, beautiful, charming and socially ambitious, who was a *dame du palais* throughout the Empire, was daughter of Madame Auguié, one of those *premières*

[14] Madame de Rémusat, *Mémoires*, 3 vols., 1880, I, 409.

femmes de chambre de la Reine whom Madame de Boigne described as 'very beautiful ladies from the highest bourgeoisie'.

The Duchesse de Montebello, daughter of Senator Guéheuneuc a former *valet de garde-robe du Roi*, having been a *dame du palais* of Josephine, became *dame d'honneur* of the Empress Marie-Louise in 1810. By making the non-noble widow of Maréchal Lannes head of the household of his Habsburg Empress, the Emperor wanted to reassure the army and what he called 'the national party which was alarmed by this marriage, by the number and rank of the chamberlains by whom she was surrounded as if they were a step towards what some called counter-revolution'.[15] He later regretted his choice. Another characteristic of the new court was that it was open to the *petite noblesse* which had been excluded from Versailles, like Napoleon himself and Duroc. Josephine's first husband could not be presented; now she was receiving presentations and her daughter Hortense had one of the principal salons of the court.

Nevertheless the influence of the court of Louis XVI grew with time. During the Empire the proportion of non-noble officials fell from 35 to 18.5 per cent: the proportion from the *noblesse présentée* rose from 22.5 to 32 per cent. From the start birth was an important factor. In 1804 Monsieur de Courtomer (a member of the *noblesse présentée* who had enjoyed the *entrées de la chambre* under Louis XVI) assumed that he did not have to explain his ancestry to Talleyrand and used it as an argument for obtaining court office. That year he became a chamberlain and continued to serve until the Hundred Days. Officials from the old *noblesse présentée* tended, like Talleyrand, Narbonne and Ségur, to come from the second rank of court families or to be younger sons. Comte Just de Noailles, younger son of the Prince de Poix, became a chamberlain; Prince Ferdinand de Rohan, younger brother of the Cardinal de Rohan of the Diamond Necklace Affair, who was made *premier aumônier* of the Empress, literally worshipped Napoleon.

Although court officials could come from any background, a remarkably high proportion came from the old *parti de la reine*, which may be a sign of its lack of enthusiasm for Louis XVI and his brothers.

---

[15] *Boigne*, I, 36; Jean Tulard, *Napoléon à Sainte-Hélène*, 1981, p. 95 (quoting Las Cases).

Mercy-Argenteau, nephew of the Austrian ambassador to Louis XVI, was a chamberlain devoted to Napoleon I. Many chamberlains (the Comtes de Choiseul, de Beauvau, de Pange and d'Haussonville) came from noble families of Lorraine, a recently annexed province which felt more loyalty to the Habsburgs (descended from their last hereditary dukes) than the Bourbons. The Queen's chief minister in exile, the former *ministre de la maison* the Baron de Breteuil, who often saw Napoleon, tried to persuade royalist nobles to serve Napoleon.[16] His granddaughter Madame de Montmorency was a *dame du palais* famous for the number of her lovers and the sharpness of her tongue. Another relation married the chamberlain, the Comte de Choiseul.

Although the court always remained open to non-nobles, birth was becoming more important. After Talleyrand's disgrace in 1809 he was replaced by the Comte de Montesquiou, a noble who claimed descent from the Merovingians and had been *premier écuyer en survivance* of Monsieur before 1791. The Montesquiou received almost as many favours from Napoleon I as the Polignac from Louis XVI. The count was *grand chambellan*, his wife *gouvernante des enfants de France* (the King of Rome called her *maman quiou*). Two of their sons and a brother of the Comte were chamberlains, another son was an ordonnance officer and a niece married a cousin of the Emperor, the Duc de Padoue, and became a *dame du palais* (see appendix, p. 209). They had colonised the court more successfully than any non-noble family and could hope for great things in the future.

They also entertained on behalf of the Emperor in their *hôtel* near the Luxembourg. In 1810 a visiting Austrian chamberlain, Count Clary, wrote of one of their Friday concerts: 'the whole town was there, at least two hundred people ... ministers, cardinals, a lot of foreigners, in fact a horde. It is like that at the Montesquiou every Friday; people go there *en frac* [whereas uniform or the *habit habillé* were obligatory at court]. They and their sons are extremely polite.' The court was becoming so aristocratic that in 1812 Félix de Faudoas, was described on the *grand chambellan*'s list of applicants for the post of chamberlain as 'a man of good family related to all the great families of France'.

---

[16] AN 349 AP, Montesquiou papers 19, Courtomer to Talleyrand, 1804; General Bertrand, *Cahiers de Sainte-Hélène*, 3 vols., 1949–59, II, 454.

The phrase refers to 'the great families' of pre-revolutionary, not Napoleonic France.[17]

There was continuity in the technical staff as well as the higher ranks of the court. The court of France had always been a hunting court, and three officials and many servants of the king's hunt entered the Emperor's. The father of the *grand veneur* Maréchal Berthier had drawn up maps of the royal hunting forests for Louis XVI. The King's loader (*porte-arquebuse*), Monsieur de Beauterne, whose ancestors had held the same position since the reign of Louis XIII, became the Emperor's loader and followed him on campaign. The man who ran the hunt was Alexandre de Girardin, son of a patron of Rousseau, and the organiser of Barras's hunts at Grosbois.[18]

The *premier médecin* Baron Corvisart in 1805 based his department on the precedent of the court of Louis XVI, as did Ségur when organising the ceremonial for the birth of the King of Rome.[19] Many artists of the Napoleonic court were also products of Versailles. Baron Denon, a friend of the Emperor who organised almost all the artistic patronage of his reign, had been a *gentilhomme ordinaire du Roi*. He frequently attended the *lever* and *coucher*, and followed the Emperor's armies in search of loot for the palaces and museums of France.

Isabey, who had painted miniatures of Marie-Antoinette's ladies and relations, became the artist most intimately connected with the court of Napoleon I. He designed the official costumes, helped to organise the coronation ceremonies and as *dessinateur du cabinet et des cérémonies* and *premier peintre de la chambre* of the Empress Josephine, was always available to draw the imperial family and their court: he later became drawing-master of the Empress Marie-Louise as well. Brongniart, a fashionable architect and decorator of the reign of Louis XVI (he built the Hôtel de Montesquiou), became *inspecteur du mobilier de la couronne* under Napoleon I and helped to organise the refurnishing of the royal palaces. Jacob-Desmalter, *menuisier-ébéniste, fabricant de meubles et bronzes de LL. MM. II. et RR.*, was one of the chief suppliers

---

[17] Prince Charles de Clary et Aldringen, *Trois mois à Paris lors du mariage de l'Empereur Napoléon Ier*, 1914, p. 276, letter of 26 May 1810; AN 349 AP 1, *Liste des personnes qui sollicitent l'honneur d'être chambellans de S.M. l'Empereur et Roi*, entry for Felix de Faudoas.

[18] Yvonne Bézard, 'Les Porte-Arquebuses du Roi', *Revue de l'histoire de Versailles*, April 1924, p. 169; Frédéric Masson, *Jadis et aujourd'hui*, 1908, p. 316

[19] Paul Ganière, *Corvisart médecin de Napoléon*, 2nd edn 1985, p. 82; André Castelot, *Napoleon's Son*, 1960, p. 28.

of furniture for the court under Napoleon I, as his father had been for that of Louis XVI.[20] Dugourc designed fabrics for the court, as he had before 1792. Goubaud, who had been attached to Louis XVI's aunts during the emigration, became *peintre des enfants de France* under the Empire. There was no artistic conflict equivalent to the political struggles of the period. Nor were there parallels to the Whig and Tory artists of early eighteenth-century England. Indeed there was less of an artistic break in 1792 or 1814 than there had been with the transition to neoclassicism at the end of the reign of Louis XV. The Empire style was simply an exaggeration of the fashionable taste of the day. Perhaps because they had suffered so much from political upheavals, French artists were eager to produce flattering images of whoever was in power.

There was also a degree of continuity, whose importance is hard to assess, among the servants. Many servants of the old court either entered or provided information for the new one. They needed a court as much as Ségur or Talleyrand. For example Gy, born in Versailles in 1772, served in the royal stables from 1784 to 1792, and joined the First Consul's stables in 1803. The career of Bouvrier Baugillon is a phenomenon of continuity. He worked in the *menus-plaisirs* under Louis XVI, served the Convention and became a porter of the Tuileries in 1795, a post he still held, six changes of regime later, in 1831.[21]

Madame Campan, a former *première femme de chambre* of Marie-Antoinette, was a more important link between the regimes. She spent the reign of terror in the country and in 1794 opened a girls' school in the old Hôtel de Noailles in Saint-Germain. It became the smartest in France, with pupils from the old nobility as well as the new rich. Under the Empire she became head of the school for daughters of officers of the Légion d'honneur at Saint-Denis. She passed on the names of former servants in the Queen's household who wanted to serve in the Emperor's, and provided information about the etiquette of Versailles.[22]

Dumoutier, a former *huissier de la chambre* (usher) of Marie-Antoinette, performed the same functions for Josephine. Since so many people

[20] Madame Basily-Callimaki, *Jean-Baptiste Isabey*, 1883, pp. 69, 84, 97; *Alexandre-Theodore Brongniart*, Musée Carnavalet, 1986, pp. 67, 235; Denise Ledoux-Lebard, *Les Ebénistes parisiens*, 1951, pp. 136–56.
[21] AN 03 451, *Registre Matricule du Service du Grand Ecuyer au 1er juillet 1824*; AN 03 154, *Registre Matricule des Employés des Châteaux et Maisons Royales*, 1831.
[22] Campan, *Correspondance*, I, 263.

from different backgrounds went to court, a good *huissier* who could remember names and faces was indispensable. Dumoutier's daughter married a son of the great court cabinet-maker Riesener, served as a *lectrice* of the Empress and was briefly a mistress of the Emperor. Basinet, a former *maître d'hôtel* of Madame Adélaïde and Madame Victoire, held the same position in the household of the Emperor's sister-in-law, Queen Hortense.[23]

Servants are usually treated as part of the background: their own books (Hue and Cléry in Louis XVI's household, Madame Campan in Marie-Antoinette's, Constant, Marchand, Roustam and Saint-Denis in Napoleon's, wrote memoirs) concentrate on their masters' lives rather than their own. There was naturally a strong sense of hierarchy at court and servants were at the bottom of it. They could not rise to more elevated positions: once a *premier valet de chambre* or *huissier*, always a *premier valet de chambre* or *huissier*. Only a change of regime allowed mobility, as in the cases of Maréchales Ney and Lannes.

On the other hand, as in private households, some servants had strong personalities and established close relations with their masters or mistresses. The son of Thierry de Ville d'Avray, who also became a *premier valet de chambre*, wrote of 'a sort of intimacy which gave the servant a great influence', if only because he could talk to the king so easily (however, he gives no examples). Marie-Antoinette's last communication with her family was through Monsieur de Jarjayes, the husband of one of her *premières femmes de chambre*. Madame de Gourbillon dominated Marie-Joséphine and obtained large sums of money from her. Napoleon used servants and his *premier valet de chambre* Marchand as sources of information in 1814 and during the Hundred Days. Boniface de Castellane, an officer in the Grande armée, found that giving presents to the Emperor's *huissiers* and *valets* paid off. Once, on the banks of the Vistula at the start of the Russian campaign of 1812, an *huissier* shut the doors of the *salon de service* so that Castellane had the chance to talk to the Emperor alone and at his ease.[24] Just as the old royal furniture installed in the Tuileries and Saint-Cloud, and the palaces themselves, may have helped to add confidence and

---

[23] André Gavoty, *Les Drames inconnus de la cour de Napoléon*, 1964, p. 24; Cochelet, *Mémoires sur la Reine Hortense*, 1907, p. 58.
[24] TVA, Vicomte de Thierry de Ville d'Avray, *Premiers Valets de Chambre*, ff. 23, 26; *Castellane*, I, 99, entry for 6 June 1812.

formality to the new court, so the servants recruited from former royal households may have imposed their own traditions and standards of behaviour on their new masters.

Servants also revived the abuses and corruption which had been a feature of the old court. Duroc had the reputation of having established perfect order in the Emperor's household. A chamberlain, the Comte de Rambuteau, remembered: 'It is impossible to run a large household with more order than the *grand maréchal*. Our *valets de chambre* only received new candles when they presented the burnt ends of old ones'. However, the reputation of the Napoleonic court for economy may be as exaggerated as that of the Napoleonic police for omniscience. In 1809 the Emperor complained to the *intendant-général*, 'Monsieur Daru my household is full of abuses.' According to the memoirs of his *mamelouke* (a personal servant dressed in oriental costume) Saint-Denis, the kitchens were especially corrupt.[25]

The political and social reasons for the return of a court in 1800–4 have already been discussed. However, Napoleon's personal tastes were also important. As early as 1802 perturbed agents of Louis XVIII had reported that 'he practices every form of royal luxury'.[26] The habit stayed. Although he usually wore a plain guards uniform (perhaps in order to stand out against the dazzling military uniforms around him), at the grandest court and public ceremonies he wore an extraordinary confection of plumes, satin and lace, the *petit costume de l'Empereur*: it was unlike anything worn by contemporary monarchs. His court would also have no parallel in the Europe.

[25] Comte de Rambuteau, *Mémoires*, 1905, p. 76; AN 02 1, *Ordre de Sa Majesté du 16 février 1809*; Louis-Etienne Saint-Denis, *Souvenirs du Mameloucke Ali*, 1926, p. 313.
[26] Comte Remacle, *Relations secrètes des agents de Louis XVIII à Paris sous le Consulat*, 1899, p. 141, report of 11 October 1802.

CHAPTER 4

꙾ ꙰

Power

Cet habit rouge est un baptême qui rend propre à tout.

Diary of Boniface de Castellane, 11 December 1813, referring to
a chamberlain's uniform

There had been no need to write down etiquette for the courtiers of
Louis XVI. They had known instinctively what to do at the King's
lever or *coucher* and that, in the language of the court, *on* meant the
King, Monsieur the King's younger brother and *bonté* weakness. The
court of Napoleon I, however, was a conscious innovation rather than
an unconscious accumulation of traditions. The Emperor himself, and
the officials of the court, needed guidance. The publication of the first
edition of the *Etiquette du palais impérial* in December 1804 was eagerly
awaited by the court 'to know what we are meant to do', as one lady-in-
waiting put it.[1]

It is one of the few written records of a court in action, thanks to
which, and to the innumerable memoirs of the period, far more is known
about the daily routine of Napoleon I than that of Louis XVI. About
Louis XVI little is certain beyond the fact that he had a *lever* and *coucher*,
and worked as hard as he hunted. Aimée de Coigny, whose first husband
was the Duc de Fleury, one of the *premiers gentilshommes de la chambre*,
writes in her memoirs that she often used to meet Louis XVI in the
early morning coming out of his library, where he had already dealt
with a huge correspondence.

Whereas Louis XVI went to mass every day, Napoleon I only went
once a week. He spent most of the day and part of the night (between
two and five a.m.) working with his ministers and secretaries. However,

---

[1] Frédéric Masson, *Revue d'ombres*, 1907, p. 75, Madame Saint-Cyr (lady-in-waiting to Princess
Caroline) to Madame Charpentier, 12 November 1804.

the court provided the framework of his life. He gossiped with his *prem-ier valet de chambre* Constant and his *mamelouke* Roustam, a Georgian slave whom he had brought back from Egypt, while they bathed, shaved, dressed and perfumed him between seven and eight in the morning.[2] The *lever* was no longer a physical process but an occasion when the Emperor received the homage of his courtiers. It took place in the Emper-or's apartment overlooking the Tuileries garden.

The *lever* is the moment when H.M. leaves his private apartment to enter his outer apartment ... it usually takes place in the hour after H.M. has been dressed. At the moment of the *lever* the chamberlain in waiting scratches [a custom inherited from Versailles] on the door of the Emperor's private apart-ment and gives him a list of the people who have come to the *lever*.

The first people admitted were the heads of the six court services, known as the *grands officiers* and the *colonel-général* of the guard, aide-de-camp, chamberlain, *préfet du palais* and so on in waiting. After them came the *grandes entrées*, that is to say princes, cardinals, ministers, other senior officials and a few *savants* awarded them by special favour. The same process took place in reverse after ten o'clock in the evening at the *coucher*.[3] Thus, although they had been transformed, the *lever* and *coucher* were still important events in the life of the French court; and the Emperor talked to his court officials before and after everyone else.

On St Helena Napoleon boasted that he had eliminated the glorifica-tion of the monarch's physical person from court life. In fact, like many other pre-1792 traditions, it did eventually reappear: Versailles could not be destroyed in a decade. Usually Napoleon ate alone in ten minutes on a table set up in his private apartments. The meal was supervised by the *préfet du palais* in waiting and followed by games with his nephews and nieces and after 1811 his son, the King of Rome. Dinner was slightly longer and more formal, and was shared with the Empress (and on Sundays with all the Imperial Family in Paris), and served by pages.[4] However, once or twice a year, like the kings of France although much less frequently, the Emperor ate in public served by

[2] Aimée de Coigny, *Journal*, 1981, p. 89; Baron Fain, *Souvenirs*, 1909, pp. 64–73, 191–6; Rous-tam, *Souvenirs*, 1911, p. 204; Frédéric Masson, *Napoléon chez lui*, 1893, pp. 82–4.
[3] *Etiquette du palais impérial*, 1808, pp. 93–4, 98.
[4] Louis Etienne Saint-Denis, *Souvenirs du Mamelouke Ali*, pp. 24–7; *Bausset*, I, 205.

his court officials. The *grand chambellan* offered a basin in which the Emperor washed his hands. The *grand écuyer* held his chair, the *grand maréchal du palais* presented his napkin, the *grand aumônier* blessed the meal, pages waited at table, and her court officials performed the same functions for the Empress. When the Emperor wanted a drink, the *premier préfet du palais* poured wine and water into a glass which the *grand maréchal du palais* offered to the Emperor.

On Thursdays, and before mass on Sundays, more people came to the *lever* which was held in the *salle du trône* in the state apartments. On those days senior officials and officers down to the rank of prefect and colonel, and their wives, could be presented by the chamberlain in waiting to the Emperor and, in her apartments, to the Empress. After mass on Sundays there were receptions like those of the Consulate in the state apartments for officers and officials down to the rank of *chef de bataillon* and *sous-préfet*.[5]

Presentation at court was also possible for members of the old nobility who did not have official positions (some requests for presentation were refused by the Emperor, because the applicant's rank was low or his or her reputation equivocal). It was a political gesture which implied a desire to serve the Emperor. Monsieur de Rambuteau, the son of a Burgundian noble (who, although detesting the revolution, had never emigrated), had himself presented to the Emperor in 1806. In 1809 he received his reward when he became a chamberlain. People presented were inscribed on the official *registre de la cour*, and thereafter received invitations to balls, concerts and plays. The number of people on the register in the category of *hommes et dames présentées*, with no official positions, rose from 96 in about 1807 to 585 in about 1812; in comparison there were 449 court officials and their spouses and only 309 members of the Senate, the Legislative Body and the Conseil d'État and their spouses. The nobility and the imperial households were becoming more important than the official world in the social life of the court.[6]

Between 1809 and 1815, the only years for which a record survives, 560 people were presented at court. The Napoleonic court was extremely cosmopolitan, and 34 per cent of those presented were foreign.

---

[5] *Etiquette du palais impérial*, pp. 95, 99, 110–11.
[6] Comte de Mérode-Westerloo, *Souvenirs*, 2 vols., Brussels, 1864, I, 197; Comte de Rambuteau, *Mémoires*, pp. 19, 46; AN 349 AP 5, *Registre de la cour*.

Of the 371 French people, 39 per cent came from the old *noblesse présentée*, 38 per cent from the *noblesse non-présentée* and 23 per cent were non-noble.[7] As with the composition of the imperial households, although non-nobles and members of the *noblesse non-présentée* were now admitted to honours from which they had been barred before 1790, the *noblesse présentée* remained numerically the most important group.

The formal pattern of the Emperor's existence, the *lever* and *coucher* and deferential household, followed him wherever he went, even in the least courtly situations. When he rushed back to Paris from Moscow, through an avenue of dying men, in December 1812, he was in a carriage or sledge with the *grand écuyer* Caulaincourt, as etiquette required. Outside were his *mamelouke*, Roustam, two grooms and a Polish officer. Duroc, *grand maréchal du palais*, and General Mouton Comte de Lobau, one of the Emperor's favourite aides-de-camp, followed in one carriage, Constant, his *premier valet de chambre*, and Baron Fain, his secretary, in another. The rest of the household, to whom he had distributed large sums of money to help them return to Paris, followed behind. Throughout the journey the Emperor's servants managed to provide him with decent food and clothing. Wherever he stopped, even if it was a peasant's hut, was called *le palais* and the *étiquette du palais* applied.

The routine of the court was maintained while he was away in Russia. Every Sunday after mass at the Tuileries or Saint-Cloud, the Empress had to receive 'the members of the highest authorities, the ladies and gentlemen who have been presented'.[8] The Emperor was aware of the rumours and intrigues which had been caused by Marie-Antoinette's love of informality. He insisted that both his wives should live as formally as possible. The Empress Josephine, who had inherited innumerable relations and acquaintances from her dramatic, disreputable past, did not always obey. It was easier to control the Empress Marie-Louise who arrived from Austria in 1810 at the age of 18. She lived in her private apartments, seeing few people apart from her doctor Corvisart,

---

[7] AN 349 AP 1, *Liste des Personnes présentées à S.M.l'Empereur et Roi depuis le 12 fevrier 1809 jusqu'au* ... (4 June 1815).

[8] Comte de Caulaincourt, *Mémoires*, 3 vols., 1933, II, 205–6; *Castellane*, I, 195, diary for 26 November 1812; Edouard Gachot, *Marie-Louise intime*, 2 vols., 1911, I, 201–2, Duroc to Duchesse de Montebello, 8 July 1812.

her drawing-master Isabey and her beloved *dame d'honneur* the Duchesse de Montebello, whom she considered the perfect woman. Yet her life was never too secluded for the Emperor. He wrote in 1814 that she should keep princes, ministers and her own ladies 'away from you. In this country people ask for nothing better than to eat you alive.'[9]

The palaces as well as the court life of the Emperor were grandiose and ultra-monarchical. Since the court elevated the official rank rather than the physical person of the monarch, the throne-room, rather than the King's bedroom, was now the centre of the state apartments and the focus of the court. There had been no formal throne-room under the Bourbons, who only used a throne for ceremonies of the order of the *Saint-Esprit* and the reception of non-European ambassadors – for example those sent by Tippoo Sahib to Louis XVI in 1788. In Fontainebleau and the Tuileries a throne-room was installed in the old *chambre du Roi* of Louis XVI. It was always preceded by a hierarchy of antechambers to which different ranks of officials were admitted. A throne-room was even created in a small country palace such as Laeken outside Brussels.

The Emperor liked grand palaces as much as splendid clothes and aristocratic chamberlains. 'Beauty according to him only resides in grandeur' recorded Fontaine on 3 March 1808 after listening to his news on joining the Tuileries to the Louvre: the court had certainly changed since the days of the Petit Trianon. A deceptively simple sentence in the law of 19 May 1804 setting up the new civil list stated 'The Emperor visits the departments; in consequence imperial palaces are established in the four principal parts of the Empire.' As a result the Emperor had a justification for acquiring more palaces than any contemporary European, or previous French, monarch. By 1812 he had palaces at Marrac in the Pyrenees, Bordeaux, Strasbourg, Laeken and Antwerp, as well as the traditional constellation around Paris, Fontainebleau, Compiègne, Versailles and Rambouillet. In addition he inherited palaces from former rulers in Rome, Tuscany, Parma, Piedmont and Holland, and acquired 8 as King of Italy. He had 44 in all.

[9] C. F. Palmstierna (ed.), *Marie-Louise et Napoléon. Lettres inédites*, 1955, p. 125, Napoleon to Marie-Louise, 3 March 1814.

Fontaine wrote of the Emperor 'He demands magnificence, gold, Gobelins tapestries and large pictures', and as usual he obtained what he wanted.[10] All his palaces were refurnished in the Empire style, with Gobelins tapestries, Savonnerie carpets, Sèvres vases, Thomire bronzes and furniture by Jacob-Desmalter. Traditional French royal splendour was redefined to glorify the Emperor's rank and dynasty. After the early years of his reign, instead of buying back the old royal furniture, he preferred to order new furniture with the rigid lines and strident gilding characteristic of the ultra-monarchical Empire style, and his palaces were covered with Napoleonic dynastic emblems: N's, bees and eagles. Foreigners were amazed. Count Clary found that the Grand Trianon, a relatively small pavilion in the park of Versailles which was intended for relaxation, was 'furnished with fairy-tale luxury. I am sure the Orient has never seen anything so fine in bronzes, embroidered velvet, porcelain, pictures, parquet, fire-places and everything is in the best taste.' In comparison Clary's master, Napoleon's father-in-law the Emperor Francis I of Austria, had only three principal residences, the Hofburg in Vienna (which Napoleon thought a hovel), Schönbrunn and Laxenburg; in the summer, as a former chamberlain of Napoleon I the Comte de Sainte-Aulaire noted with stupefaction, he lived in a small house at Luberegg in Upper Austria like a private person.[11]

Napoleon's other palaces were equally magnificent, as can be judged by a visit to the dazzling state apartments (and the Empress's cashmere-draped boudoir) at Compiègne today. English visitors after 1814 were especially struck by the now-vanished palace of Saint-Cloud: 'The interior presents a scene of astonishing elegance and splendour ... the style of furnishing and ornamenting within is very princely and magnificent and the furniture is superb ... the Graces themselves might not scorn to repose upon the sofas.'[12] The Duchess of Rutland noticed that in the Tuileries: 'At every corner is a large N; the draperies are covered with bees and each piece of furniture is surmounted with an imperial eagle.' They were hung with splendid pictures: Duroc wrote that French

[10] *Archives parlementaires*, 1866, VIII, 344, law of 19 May 1804; P. L. F. Fontaine, *Journal*, 2 vols., 1987, I, 200, 204, entries for 3, 23 March 1808.
[11] Prince Clary et Aldringen, *Trois mois à Paris*, p. 177, letter of 24 April 1810; Comte de Sainte-Aulaire, *Souvenirs*, 1927, p. 35.
[12] Seth William Stevenson, *Journal of a Tour through Part of France ... made in the Summer of 1816*, Norwich, 1817, p. 187, diary for 2 June 1816; Thomas Raffles, *Letters during a Tour through some Parts of France ... in the Summer of 1817*, Liverpool, 1818, p. 92.

museums should be prepared to cede any pictures the Emperor required 'for the decoration of the palaces'.[13]

In addition to reintroducing much of its etiquette, and employing part of its personnel, Napoleon I showed his respect for the old French monarchy by planning to move into its supreme symbol, Versailles. Having endured neglect and the installation of a museum of French painting under the republic, Versailles began to be restored in 1808. Six million francs were allocated to it in 1810. Duroc wrote to Baron Costaz, the head of the *bâtiments de la couronne*, that 'H.M., Monsieur, desires to inhabit Versailles as it is, keeping everything as it is and making no notable changes or new constructions... as Louis XVI inhabited it.' In the same year Comte Daru, *intendant-général de la maison* told the Legislative Body 'Versailles is necessary for the splendour of the imperial throne.' By 1811, however, the Emperor had changed his mind. The Versailles of Louis XVI was no longer good enough. He planned to build a new façade on the side looking towards Paris: 'H.M. wants grandeur', wrote his *premier architecte* Fontaine.[14]

Napoleon's court reflected his view of monarchy. He claimed to be a child of the revolution and maintained a façade of constitutionalism by preserving the Senate and the Legislative Body. In reality, however, he was an autocrat bent on increasing the power of his dynasty. Like the military monarchs of Eastern Europe such as the Tsar of Russia and the Emperor of Austria, he wanted the monarchy and the court to be the principal institutions in the country. Louis XV and Louis XVI had accepted the independence of institutions such as the parlement, the Conseil d'Etat and later the National Assembly, and had tried to keep their court as a separate domestic and social sphere. Napoleon believed, as he declared in fury to the Legislative Body on 1 January 1814: 'Everything resides in the throne ... I alone represent the People ... France needs me more than I need France.'

Napoleon's court was more isolated than its predecessor. At Versailles under Louis XVI Arthur Young had found 'men whose rags betrayed them to be in the last stages of poverty' wandering through the King's bedroom. The *capitaines des gardes* had believed that the public should

---

[13] *Journal of a Trip to Paris by the Duke and Duchess of Rutland*, 1814, p. 19; Jean de La Tour, *Duroc grand maréchal du palais*, 1908, p. 285, Duroc to Daru, 7 March 1811.

[14] Clary, *Trois mois à Paris*, p. 173, letter of 24 April 1810; AN 400 AP 4, Duroc to Costaz, 18 January 1810; *Moniteur*, 1810, p. 130; Marie-Louise Biver, *Pierre Fontaine*, 1964, p. 157.

be allowed as close as possible to the King, and that 'you must never prevent recourse to the Sovereign'. In contrast, in the Tuileries under Napoleon, the public was only admitted, on Sundays, to the *salle des maréchaux*, the large room in the central pavilion which was lined with portraits of marshals and busts of generals (see plate 12). The state and private apartments were closed, and the police had orders to keep petitioners away from the Emperor at parades.[15]

Everyone who went agreed that the court was magnificent. The splendour and formality of the receptions, where the Emperor was surrounded by a constellation of courtiers and officers in full uniform, were so terrifying that some women fainted from fear when they were presented. At the New Year reception in 1811 one officer was so overawed that he could not distinguish who was around the Emperor.[16]

However, although he could be charming when he wanted, the Emperor was also one of the rudest monarchs in history. Madame de Rémusat, a favourite lady-in-waiting of Josephine (and niece of Louis XVI's foreign minister Vergennes), described in her memoirs the first appearance of *grands seigneurs* at the Emperor's court. When they breathed the atmosphere of a palace again and saw orders, privileges and a throne, they thought they were back in the world of their youth. 'But soon a severe remark, a brutal and novel will-power suddenly and for ever told them that everything was different in this court which was unique in the world.'

Napoleon I tried to set court officials against each other and enjoyed telling them that their spouse was unfaithful. He insulted Talleyrand, taunted Caulaincourt and asked Bertrand to provide Madame Bertrand as his mistress. An example of his wounding behaviour is his refusal to take Berthier, one of his oldest comrades in arms, back to Paris from Russia, as Berthier implored. According to people listening outside, the Emperor said, 'it is impossible; you must stay with the King of

---

[15] Emile de Perceval, *Le Vicomte Lainé*, 2 vols., 1926–7, I, 219n, note of Lainé; Arthur Young, *Travels in France during the Years 1787, 1788 and 1789*, 1929, p. 89, diary for 23 October 1787; AN C 218, Maréchal de Beauvau to Prince de Poix, 17 June 1786; AN 400 AP 4, Duroc to Prefect of Police, 8 January 1808.
[16] Haus- Hof- und Staatsarchiv Vienna (henceforward referred to as HHSA), Nachlass Montenuovo, Duchesse de Montebello to Marie-Louise, August 1814; General François Dumonceau, *Mémoires*, 3 vols., Brussels, 1958–64, I, 319.

Naples. I know very well, myself, that you are good for nothing; but
nobody believes it and your name has some effect on the army.' He
was also rude at court receptions. He insulted the British ambassador
in 1803, the Austrian in 1808 and the Russian in 1811 — a sign that
war with each power was imminent. On New Year's Day 1811 he
said to the *grands vicaires* of Paris, according to Stendhal: 'I do not
trust you; the religion I profess is as different from yours as heaven
from hell. I have my eyes on you ... remember that I have a sword.'[17]
Such words had all the more impact because they were so different
from the good manners which all other monarchs, particularly the Bourbons, felt obliged to show at court.

The Emperor's bad manners were not the only source of strain at
his court. It was run with military discipline. 'The ceremonial was executed as if it was controlled by drum-beat', remembered Madame de
Rémusat. Everything proceeded at such a pace that Talleyrand, who
had a club-foot, had difficulty in keeping up with the Emperor. Meals
were finished in ten minutes. Count Clary, when he went hunting with
the court at Compiègne, was embarrassed to find that he was still drinking coffee after the Emperor and his courtiers had finished breakfast.[18]

The dread of seeing relations' names in the lists of dead and wounded,
and the anxiety over whether the Emperor could remain victorious for
ever, were an even greater source of strain. Moreover, unlike the courtiers of Versailles, many courtiers of Napoleon I had little in common.
They came from different backgrounds, and sometimes countries, and
had different tastes and assumptions. In letters of the time Talleyrand
and Queen Hortense described the court of Napoleon I as *triste*, a word
seldom used of Versailles. They may have been right. In contrast to
courtiers' ruthless pursuit of even the smallest attic at Versailles, few
courtiers of Napoleon I cared to use their apartments at the Tuileries.
Madame de La Rochefoucauld (whom the Emperor called 'a little cripple,
as stupid as she is ugly') did not occupy her apartment as *dame d'honneur*
of the Empress Josephine; the Duchesse de Montebello, *dame d'honneur*

---

[17] Mansel, *Eagle in Splendour*, p. 112; Madame de Rémusat, *Mémoires*, 3 vols., 1880, II, 39;
Castellane, I, 202, diary for 5 December 1812; Stendhal, *Oeuvres intimes*, Angers, 1955,
pp. 1030–1.
[18] Rémusat, *Mémoires*, II, 32; Clary, *Trois mois à Paris*, p. 11, letter of 21 March 1810.

of the Empress Marie Louise, did only because the Emperor ordered her to.[19]

The court was magnificent from a distance but lost by being seen at close quarters according to Countess Potocka, an admirer of the Emperor. Many court balls looked impressive. But in 1806 when Madame de Boigne, a royalist, attended one she thought the Emperor in his *petit costume* looked dreadful, like a theatre king. She also noticed his rudeness to the ladies of Paris who, for once, had been admitted to the palace. She concluded: 'I had seen other monarchs, but none who treated the public so cavalierly'.[20] Few court officials, except perhaps Ségur and Duroc, liked the Emperor.

What the court lacked in pleasure and personal feelings for the monarch and his family, however, it gained in political importance. Since it was the centre of an empire which stretched from Hamburg to Rome and dominated the rest of the continent, it was a source of even more power and promotion than the court of Louis XIV had been. The Kings of Bavaria, Saxony and Württemberg, and a horde of lesser princes such as the future Leopold I of the Belgians, attended the Emperor's *levers* in 1809, to the great satisfaction of his chamberlains. As Metternich's latest biographer points out, in 1810 Metternich spent six months in Paris when he was foreign minister of Austria, drawn by the magnetism of Napoleon and the glamour of his court.

The court became increasingly important after 1809, for four reasons. The Emperor was in Paris and at peace; his appetite for power and splendour was increasing; his court now consisted of about 3,000 people and was almost as large as the central bureaucracy; and he was marrying again. The Empress Josephine, modest, charming and kind, had tried to make the court as agreeable as possible. However, her lack of sons by the Emperor made their divorce almost inevitable. It took place in December 1809 and in April 1810 he married the Archduchess Marie-Louise: her wedding procession from Vienna to Paris was modelled on that of her great-aunt Marie-Antoinette 40 years earlier. That year the *entrée* to the *salle du trône* was taken away from *présidents de*

---

[19] *Revue des deux mondes*, November 1935, p. 789, Talleyrand to Caulaincourt, 10 December 1807; Jean Hanoteau (ed.), *Les Beauharnais et l'Empereur*, 1936, p. 155, Hortense to Eugene, 20 September 1805; *Madame de Rémusat*, II, 342; Jean Tulard (ed.), *Napoléon. Lettres d'amour à Joséphine*, 1981, p. 262, Napoleon to Josephine, 13 March 1807.
[20] Countess Potocka, *Memoirs*, New York, 1900, p. 128; *Boigne*, I, 189.

section in the Conseil d'état, important government officials often from a revolutionary background, and given to dukes (even if, like the young Duc de Montebello son of Maréchal Lannes, they had no official position). His flattering, servile court was becoming the only world the Emperor knew. Stendhal thought that after 1810 the Conseil d'Etat lost influence to the court, which corrupted the Emperor and helped turn his vanity into a disease.[21]

The direction in which the court was heading was shown by the return of the *habit habillé*. The court costume of Versailles had no longer been obligatory at the Tuileries after 1789. Often thought to have been brought back by the Bourbons in 1814, in fact like many *ancien régime* customs it was reintroduced by Napoleon I. At first it was restricted to men without official positions. Years later Rambuteau remembered the white silk coat, covered in spangles, which he wore to one *fête de Saint-Napoléon*, before he became a chamberlain and acquired a uniform. However, in 1811 the Emperor decided that henceforth the *habit habillé* would be worn at grand court entertainments. It first appeared at a ball given by his sister, the beautiful Princess Pauline. Only the genius of Napoleon I could have persuaded battle-scarred former republicans, such as Marshals Ney and Junot, to wear costumes of pink or green silk.[22] In part this decision was intended to encourage the commerce of Lyons, which the Emperor was also trying to help with lavish orders for silk hangings for his palaces. But it is also an indication of his growing taste for a courtly and anachronistic style of monarchy.

There was no longer a difference between the household and the government in the etiquette of the court. Comte Regnault de Saint Jean d'Angély, secretary of state of the imperial family, wrote to Cardinal Fesch in 1811 that 'it must be stated that the Grand Dignitaries [Cambacérès, Lebrun, Talleyrand and Berthier] are the first officers of the household of the Emperor and that the Ministers and the Grand Officers of the Empire are also in the household of the Emperor as they all have presentations to make to the Emperor inside the Palace.' Under the consulate Napoleon had been surrounded by ministers, senators

---

[21] Guillaume de Bertier de Sauvigny, *Metternich*, 1986, p. 125; FM 116 (*Registre* of Comte de Ségur), Duroc to Ségur, 14 August 1810; Stendhal, *Napoléon*, I, 184, 200.

[22] *Rambuteau*, p. 20; *Castellane*, I, 82, diary for January 1811.

and councillors of state and a foreigner had said 'there is a power but there is no court' (see figures 2 and 3). Now an etiquette had been established 'in accordance with what used to exist in the former French monarchy and with what exists in the other courts of Europe.'[23] The government machinery of ministers, Conseil d'état and prefects still existed. However, personal service of the Emperor in his household was becoming equally important.

This process had been going on since 1800. The Emperor's aides-de-camp, in particular his favourite Duroc, who was devoted, competent and discreet, had played an important part in confidential negotiations with the King of Prussia, the Tsar of Russia and the King of Spain. Savary and Caulaincourt, two aides-de-camp, organised the kidnap of the Duc d'Enghien in 1804. Cardinal Fesch, the *grand aumônier*, was in effect head of the Catholic church in France. He was promoted to the sees of Lyons (1802) and Paris (1809), concurrently, and the coadjutorship of Regensburg (1806). He was not the only important priest at court. Duroc helped his cousin the atheist Abbé de Pradt to become one of the Emperor's *aumôniers*. The Emperor frequently talked to him at the *lever* and he soon became Bishop of Poitiers and the Emperor's spy on royalist priests in the west of France. On St Helena Napoleon remembered that 'this means of having a channel of information on many matters without passing through any ministry, and only through the Duc de Frioul [Duroc], who enjoyed his entire confidence, pleased the Emperor'. Like many other monarchs Napoleon distrusted his own ministers and liked to use his court as an alternative government. He took de Pradt to Bayonne and Spain in 1808, to help persuade the Spanish Bourbons to give up the throne, and later promoted him to Archbishop of Malines.[24]

Whereas under Louis XVI ministers' antechambers, or the salon of the Duchesse de Polignac, had been the places to go if a job or a favour was wanted, now it was the Emperor's *lever* and *coucher*. The Comte de Chabrol attributed his promotion to Prefect of the Seine – the man in charge of Paris – to the fact that the Emperor noticed him one day in 1812 at the Tuileries. Stanislas de Girardin, brother of Alexandre

---

[23] FM 116, Regnault de Saint Jean d'Angély to Cardinal Fesch, 4 October 1811.
[24] Napoleon I, *Correspondance générale*, 32 vols., 1858–70, XXXI, 99.

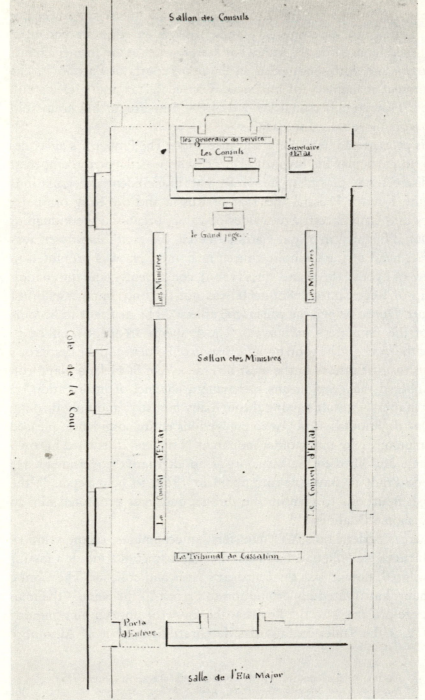

Sallon des Consuls

les généraux de Service

Les Consuls

Secretaire d'Etat

le Grand juge

Les Ministres

Les Ministres

Cote de la Cour

Sallon des Ministres

Le Conseil d'Etat

Le Conseil d'Etat

Le Tribunal de Cassation

Porte d'Entrée.

salle de l'Eta Major

2 The state apartments in the Tuileries under the consulate (Archives Nationales Papiers Fontaine 439 AP 1 doss. 4) Before he became Emperor, Napoleon was surrounded on public occasions by servants of the state: generals, ministers and councillors of state. There is no sign of his family or a court.

1 L'EMPEREUR.
2 L'IMPÉRATRICE.
3 MADAME.
4 La Reine d'Espagne.
5 Le Roi de Hollande.
6 La Reine de Hollande.
7 Le Roi de Westphalie.
8 La Reine de Westphalie.
9 Le Prince Borgèse.
10 La Grande Duchesse de Toscane.
11 Le Roi de Naples.
12 La Duchesse de Guastalla.
13 Le Vice Roi d'Italie.
14 La Reine de Naples.
15 Le Grand Duc de Bade.
16 Le Grand Duc de Wurtzbourg.
17 La Vice Reine d'Italie.
18 La Grande Duchesse de Bade.
19 Les Grands Dignitaires.
20 Le Corps Diplomatique.
21 Les Ministres.
22 Les Princes Etrangers.
23 Le Grand Maréchal du Palais.
24 Le Grand Maître des Cérémonies.
25 Les Grands Officiers de la Maison, les Pages et les Officiers de Service.
26 Les Dames du Palais et les Dames des Princesses.
27 Les Officiers de la Maison.
28 Les Personnes de la Cour.
29 Tables de Service.
30 Tables de desserte.
31 Passage pour le Service.
32 Tribunes hautes occupées par les personnes invitées de la Ville.

3 Plan of the banquet in the theatre of the Tuileries on the day of the Emperor's marriage to Marie-Louise, 2 April 1810 (Percier and Fontaine, *Description des cérémonies et fêtes pour le mariage de Sa Majesté l'Empereur Napoleon*, 1810, photo Bibliothèque Nationale)
As Emperor, Napoleon was always surrounded by his family and court. Whereas members of the public could watch the Bourbons dine, only 'the people invited from the City' and the court could watch the Bonapartes.

de Girardin, had been a supporter of the revolution and a deputy in the Legislative Assembly. Under the Empire, like many other former revolutionaries, he discovered a taste for court life, of which his diary is an excellent record. As *premier écuyer* of the Emperor's elder brother Prince Joseph, he was furious when his master's promotion to be King of Naples in 1806 and King of Spain in 1808 meant that King Joseph chose his new subjects to run his stables. Girardin resigned in pique in 1808, although when King Joseph returned to Paris he did everything in his power to see his former master again.

Girardin decided to become a prefect instead, and used the court to realise his ambitions. First he asked for advice and help from the two most influential men at court, Duroc and Berthier (the third, Caulaincourt, was serving as ambassador in St Petersburg). Then he began to attend the *lever* and the *coucher* regularly. He noted in his diary when Napoleon as 'a very great favour' asked for his news one evening. Finally on 21 March 1812 Napoleon at a *lever* announced that he had been appointed to 'one of the most important prefectures of the Empire, Rouen'. It paid to go to court under the Empire.[25]

The promotion of the chamberlains also revealed the political importance of the court. Rambuteau was delighted by his position. It meant that he was 'greatly flattered by everyone who approached the Emperor, ministers, princes, princesses, marshals, ambassadors, *grands officiers*, an entire court chasing after the master's notice and prompt to detect even the slightest appearance of favour'. They were 'constantly in contact with the Emperor and people in office'. Three chamberlains were on duty in the palace every week. They arranged private audiences, presented people to the Emperor and Empress and wrote letters in their name. They followed the Emperor to meetings of the Conseil d'état and indeed almost everywhere except his private apartments. They talked to the Emperor in the evening when the *petites entrées* (senior officials and *savants* who had the right to come to the Empress's apartment after dinner) were admitted, often about the court of Versailles and the merits of its etiquette. The Empress Marie-Louise wrote about them in her diary: she was fond of the Comtes de Pange and de Sainte-

[25] Jean Tulard, *Napoléon et la noblesse d'empire*, 1979, p. 134; FM 266, souvenirs of Stanislas de Girardin, 14 February, 15 May, 1 December 1811, 21 March 1812.

Aulaire but called Comte de Béarn *monsieur l'embarras*. During winter they had to stay in Paris whether they were in waiting or not.[26]

The Emperor's autocratic view of monarchy meant that he used his chamberlains, the courtiers most closely attached to his person, for political purposes. First he used the position to attach wealthy members of what was called 'the former opposition' to his court. He was then able to use them as a source of information about royalist intrigues: he found the stupidest were often the most informative.

For there was still an aristocratic opposition which regarded the Emperor as a dangerous, dishonest usurper. Its centre was the Faubourg Saint-Germain in Paris, the royalist counter-court to Napoleon's brilliant court in the Tuileries. A surprisingly large number of royalist nobles, the Luynes, the Duras, the Montmorency had recovered, or acquired, *hôtels* there. These nobles were important because they still had large estates (the Duc de Duras acquired Ussé on the Loire during the Empire) and the glamour of their names. They created a private royalist world with its own jokes and loyalties, which was frequented by foreign ambassadors as well as the old nobility.

Some court officials went there as well, since they were often related to royalists. The sister of the Comtesse de Montesquiou, for example, was mother of the royalist Sosthènes de La Rochefoucauld and most of the Noailles remained royalist, although Comte Just de Noailles was a chamberlain. The royalist salon of Madame de Laval was frequented by officials of the Empire such as Narbonne and Talleyrand. In some aristocratic salons chamberlains were made to feel ashamed of their uniforms and jokes circulated against the Bonapartes. When the Emperor married Marie-Louise, people in the Faubourg Saint-Germain sneered: *C'est par ce mariage que l'Empereur s'allie [salit] les Bourbons.*[27]

Many royalist nobles resisted the Emperor's offers of employment. For example at a family conclave in the Hôtel de Tingry the Montmorency vowed to shun Napoleon's court and never to enter his service,

---

[26] *Rambuteau*, pp. 53, 83; Abbé Moulard, *Le Comte Camille de Tournon*, 3 vols., 1927–32, I, 52n., Camille de Tournon to Madame de Tournon, 7 February 1806; Comte Thiard de Bissy, *Souvenirs*, 1900, pp. 9, 21; Marie-Louise, 'Carnets de voyage', *Revue de Paris*, 1 March 1921, pp. 44–5.

[27] AN AF IV 3177, *Minutes des actes de la Secrétairerie d'Etat*, 21 December 1809; Comte de Montholon, *Récits de la captivité de l'Empereur Napoléon à Sainte Hélène*, 2 vols., 1847, II, 24–5; Clary, *Trois mois à Paris*, p. 90, letter of 5 April 1810.

despite the pleas of the Baron de Breteuil. The most eloquent royalist
in the family was Mathieu de Montmorency, son of Madame de Laval.
At the beginning of the revolution he had been dismissed as one of
Artois's *capitaines des gardes* for his advanced political views but had
now become a fervent royalist and Catholic: he was later head of the
secret society, the Chevaliers de la foi, and the most important royalist
conspirator against the Empire. The Ducs de Duras and Fitzjames and
Sosthènes de La Rochefoucauld also refused court office under the
Empire.[28]

Even some court officials remained royalist at heart. The daughter-in-
law of the Duc de Luynes, Madame de Chevreuse, had become a *dame
du palais* in 1806. In 1808 she refused to attend the captive Queen
of Spain, saying that it was bad enough being a slave without being
a gaoler as well. She was exiled to the provinces for the rest of her
life. In 1812 Charles de Gontaut, a chamberlain, married a member
of the royalist family of Rohan-Chabot (one of whom was also a
chamberlain). As Talleyrand noticed, on the wedding announcements
sent to officials of the Empire the words *chambellan de l'Empereur*
were added in pencil. In other words one court official preferred to
please the royalist nobility by not printing his official imperial title rather
than to demonstrate his allegiance to the new regime by printing it.[29]

Nevertheless some chamberlains became attached to the regime and
had brilliant careers. Formed and vetted by the Emperor, they would
be ideal instruments of his will outside the court.

This use of the chamberlains suited the old nobility. Many of them,
in Belgium, Piedmont and the Rhineland as well as France itself, were
keen to serve in the army or the administration now that normality
had returned and France was no longer a republic. In addition to the
nobles' traditional desire for glory and distinction, many needed to restore the family fortunes after the disasters of the revolution.

In 1804, however, they often found that the administration and the
army were run by people younger and poorer than themselves. It was

[28] Edouard Herriot, *Madame Récamier et ses amis*, 2 vols., 1905, 2nd edn, I, 126, *Récit d'Adrien de Montmorency*; *Journal des débats*, 10 January 1810; cf. Charles-Otto Zieseniss, *Napoléon et la cour impériale*, 1980, p. 378.
[29] Constantin de Grunwald, 'Metternich à Paris en 1808–09', *Revue de Paris*, 1 October 1937, p. 56, despatch of 3 June 1808; Emile Dard, *Napoléon et Talleyrand*, 1935, p. 294n, Talleyrand to Duchesse de Courlande, 23 November 1812.

galling to serve as their subordinates. The position of chamberlain (or *écuyer*, aide-de-camp or *aumônier*) gave them the official status necessary to justify entering government service in a position of importance. One chamberlain, the Comte de Bondy, son of a pre-1789 tax official, grew to love and admire the Emperor: he believed that the Emperor's knowledge was 'really universal'. Bondy also came to know Talleyrand, Ségur, Rémusat and the unofficial prime minister the Duc de Bassano, who as *ministre secrétaire d'état* was a member of the household. Bondy often had so many people to present and letters to answer that he felt exhausted.

Nevertheless, service at court was worth the strain since it was a means to restore his family's fortunes. Bassano, who had become a friend, told Bondy in 1809 that 'I could only accept a very grand and very honourable position, being in the Emperor's household.' In the summer of 1809, during the campaign against Austria, he was in charge of the plays put on in the palace theatre, while the Emperor was in residence in Schönbrunn, and often had the opportunity to talk with Napoleon during meals. A few months later he had become a baron with an income of 4,000 francs a year on the *domaine extraordinaire* and, as Prefect of the Rhône, the man in charge of Lyons. He also used the position to advance his own and his wife's relations in the administration. It is not surprising that he wrote that his family was bound 'to all eternity to serve the Emperor and his family'.[30]

Other chamberlains also did well. His colleagues, the Comtes de Mercy-Argenteau and Germain, and the *écuyer*, the Baron de Saint-Aignan, became ambassadors to Bavaria, Wurzburg and the smaller Saxon courts respectively. Las Cases, the future memorialist of St Helena, at the Emperor's wish became a *maître des requêtes* and was sent on missions to Illyria and the French provinces. Rambuteau became Prefect of the Simplon, Miramon of the Eure and d'Arberg of Seine et Oise.

The court also extended its influence into the army. The Comte de Lauriston, a descendant of John Law the disastrous Scottish financier of the Regency, had been at the same military college as the Emperor.

---

[30] AN 177 AP 3 (letters of the Comte de Bondy), Monsieur to Madame de Bondy, 9 May 1805, 7 April 1808, 16 June, 13 July, 4 October 1809; cf. Comte de Sainte-Aulaire, 'Souvenirs sur Napoléon I', *Revue de Paris*, May 1925, pp. 482–3.

After he became an aide-de-camp in 1800 he had a brilliant career which took him from Ragusa to Spain. He served as ambassador to Denmark and Governor-General of Venice and became a count and a general. In 1811 he was appointed ambassador to Russia in replacement of Caulaincourt, whom he had never forgiven for obtaining the post of *grand écuyer* in 1804. His wife was a *dame du palais* throughout the Empire.

Another aide-de-camp, Bertrand, was sent on missions of inspection throughout the Empire, received estates from the *domaine extraordinaire* and the title of count, became Governor-General of the Illyrian Provinces in 1811 and *grand maréchal du palais*, after Duroc's gruesome death on the battlefield in 1813. The Emperor's courtiers obtained some of the best jobs in the army as well as the administration and diplomacy. To the fury of the minister of war, from 1810 the Emperor's trusted aide-de-camp Comte Mouton (plate 24) had the job of checking all his reports. In 1812 Lobau and another aide-de-camp, Comte Durosnel, became *aides-majors-généraux* respectively of the infantry and cavalry of the *grande armée*. In 1813 the Comte de Mathan, mayor of Caen, who had become a chamberlain when the Emperor passed through Caen, became a *colonel-major* without having served in the army since the revolution.[31]

Narbonne was another noble whose return to office shows the importance of the Emperor's court. Since his return in 1801 he had been leading a life of leisure in Paris surrounded by his books, his friends and Madame de Laval, who had succeeded Madame de Staël as his mistress. After ten years he had been reunited with his younger daughter, who had been left in the care of a family of peasants near Madame Adélaïde's chateau at Bellevue: they had to be paid to give her back. He married her to Rambuteau. Like many other courtiers of Napoleon I, and unlike the nobles of the Faubourg Saint-Germain, he was in debt and needed to restore the family fortunes; but all his efforts to obtain active employment were unsuccessful, probably due to the secret hostility of his intimate friend Talleyrand. Talleyrand was jealous of Narbonne's charm, intelligence and ability: he said that Narbonne had 'too much zeal'.

[31] Comte Emmanuel de Las Cases, *Las Cases mémorialiste de Sainte-Hélène*, 1959, p. 125; *Castellane*, I, 131, 241, diary for 12 August 1812, 11 December 1813.

In early 1809 Talleyrand's criticism of the Emperor's policies in Spain and reconciliation with his former enemy, the minister of police Fouché, led to his disgrace. After a celebrated scene when the Emperor called him 'shit in a silk stocking', he lost his post as *grand chambellan*. A few months later Narbonne resumed his former rank in the army. It is characteristic of the personal contacts which crossed political boundaries that he was helped by Berthier, whom he had known at Versailles and the Tuileries under Louis XVI, and Fouché who had been his mathematics teacher at the collège de Juilly before becoming a mass-murderer during the revolution. Narbonne, one of the few courtiers who held high office under both Louis XVI and Napoleon I, became a favourite aide-de-camp of the Emperor: he was the first person to present Napoleon with letters placed on an upturned hat and this usage of Versailles was swiftly adopted at the court of Napoleon I.[32] He replaced Talleyrand as the Emperor's favourite conversational partner, by night as well as by day, and proved that the antechambers of Versailles could produce greater independence of spirit than the campaigns and assemblies of the revolution. The Emperor remarked: 'In order not to be flattered, even on campaign, I had to take as an aide-de-camp a courtier, a wit from the old court.'[33]

Narbonne, the quintessence of 'the old court' had reason to feel at home at the new one, despite its uncomfortable atmosphere. His son-in-law Rambuteau was a chamberlain, Rambuteau's sister Madame de Mesgrigny was a *sous-gouvernante* of the King of Rome, her husband was an *écuyer* and they were often all in waiting at the same time. Through his service at court Narbonne became a political figure again, consulted on the most important matters. He was Governor of Raab during the campaign of 1809, minister to Munich in 1810, and Napoleon's last envoy to Alexander I before the invasion of Russia.

Politics under the Empire were essentially court politics. Before the divorce there had been the struggle between what Talleyrand called *le côté famille* and *le côté de l'Impératrice*. The Empress's children and relations, the Beauharnais, were rivals with the Emperor's family for thrones, offices and favour. After 1809 the court witnessed a contest for the Emperor's favour between Bassano and Talleyrand and

---

[32] *Rambuteau*, pp. 22–5, 43; *Castellane*, I, 60, diary for June 1809.
[33] M. Villemain, *Souvenirs contemporains d'histoire et de littérature*, 2 vols., 1855, I, 170.

Caulaincourt. Bassano was devoted to the Emperor and did nothing
to restrain his ambitions. He was encouraged by his wife, a tall ambitious
dame du palais. The fact that she was the daughter of a Dijon doctor
did not prevent the Prince de Ligne from admiring her almost as fervently
as he had once admired Marie-Antoinette. He wrote that she was beautiful, amiable, amusing and charmingly malicious. The Duchesses de
Bassano and de Montebello 'both appear to me just as perfect for style,
grace and manners as the real Duchesses of the past and the latter
were much less attractive'. The salon of the Duchesse de Bassano was
the most influential in Paris, and puppet shows were performed mocking
Talleyrand's and Caulaincourt's love of peace. Conversation favoured
war with Russia. The Empire was now such a courtly, military monarchy
that Madame de Noailles remarked: 'At this time we talk about chivalry
as much as during the revolution people talked of liberty.'[34]

Despite his official disgrace, and his secret contacts with Russia and
Austria, Talleyrand continued to attend the court; he used it to learn
the latest news and to assess his standing with the Emperor. In 1812
the Emperor decided to appoint him ambassador to Warsaw. Such an
able diplomat, who had many Polish friends, might be able to persuade
the Poles to support the invasion of Russia – although the Emperor
felt such distaste for the Poles' 'republican spirit' that he could not
bring himself to promise the restoration of Poland.

When the Emperor kept Talleyrand late at the *coucher* one evening,
the Duchesse de Bassano was afraid that it might mean Talleyrand's
return to favour and replacement of her husband as foreign minister.
She enjoyed her position too much to yield it without a struggle. One
of her great friends and constant guests was the chamberlain Rambuteau. As Narbonne's son-in-law he was equally horrified at Talleyrand's
return to favour. He wrote in his memoirs 'I undertook the task of
innocently spreading the news' that Talleyrand would accompany the
Emperor to Dresden, before it was officially announced. He told a group
of foreign diplomats while they were playing billiards. The Emperor
was furious and appointed the ineffective Abbé de Pradt instead.[35]
Talleyrand in Warsaw might have meant greater help for the Empire

---

[34] Paul Morand, *Le Prince de Ligne*, 1964, p. 89; Madame de Chastenay, *Mémoires*, 2 vols.,
      1896–7, II, 131.
[35] *Napoleon I*, XXXI, 101; *Caulaincourt*, III, 435, 442; *Rambuteau*, pp. 66, 85.

from the Poles in the campaign of 1812, and from him in 1813–14. Narbonne and the Bassanos had won.

The Emperor's court reached its apotheosis at Dresden in May 1812. As his armies streamed towards Russia, Napoleon I held a court of Kings in the capital of Saxony, attended by the Emperor of Austria as well as the King of Prussia. He behaved as the host and his court officials arranged the accommodation and entertainment. The days passed in concerts, banquets, visits and receptions. The Empress of Austria was dismayed to see that 'the Queen and all the princesses were forced to pay their court to him like men: to rise and sit down when he wanted. In general it is hard to imagine either the servile fear shown towards him at the court of Saxony or the hatred of the people.' Napoleon I was so charming and compelling that her husband Francis I wanted to accompany him on the invasion of Russia. Only her tears and Metternich's arguments prevented the Emperor of Austria from witnessing the burning of Moscow.[36]

During the nightmare of the retreat from Moscow, at the age of 57, Narbonne never lost his spirits. His aide-de-camp Castellane wrote: 'He is one of the small number of great-hearted men whose courage increases with our disasters.' He had the company of an attractive French harpist whom he had found in Moscow, he kept up a stream of funny stories and was powdered every morning sitting on a plank of wood, 'as if he was in the most agreeable boudoir'. He won the admiration of the entire army. It is true that the Emperor's household was in a privileged position compared to the rest of the army and, thanks to Duroc, almost always had something to eat.[37]

In November 1812 an unemployed general called Malet managed to seize control of Paris and imprison the Duc de Rovigo, who had replaced Fouché as minister of police, for a few hours. The Malet Affair revealed the fragility of the Empire to the Emperor as well as his subjects. In 1813–14, as the Emperor suffered repeated defeats on the battlefield and opposition grew in France itself, he increasingly used his court officials as political agents, as if he felt they were more trustworthy than other people. In 1813 the *grand chambellan* Montesquiou com-

---

[36] Baron de Bourgoing, *Le Coeur de Marie-Louise*, 2 vols., 1938–9, I, 83, Empress of Austria to Archduchess Beatrice, 6 June 1812; Bertier de Sauvigny, Metternich, p. 140.

[37] *Castellane*, I, 186, 203, 206, 13 November, 6, 8 December 1812.

plained to Caulaincourt that so many chamberlains were away serving as diplomats, prefects or officers that there were not enough available to serve at court.[38] Soon he himself and Ségur were sent away on missions to the provinces.

Some of the Emperor's aides-de-camp received important military commands in Germany, for example, Lemarois at Dusseldorf. Narbonne was used in negotiations with the Pope and the King of Prussia and then became ambassador to Vienna. He rapidly realised that Austria was turning against Napoleon, but his pleas for peace annoyed the Emperor and he was sent to govern Torgau, where he died from a fall from a horse. His old rival Talleyrand wrote in triumph to the Duchesse de Courlands: 'Have you heard, *chère amie*, the terrible news? Narbonne is dead. What a disaster! To go and die from a fall at Torgau!' He had no desire to make such a mistake himself, and was already talking with royalists such as Bruno de Boisgelin, son of a *maître de la garde-robe du roi*.[39] He may also have been corresponding with his uncle the *grand aumônier* of Louis XVIII.

Narbonne was replaced as the Emperor's favourite aide-de-camp by the young and charming Comte de Flahault, the idol of the salons of Paris and the lover of Queen Hortense. As an aide-de-camp of the Emperor, Flahault was able to live in splendour and to influence policy: he became a lieutenant-general, a count and one of the Emperor's representatives in negotiations with the allies.[40]

Even the Empress's *dames du palais*, normally considered companions or maids, now began to play a role in politics. Madame de Brignole was famous for her ambition and intelligence: she had been one of the patrons of the pro-French party in Genoa in the 1790s. Moreover, she was a friend of Talleyrand and of one of the Pope's most important advisers Cardinal Consalvi. Relations between the Emperor and the Pope were so bad that the Pope had excommunicated the Emperor and the Emperor had imprisoned the Pope. Much of the church supported the Pope, including the *grand aumônier* Cardinal Fesch, who left the court for his diocese in 1812. In November 1813 the Emperor used Madame de Brignole to try to arrange a concordat with the Pope,

[38] AN 195 AP 12, 72, Montesquiou to Caulaincourt, 26 September 1813.
[39] Dard, *Napoléon et Talleyrand*, pp. 217, 293, Talleyrand to the Duchesse de Courlande, 2 December 1813; *Coigny*, p. 181.
[40] Françoise de Bernardy, *Son of Talleyrand*, 1956, pp. 98–105.

who was a prisoner in a wing of Fontainebleau. The attempt did not succeed. A few months later he hoped to persuade Maréchal Augereau to fight harder by pressure from the Empress and other *dames du palais* on the Maréchale.[41] The Emperor also used the social life of his court as a political weapon. He ordered Duroc to establish lists of the ladies going to court and of the officers in Paris, and invite them to the *petits cercles* in order to get to know them, 'my intention being to draw the army closer to me'.[42]

The campaign ended in catastrophe. In 1814 the allied armies closed in on the French Empire. The Emperor, with his campaign household (headed, after November 1813, by the new *grand maréchal du palais* Bertrand), fought brilliantly but could not resist the pressure of numbers. Royalist hopes revived and royalist agents began to distribute Louis XVIII's proclamations throughout France. The Abbé de Pradt spoke for many people, at court as well as in opposition, when he said that there was one emigré whom it was time to recall in France and that was common sense.[43] The Empress's court in Paris began to look very empty indeed. The Emperor's prestige diminished; and his court officials went over to the attack.

[41] *Senfft*, p. 175; Arthur Lévy, *Napoléon intime*, p. 618, Napoleon to Marie-Louise, 23 February 1814.
[42] AN 184 AP 2, *Instruction particulière au grand maréchal*, ?1813.
[43] *Boigne*, I, 212.

CHAPTER 5

❧ ❦

The year of two courts

Un gentilhomme qui ne se montre pas à la cour n'existe plus.
M. N. Balisson de Rougemont, *Le Rodeur français ou les moeurs
du jour*, 14 August 1814

Years of subordination had not destroyed court officials' ability to think
for themselves. Indeed many believed that they were more than servants
and that, in a crisis, they had a duty to defend their master's or mistress's
interests, even against their orders. This explains why many court
officials had emigrated to Coblenz to fight for the traditional French
monarchy despite Louis XVI's opposition to emigration, while others
had tried to defend the royal family in the Tuileries on their own initiative.

Court officials felt especially independent in their relationships with
female members of the ruling family. Marie-Antoinette, who was not
as capable as she wanted to appear, could be manipulated by her
officials, such as her *grand aumônier* Mgr de Fontanges, Archbishop
of Toulouse, at the beginning of the revolution. Even physical manipula-
tion was not unknown. On 20 June 1792, during the first invasion
of the Tuileries that summer, her courtiers, led by her *chevalier d'honneur* the Duc de Choiseul, defied her demands to join the King and
dragged her to another room. Courtiers could also give orders to the
Bonapartes. In early 1814 the Emperor's mother wrote to her beautiful
daughter Princess Pauline that, since she was lucky enough to have
courtiers devoting themselves to her service, she should follow their
advice.[1]

---

[1] AN C 222 f. 5, account of 20 June 1792, found in Madame de Tourzel's apartment; Collection
Brouwet, *Napoléon et son temps*, 3 vols., 1934, number 36, Madame Mère to Pauline, 5 March
1814.

Court officials in the households of the Emperor and Empress were of much greater importance, since they were at the centre of events in a personal monarchy, and they also took initiatives. Caulaincourt was always pressing the Emperor to make peace. He was so closely associated with a policy of peace that in November 1813 the Emperor made him minister of foreign affairs in place of Bassano, to reassure the public.

In the Empress's household people went further. There was a 'regency party', led by her *dame d'honneur*, the Duchesse de Montebello, and her doctor, Baron Corvisart. According to their enemy Madame de Montesquiou, other members were Talleyrand, Caulaincourt and Flahault: 'the party of the regency, always alert, always active ... revived each time the Emperor left the court, and simply vegetated when he returned'. The Duchesse de Montebello was forceful and forthright. She told the Empress she was not 'imposing enough'; and her advice was not restricted to manners.[2]

The 'regency party' believed that the Emperor would never accept a reasonable peace. Therefore the Empress should become regent for her son as Napoleon II – as she was in 1813 and 1814 for Napoleon I. It is almost certain that, to drive them apart, the Duchesse de Montebello and Corvisart tried to persuade the Empress not to sleep with the Emperor. Talleyrand also favoured a regency and fear of his intrigues made Napoleon insist that the Empress, her court and the government leave Paris at the end of March 1814, when the allied armies drew near. In the crucial days in early April 1814, when the Empire was collapsing, the Emperor and Caulaincourt wanted the Empress to come from her temporary refuge at Orléans to join him at Fontainebleau, although the Emperor did not give a formal order. The Duchesse de Montebello and Corvisart helped dissuade her, although the Emperor's desire for her to obtain Tuscany rather than Parma was also a factor. Most of her other court officials, like her *premier écuyer* Prince Aldobrandini and her *chevalier d'honneur* the Comte de Beauharnais, drifted away. The only court official still loyal to Napoleon I was Madame de Montesquiou. She loathed the Duchesse de Montbello, who had spread rumours about her niece's behaviour when escorted by Cossacks.

[2] *Caulaincourt*, I, 160; Comtesse de Montesquiou, 'Souvenirs', *Revue de Paris*, May 1948, p. 64; HHSA NM, Duchesse de Montebello to Marie-Louise, 30 November 1814.

She was prepared to be blunt with the Empress but her advice had little effect.[3] The Empress went with a reduced court to Rambouillet, where she met her father. She was exposed to even more pressure hostile to Napoleon, and agreed to leave for Vienna.

Few courtiers were prepared to stay with her. The Duchesse de Montebello and Corvisart returned to France in early June. Before he left Corvisart had profited from the Empress's isolation. He persuaded her to promise to buy him a house and to leave some of her best pictures in his care (she later had to pay his heir to send them back). Politics and money dominated the relations of even the most devoted court officials with their masters.[4]

In Vienna Marie-Louise, who had been created Duchess of Parma, was given a partly Parman and partly Austrian household by her father (although most of her servants remained French). It was headed by Count Neipperg, who became her lover. Eventually she thought and acted as Duchess of Parma rather than Empress of the French. Her last letter to Napoleon was on 1 January 1815.

The Emperor experienced a similar abandon. Once he was defeated the danger of concentrating power in his court rather than in independent institutions became clear. The tie of personal service to the monarch was easy to ignore when he was about to lose his throne. In early April 1814 his aides-de-camp and court officials began to criticise him in the antechambers of Fontainebleau. General Friant, a chamberlain and commander of the first division of the infantry of the old guard, refused to obey the Emperor's order for an attack on Paris.[5] The persuasion of Caulaincourt and Marshals Ney, Macdonald and Oudinot, as well as the pressure of events, made him abdicate on 7 April.

Courtiers began to drift away to swell the court forming around the Comte d'Artois (now known as Monsieur), who entered Paris in triumph on 12 April. Berthier, hitherto one of the Emperor's most devoted servants, left him for ever on 18 April. He wanted a rest and to preserve his honours and property. Servants like Constant and Roustam also disappeared; as the Emperor noted, no one, not even Flahault, wanted

[3] Frédéric Masson, *Napoléon et sa famille*, 15 vols., 1908–19, XI, 191, Méneval to Caulaincourt, 29 April 1815; *Caulaincourt*, III, 310, 464.

[4] AN 95 AP 14, Méneval to Fain, 13 April 1814; Paul Ganière, *Corvisart médecin de l'Empereur*, 1985, pp. 355–6, 397.

[5] Baron Jean Thiry, *La Première Abdication*, 1939, p. 190.

to accompany him to Elba. Flahault wrote that he owed himself to his mother before his Emperor.

Even the few court officials who remained loyal were now sufficiently independent to disobey the Emperor. Napoleon attempted suicide on the night of 12/13 April. When the attempt was discovered Bertrand, Caulaincourt and the Emperor's servants refused to give him more poison as he begged. They saved his life against his own orders. When the Emperor left on 20 April he was accompanied only by Bertrand, Generals Drouot and Cambronne of the Garde impériale and a few valets. His courtiers had emerged as guardians of morality and the social order. On the way back to Paris at the beginning of the Hundred Days Bertrand refused to countersign a decree confiscating the property of prominent royalists.[6]

In this bewildering year, when courts sped in and out of the Tuileries with the rapidity of changes of government in the third republic, Napoleonic court officials also acted independently in Paris. Talleyrand took the initiative in setting up a provisional government on 1 April. Rémusat the *premier chambellan*, the Abbé de Pradt (who became *grand chancelier de la Légion d'honneur*, one of the least appropriate appointments of the first restoration), Jaucourt former *premier chambellan* of King Joseph, the chamberlain Germain and many others joined him: Maréchale Ney, a *dame du palais* of the Empress, gave a ball for the Tsar of Russia a few days after he entered Paris.

Most Napoleonic court officials blamed the Emperor himself for the destruction of the Empire. They felt absolved of their duty to remain loyal and hoped to become officials in the new court of the Bourbons. A *préfet du palais*, de Bausset, wrote from Rambouillet where he was in attendance on the Empress Marie-Louise (whom he later followed to Vienna), 'If I remained in the royal household I would keep all my rights.' These officials were so determined to stay at court that they should have been inscribed on the inventory of the palace, remembered a companion of Queen Hortense.[7] The Senate and Legislative Body supported Talleyrand with an enthusiasm caused in part by their resentment of the Emperor's autocratic, court-centred monarchy.

[6] AN 95 AP 14, 64, Berthier to Caulaincourt, 9, 22 April; Earl of Kerry, *The First Napoleon*, 1925, p. 71, Flahault to Madame de Souza 16–19 April 1814; *Caulaincourt*, III, 357–67.
[7] Comte d'Hérisson, *Un Secrétaire de Napoléon Premier*, 1894, p. 197, Bausset to Mounier, 14 April 1814, to Vitrolles, 28 April 1814; *Cochelet*, p. 119.

The imperial household continued in official existence, drawing its salaries, under the control of Baron Mounier (*intendant des bâtiments de la couronne* from 1813 to 1830) until the middle of May. At the same time another example of court officials' initiative was provided by the spontaneous resurrection of the old court, before the return of the King. Without orders, out of a mixture of duty, love and ambition, officials from the old royal households, or their heirs, left their estates in the country or their *hôtels* in the Faubourg Saint-Germain and returned to the Tuileries. Neither death nor revolution nor the 14 years of rule by Napoleon had been able to break their ties to the court of France.

Among them were the Duc de Duras, who began his career as the most important *premier gentilhomme* of the restoration by organising Louis XVIII's receptions in London in April. The Marquis de Dreux-Brézé, full of importance and precedents (he was to be consulted as an expert on court ceremonies by the King and the Prince de Condé although they were much older than he), replaced Ségur as *grand maître des cérémonies*. He organised the ceremonies for the King's arrival with the help of the Emperor's architect Fontaine and the revived *menus-plaisirs* under Belanger and Dugourc, artists who had worked in the households of Artois and Provence before 1791.[8] Others who rushed to the Tuileries included the Comte d'Escars, brother and successor of the *premier maître d'hôtel*; the Baron Thierry de Ville d'Avray, son and successor of a *premier valet de chambre* and *intendant du garde-meuble*; and the Duc de Maillé, son and successor of a *premier gentil-homme* of Artois. The return of the King transformed their lives.

On 3 May, using the Emperor's carriages which had been hastily painted over with his own coat of arms, Louis XVIII drove down the Rue Saint-Denis to Notre-Dame for a Te Deum and then on to the Tuileries. He was accompanied from England by about 50 court officials and servants. Among them was his most intimate and trusted court official, the Duc de Gramont, *capitaine des gardes*. He was the only courtier to have a personal apartment in the Tuileries as well as the official apartment he used when in waiting and was the man whom

[8] Hérisson, *Un Secrétaire*, p. 211, Mounier to Vitrolles, 28 April 1814; Fontaine, 27 April 1814; AN 03 120, Condé to *contrôleurs-généraux de la maison*, 2 March 1815; AN 03 527, *Relation des Obsèques de la Duchesse Douairière d'Orléans*, 23 June 1821, f. 6.

the royal family treated with the greatest respect and favour. Other courtiers were the *grand aumônier* Talleyrand-Périgord, now 'an old woman almost in his second childhood' and Blacas, *grand maître de la garde-robe*, who was appointed *ministre de la maison du Roi*.[9]

Blacas was one of the most important court officials of the restoration. Born in 1771, he was younger and less grand than the others. He came from an ancient *provençal* family, never presented at Versailles, and was the first provincial noble to obtain high court office under Louis XVIII (however his marriage to Mademoiselle de Montsoreau in April 1814, a few days before their return to France, made him a close relation of numerous court officials, see appendix, p. 210). When other court officials wanted to annoy him (which often happened, since they were jealous of his favour with the King), they said they did not know who he was. He was one of the most original connoisseurs of the period, a patron of Ingres and Champollion, the owner of magnificent classical antiquities, one of the first European collectors of Islamic art and a stimulus to the study of *provençal*. He was also an able diplomat, who knew how to win the confidence of monarchs and ministers and a fervent royalist, who told the secretary-general of the *ministère de la maison*, Vicomte de La Boulaye, that he was prouder of being *grand maître de la garde-robe* than of being a minister.

Although keen to maintain the theoretical powers of the monarchy, and to date his acts from 'the nineteenth year of our reign', Louis XVIII believed in the charter he granted in June. France was now a constitutional monarchy and the King left most decisions to his ministers. There was no equivalent to Napoleon's concentration of power in his own hands and the court and the government became distinct again. The King's *déjeuner* and the *ordre* (when he gave the password to commanders of the guard in the evening), were social, not political and career-making, occasions (see Chapter 8). He did not have a *lever* and *coucher* and rarely intervened to decide individual promotions. Therefore Blacas, the King's favourite minister, was at the centre of politics, hounded with requests for office, money, favours of any kind: he often

---

[9] AN 03 2007, *Etat des Logements*; Xavier de Montépin, *Souvenirs intimes et anecdotiques d'un garde du corps des Rois Louis XVIII et Charles X*, 5 vols., 1857, v, 40; Bibliothèque Victor Cousin, Fonds Richelieu (henceforward referred to as BVC FR) 72 f. 218, Marquis de Bonnay to Richelieu, 4 November 1816.

worked until three o'clock in the morning.[10] But he was not, as Bassano had been, an unofficial prime minister: Talleyrand, Minister of Foreign Affairs, and the Abbé de Montesquiou, minister of the interior (a relation of the *grand chambellan* of Napoleon I) were more important.

As *ministre de la maison du Roi* he worked directly with the King, and the organisation of the court reflected their personal preferences. In 1814, although there was a change of regime, there were no purges and the army, the administration and the Legislative Body remained essentially (and, in the case of the latter, entirely) the same. The court, however, did not. As in the eighteenth century, the King wanted it to be a domestic and social institution rather than a political weapon and he expressed the desire 'to recall for preference the former' (officials). This was due both to love of the traditional *maison du Roi*, and to the *charges* system. The royal family felt that since it based its claim to the throne on hereditary right it should respect other people's, and the *charges* of the *maison du Roi* had still not been repaid. They still had rights which had to be taken into consideration. Blacas himself signed a contract whereby the Marquis de Rochemore, the new *maître des cérémonies*, promised to pay his predecessor, the Comte de Nantouillet, 6,000 francs a year compensation.[11]

In the *maison du Roi* the organisation of each service was left to its head, as was usual in large households, where senior servants selected and directed their subordinates. Blacas intervened only to ensure economies, so that all departments (except his own, the *garde-robe*) were smaller than they had been in 1792. Therefore the enormous domestic departments which had been such a feature of the old court of Versailles, were restored. Blacas ran the *garde-robe* with a staff of 33. The *chambre* was much the same as in 1792. The four *premiers gentilshommes*, the Ducs de Duras, de Fleury, d'Aumont and de Richelieu, were sons or grandsons of former *premiers gentilshommes*. They still dealt with requests for presentation and audiences, and with the deluge of petitions addressed to the King.

The *premiers valets de chambre* were still extremely important. They had an apartment which communicated directly via a private staircase

[10] Vicomte de La Boulaye, *Mémoires*, 1975, pp. 265, 270.
[11] AN 03 529, *Vues générales sur la formation de la Maison du Roi*, 1814; AN 154 AP v 23, 2, contract of 4 November 1814, signed by Blacas, Nantouillet and Rochemore.

with the King's bedroom – which was convenient for secret audiences. It was through them that Decazes, who was to become one of the most important figures in French politics, first established a correspondence with the King in the summer of 1815. Of the four *premiers valets de chambre* Hue and Peronnet had served the King in exile; Thierry de Ville d'Avray and Lorimier de Chamilly, sons of two of Louis XVI's *premiers valets de chambre*, had been living in France. The *chambre* was still based on the principle that 'The King of France cannot be served like a private person by ordinary servants … the more you raise your entourage, the more you raise yourself' and almost all the people in the *chambre* were men of wealth and education. However, they were becoming an anachronism. The King had for a long time been living more like a private person. He was shaved and dressed, and had his chair wheeled, by servants from humbler backgrounds than the *huissiers* and *valets*.[12]

There were enormous differences between the courts of Louis XVIII and Napoleon I. The King's was less organised, less youthful, more religious and more domestic than the Emperor's. Food was again one of the glories of the court of France. So clean and empty under Napoleon, the Tuileries was now full of the smell of cooking. A staff of 158 in the *bouche du Roi*, under a celebrated gourmet, the Comte d'Escars, helped maintain the legendary reputation of the royal kitchens (the King of Bavaria and the Grand Duke of Hesse sent chefs to be trained there). The King's table, supplied by game from the royal forests and fruit and vegetables from the *potager du Roi* at Versailles, was one of the best in Europe and he spent far longer over his meals than the Emperor. Napoleon's *premier maître d'hôtel*, Monsieur Dunan, left to take charge of the kitchens of the Duc de Berri.[13]

Many of the kitchens which appeared in the Tuileries served the members of the royal family. For another difference from the court of

[12] Ernest Daudet, *Louis XVIII et le Duc Decazes*, 1899, p. 58; AN 03 194, *Travail de Mr. le premier gentilhomme de la chambre du Roi sur l'organisation du personnel*, 1820; Philip Mansel, 'The Court of France 1814–1830', unpublished Ph.D. thesis, London, 1978, p. 96.

[13] Sismonde de Sismondi, 'Lettres écrites pendant les Cent-Jours', *Revue historique*, IV, May 1877, p. 147, letter of 3 April 1815; Archives X, Comte de Wintzingerode to Duchesse d'Escars, 5 July 1814; AN 03 533, ff. 54–76, 110–11, *Organisation de la Maison-bouche du Roi*, 1 November 1814, 14 March 1815; M. A. Carême, *L'Art de la cuisine française au XIXe siècle*, 5 vols., 1843–7, I, xlvii.

Napoleon I was that the court of Louis XVIII was a family court. The Empire was based on the genius of one man, the restoration on the rights of a family, and during the restoration all the members of that family were unusually important. Because of Louis XVIII's and Angoulême's childlessness, all the royal family were heirs presumptive or their wives. Therefore, whereas only the Empress and the King of Rome had lived in the Tuileries, all the royal family did. As a result about one-third of the court escaped the control of the minister. Every prince had the right to choose his own servants and Blacas wrote, 'I do not concern myself in any way with the formation of the Princes' households.'[14]

Monsieur organised his household on the basis of his pre-1789 household, although on a reduced scale (124 officials and servants in the *chambre* in 1789, 55 in 1814). He solved the problem of the *charges* (as the King could have done) by paying many former holders 10 per cent interest on what they had paid for their *charges*, but not reappointing them. Monsieur had two *premiers gentilshommes*, the Ducs de Maillé and de Fitzjames. Fitzjames, described in 1809 as having 'an agreeable appearance and very good manners and . . . a decent fortune', had refused to be a chamberlain of the Emperor, although he was a brother-in-law of Bertrand, the future *grand maréchal du palais*. He was a leading member of the royalist secret society, the Chevaliers de la foi, and was to become an important politician.[15]

The presence of aides-de-camp was an innovation from the emigration. With Fitzjames they formed a group of active ultra-royalist politicians, whose position in the household of the heir to the throne increased their political impact. The section of the Tuileries inhabited by Monsieur, the Pavillon de Marsan beside the Rue de Rivoli, became a synonym for ultra-royalist intrigues. Proven royalism and noble birth were the most striking characteristics of the aides-de-camp. Of the 15 appointed by 1815, 7 had joined Monsieur in eastern France in February

[14] AN 03 706, *Maisons des Princes, brouillon* of Blacas to d'Aigremont, 16 December 1814.
[15] AN 03 886, 152 OG, *Etat nominatif comprenant les emplois et traitements de toutes les personnes qui fesoient partie de l'ancienne maison de Monsieur aujourd'hui roi*, enclosed in Belleville to Doudeauville, 23 February 1825; *Almanach de Versailles*, 1789, pp. 180–200; AN 03 3007, *Sommier des Indemnités et Gratifications pour Finances de Charges non liquidées*, 1820–5; AN AF IV 3177, *Minutes des actes de la secrétairerie d'état*, 21 December 1809.

and March 1814 before the defeat of Napoleon I. They included Jules
de Polignac the future prime minister of 1829–30, the Comte de Bruges
and Sosthènes de La Rochefoucauld, who had led a royalist demon-
stration in Paris on 31 March 1814. Only in 1815, too late, did Monsieur
appoint two non-nobles, Generals Bordessoulle and Digeon: he excused
his delay by saying that, although 40 or 50 had offered their services,
'the fear of hurting the greater number decided me to delay the choice'
– although it did not stop him choosing nobles.

In Lamartine's words Monsieur was 'almost a king by the pomp
of his household'. It contained over 250 people, when another younger
brother and heir presumptive, the Duke of York, brother of the Prince
Regent, who was commander-in-chief of the army as well, had only
four court officials and four aides-de-camp. Monsieur's green and pink
livery (and his sons' green and gold) must have been almost as familiar
a sight in the streets of Paris as the King's blue, silver and red. Since
Monsieur had 31 members of the old *noblesse présentée* in his household, whereas the King had only 19, it is not surprising that much
of the nobility looked to him for leadership.[16]

In 1815 Monsieur used his household, especially the Comte de Bruges,
'a man of capacity, of decision and above all of very firm will-power',
as a political instrument. During the first restoration Monsieur had
great influence over the King and sat in the council. He was neither
a fool nor a prisoner of old regime attitudes. He was a forceful political
operator and admired 'Bonaparte' whom (according to Lévis) he
regarded as 'our master': in April 1814 he appointed Marshals Moncey
and Oudinot to the council. His household also liked tough Napoleonic
officials. One of Bruges's nephews was an aide-de-camp of Maréchal
Soult and in early 1815 Monsieur and Bruges helped make Soult minister
of war. In return Bruges, an emigré who had served in the British army,
became *grand chancelier de la Légion d'honneur*, an appointment only

[16] Archives Historiques du Ministère de la Guerre (henceforward referred to as AHMG), xem
52, *Liste des aides de camp de monsieur*; Maréchal Macdonald, *Souvenirs*, 1892, p. 353;
Alphonse de Lamartine, *Histoire de la Restauration*, 8 vols., 1851–2, ii, 296; *Royal Kalendar*,
1821, pp. 127, 176.

a little less insulting than Talleyrand's choice of de Pradt a few months earlier for the same position.[17]

The households of Monsieur's sons, the Ducs d'Angoulême and de Berri, were smaller, younger, less reactionary and less political than their father's. They each had a few court officials and aides-de-camp, all of whom came from the old nobility: some, such as the Comte de Damas, *premier gentilhomme* of Angoulême, and the Comte de Mesnard, a *gentilhomme d'honneur* of Berri, had been with them in emigration. Each household probably contained about 150 people. All their aides-de-camp had served in the Napoleonic army and, unlike his father, Angoulême had the reputation of being surrounded by 'sensible people'.

The Bourbons were good masters who tried to protect their courtiers' rights and interests. Concern for courtiers' rights was so great that in 1820 the Duc de Berri's household passed intact to his posthumous son the Duc de Bordeaux. Thereby no one lost a job. In 1814 the Duchesse d'Angoulême's household reflected a similar concern, since it was partly recruited from her mother's. Four of her six ladies-in-waiting were daughters or nieces of ladies-in-waiting of the Queen.[18] Her secretary, Charlet, was son-in-law of one of the *gardes du corps* who had saved the Queen's life on 6 October 1789. Her *chevalier d'honneur* was Mathieu de Montmorency, head of the Chevaliers de la foi, a prominent royalist politician who had long shed the revolutionary sympathies which had caused Monsieur to dismiss him as *capitaine des gardes* in 1790.

The organisation of the inner court and of the princes' households appears to confirm Fontaine's bitter assertion that 'as it was in the old days' was the key phrase at court in 1814.[19] But the reality is shown by Fontaine's role in organising the ceremonies of the first restoration. Like many Napoleonic officials, he resented sharing office with

[17]   Comte Louis de Gobineau, *Mémoires*, Brussels, 1955, pp. 111–12; Bibliothèque Administrative de la Ville de Paris, Manuscrits 387, Duc de Lévis, *Souvenirs de cour* (henceforward referred to as BAVP Lévis), January 1824; Comte de Jaucourt, *Correspondance... avec le Prince de Talleyrand pendant le Congrès de Vienne*, 1905, pp. 139, 193, letters of 4 January, 13 February 1815; Comte Ferrand, *Mémoires*, 1896, p. 110. See AAE 681 f. 94 vo., Rivière to Talleyrand, 4 January 1815, f. 121 vo., Reinhard to Talleyrand, 4 February 1815, for other examples of the *maison de Monsieur* in action.

[18]   Marquise de Montcalm, *Mon Journal pendant le premier ministère de mon frère*, 1934, p. 152, diary for 13 April 1816; Archives du Comte Saint Priest d'Urgel, Avignon, *Mémoires du Comte d'Agoult*, f. 102.

[19]   Fontaine, 21 March 1815.

royalist rivals, and so exaggerated their influence. In fact much of the court escaped the influence of 'the old days'. The court bureaucracy remained the same, working from the Hôtel du Châtelet in the Faubourg Saint-Germain. The *secrétaire-général*, the Vicomte de La Boulaye, son of a *commissaire-général de la maison* under Louis XVI, had served in the administration throughout the Empire. Most secretaries-general of the different departments of the court, for example Feutrier (Minister of Ecclesiastical Affairs in 1828–9) in the *grande aumônerie*, remained in office under both regimes. Monsieur Leduc, father of Viollet Leduc, the restorer of French cathedrals, was secretary-general of the department dealing with the palaces from 1801 to 1831.

The more technical the department, the less likely it was to change, since there was less area for disagreement over qualifications for office. The *musique* continued unchanged with such renowned musicians as Paër, Kreutzer and Boïeldieu performing in the palace chapel on Sundays and at the infrequent court entertainments: Cherubini, who had not previously been employed since he detested Napoleon, became joint *surintendant* with Lesueur in 1816. Although all the senior officials in the *écuries* were replaced by former *écuyers* in the royal households or their sons, below them the department remained the same as under the Empire. The servants simply changed liveries, from the Emperor's green and gold to the King's blue, silver and red. The year 1814–15 was a busy one for the *écuries*. Horses and carriages left from the central depot opposite the Tuileries to Vienna with Marie-Louise, to Elba and later Rochefort on the Atlantic coast with the Emperor and to Ghent with the King.[20]

The *vénerie* is a notable example of continuity at court. The Napoleonic department, itself strongly influenced by that of Louis XVI, continued almost unchanged in 1814 under Maréchal Berthier. Beauterne was *porte-arquebuse* of Louis XVIII, as he had been of Napoleon I and Louis XVI. Alexandre de Girardin won the favour of Monsieur and his sons. Hunting was a passion for them – on one day in 1829, at the age of 74, Charles X shot 345 birds and his eldest son 298 – and they liked de Girardin because he ran the royal hunts well. In 1819

---

[20] AN o3 354, *Etat des Services de la Musique*, November 1825; AN o3 414, Donet, *secrétaire-général des écuries*, to Vernon, 20 August 1814; AN o3 388, Pradel to Vernon, 11, 17 August 1815.

he became *premier veneur* with constant access to the royal family, a brilliant climax to a career pursued at both the Napoleonic and the Bourbon courts.

The palaces provide another example of continuity in the outer structure of the two courts. There was no break in 1814, as there had been in 1789 with the eviction from Versailles. The same artists continued to be employed: in 1816 Gérard's *Bataille d'Austerlitz* was replaced on the ceiling of the old *salle du Conseil d'état*, now an antechamber to the chapel, by his *Entrée d'Henri IV à Paris*.[21] Despite his open Bonapartism, Fontaine remained the architect of the court and built the *chapelle expiatoire*, in honour of Louis XVI, Marie-Antoinette and Madame Elizabeth after 1817.

Louis XVIII said that Bonaparte had been a good concierge. Monsieur, the Duchesse d'Angoulême and the Duc de Berri 'expressed their satisfaction' over the decoration, furniture and *distribution* (arrangement of rooms) at Compiègne. Napoleonic emblems were, for a time, left undisturbed in the palaces. In August 1814 Monsieur d'Arblay of the Gardes du corps wrote to his wife Fanny Burney, 'His palace is still as it was six months ago, sprinkled with bees, N's, and eagles, which could at least have been removed from the throne on which his majesty was sitting'. Louis XVIII liked Empire furniture and continued to use Napoleon's throne until 1822. He made few changes in his own apartments except to install a tub in which he could take sulphuric baths and a corridor leading to the chapel. There was no attempt to repurchase the furniture, or revive the room-pattern of Versailles. During the restoration royal furniture of the reign of Louis XVI appealed to English collectors such as George IV and Lord Hertford, rather than its former owners.[22]

The main difference in the Tuileries was in the number of people who lived in it. Under Napoleon, because the court was not especially

[21] Musée International de la Chasse, Gien. *Livret des Chasses du Roi*, entry for 12 October 1829; AN 03 1393, *Rapport au Comte de Pradel*, 1 April 1816; AJ 19 145, *Journal du mobilier entré au château*, 1814–21 records few changes in 1814 except for the introduction of curtains.

[22] Jean Coural, *Mobilier National. Soceries Empire*, 1980, p. 22; Fanny Burney, *Diary and Letters*, 2nd edn, 7 vols., 1854, VII, 41, Monsieur to Madame d'Arblay, 30 August 1814; AN 03 2015, f. 87 vo.–93, *Inventaire du mobilier du château des Tuileries*, 1816–30, *salle du trône*; Fontaine, 18 May 1814.

agreeable, few people wanted an apartment in the palace. Under Louis XVIII, as Fontaine noted, the palace was 'full to the attics'. The Pavillon de Flore was occupied by the *grand maître de la garde-robe*, the *premier gentilhomme* and *capitaine des gardes* in waiting. The *premier maître d'hôtel* lived at the top of the palace. Court officials, servants, guards and the court pharmacy, stables and post office occupied buildings in the surrounding quarter.

Another change was the installation of *gardes du corps* in the *salle des maréchaux* and at the entrance to the King's private apartments and *cent-suisses* in their own room: the Garde impériale had only guarded the outside of the palaces. Louis XVIII's first act as King had been to restore the old *maison militaire* as it had been in 1775, before the cuts of Louis XVI. Indeed it was expanded as two new companies of *gardes du corps*, commanded by Marshals Berthier and Marmont, were added to the four traditional ones under the Ducs d'Havré, de Gramont and de Luxembourg and the Prince de Poix (his disgrace in 1795 was forgotten).

The King's plan to live half the year at Versailles reflected his court's combination of the reigns of Louis XVI and Napoleon I, since it was in accordance with the Emperor's intentions as well as a return to 'the old days'. A new pavilion to balance the Aile Gabriel was begun. Louis XVIII made his first visit on 17 August. According to Fontaine, 'The King seemed much less interested in the new arrangements and constructions than in finding several pictures, portraits and other details which can bring back the past. He then went to Trianon, whose magnificent furniture seemed unsuitable to him.' The Bourbons liked the Empire style and had almost the same taste as the dynasty they replaced. However, they did occasionally find it slightly overpowering: several years later the Duchesse de Berri rejected fabrics woven for the Empress Marie-Louise because the colours were so bright that they tired her eyes.

Fontaine claims that the court's intention to spend half the year at Versailles had a 'very bad effect' on the people of Paris, who feared the resulting loss of business. However, no other source records such reactions. What most interested the public were the jobs provided by the restoration programme. This was indeed the main reason why the government continued the works on Versailles and the Louvre in April 1814, as Napoleon was to do during the Hundred Days. Napoleon had accustomed the public to the idea of a return to Versailles as well as to the reality of a powerful monarchy and an elaborate court.[23]

The staff, although not the governors, of the palaces remained the same in 1814. The continuity in servants of the two courts is illustrated by the *caisse de vétérance* (pension fund) set up by Napoleon. After 1814 the fund continued to receive 3 per cent of salaries and to pay pensions to the employees of the court. All employees who lost their jobs in 1814 but had been employed in the Emperor's household on 1 January 1810 received pensions during the restoration.[24]

The social life and much of the ceremonial of the court also remained Napoleonic. Dreux-Brézé admitted that the decree of 24 Messidor An XII continued to be referred to 'daily' as the basis of public ceremonial, although not for traditional ceremonies such as the *grand couvert* when, once or twice a year, the King ate in public. The most important public ceremony was the reception held by the King and the royal family in the Tuileries every Sunday after mass. Even during the restoration, when religion was fashionable, courtiers paid little attention to the service, which only lasted half an hour: often they talked right through it. What mattered was to meet people, to hear the latest news and to be noticed by the King and the royal family.

There was little change in the organisation of these receptions. Like the Emperor, the King, surrounded by his principal court officials and guards officers, progressed through the state apartments after mass (which Louis XVIII, being an invalid, often heard in his bedroom), 'to allow the people who have the right to be there to pay their court to him'. The only Napoleonic servants maintained in the *chambre* were four *huissiers*, evidently in order to recognise and admit the elite of the Empire. The *entrées* to the different rooms in the state apartments continued to be given to senior officers and officials. Since the immense majority had been appointed since the revolution, the receptions of Louis XVIII were therefore the social consecration of the new France: they were not a return to the old regime. Many ultra-royalists were disillusioned. The court of France had become 'a court where we see

---

[23] Fontaine, 12 July, 12 October, 18 November 1814, 17 April 1815; Barbara Scott, 'The Duchesse de Berri as Patron of the Arts', *Apollo*, 296 (NS), October 1986, p. 347.
[24] AN 03 533 f. 73, *Ordonnance* of 3 December 1814.

walking beside us, sometimes even before us, men coming from the people whose only advantages are so-called services of which they ought to be ashamed'.[25]

The court of Louis XVIII was more accessible and more public than Napoleon I's. People presented at court (the qualifications seem to have been very broad: certainly there was no return to the practices of Versailles) were given the *entrée* to the *salle de la paix*. Remembering the hurt feelings of 1789, the minister of the interior the Abbé de Montesquiou, not Dreux-Brézé, regulated the ceremonial concerning the deputies. They were now admitted to the *salle de la paix*, one room further than under the Empire. Senior officers of the Légion d'honneur were also given special *entrées* at court.[26] Suitably dressed (boots were forbidden) members of the public were admitted into the *salle des maréchaux* and the chapel on Sundays and into the King's private apartments during the week, if he was out. The ancient royal tradition of accessibility was close to Louis XVIII's heart. A pamphlet he inspired and corrected boasted that before 1814 'it was more difficult to approach the humblest official of the palace than it is now to reach the person of the King'.[27] In 1814 when the King went through the *salle des maréchaux* he was greeted by cheers of *Vive le Roi!* and a shower of petitions. So was Charles X in 1824.[28]

In 1814 so many people attended the receptions at court that the Tuileries was fuller than at any time in its history. Everyone went, the old nobility, the Napoleonic aristocracy, returned emigrés, members of the public and the English who were flooding into Paris. The restoration court was extremely cosmopolitan. In 1814 all 'foreigners having in their own courts ranks or titles equivalent to those of the people admitted into the *salle du trône*' (that is to say ministers, cardinals, ambassadors,

[25] AN o3 527, *Copie des Ordres du Roi du 13 mars 1818* by Dreux-Brézé; AN o3 530, *Règlement sur les Entrées dans le Palais du Roi*, 1 December 1820; AN o3 194, *Travail sur la chambre du Roi*, 1814; anon., *Voyage d'un étranger en France pendant les mois de novembre et de decembre 1816*, 1817, pp. 136–7.

[26] AN o3 195, 80–3, *Décisions du premier gentilhomme*, 1814; *Journal des débats*, 30 May 1814, p. 1, 29 June 1814, p. 2; BN NAF 24062, *Procès-verbaux des séances du conseil du Roi*, entry for 20 June 1814.

[27] AN o3 519, *Consigne générale des gardes du corps* f. 8; AN o3, Intendant du Garde-Meuble to Duras, 5 August 1815; Chateaubriand, *Réflexions politiques*, 1814, p. 126; *Jaucourt*, p. 103, Jaucourt to Talleyrand, 30 November 1814.

[28] Henry Wansey, *A Visit to Paris in June 1814*, 1814, p. 92; AN 107 AP 14, Journal du Marquis de Galliffet, 1824.

marshals, dukes and a few other senior officers) received its *entrées*. On Louis XVIII's orders the English were allowed into the palace 'in any manner and at any time that they present themselves'. One Englishman was amazed that he was admitted to the chapel, although wrongly dressed, while many correctly dressed Frenchmen were turned away.[29]

Davout was the only marshal who did not go to court and it was the main meeting-place for Napoleonic generals. Even Flahault, one of the Emperor's favourite aides-de-camp, now impoverished and unemployed, went once a month. Napoleonic officers complained at court as bitterly about the lands and revenues they had lost in the territories ceded in 1814, as did former emigrés about what they had lost in France itself.[30]

Different worlds and individuals met at court for the first time. It provided the first introduction to the new ruling class for emigrés like the Duc d'Aumont, who had been serving in the Swedish army, the Duc de Richelieu, who had been governing Odessa, and the Duc d'Orléans, who had been living in Sicily. Monseigneur de La Fare (*premier aumônier* of the Duchesse d'Angoulême) returned from Vienna in 1814 and wrote, 'The Duc de Richelieu has arrived, but I have not seen him yet. I will meet him at the court. That is where I find everybody.' It was at court that Richelieu first made an impression as a political figure and met two of the six members of the ministry he was to lead in September 1815.

Louis XVIII also held receptions for the men and women presented at court on Mondays and for the Corps diplomatique on Tuesdays. These occasions provided a greater opportunity for an exchange of words, although not for a conversation, since the King did not hold conversations except during a private audience. The King in the *salle du trône*, and each member of the royal family in the main room of their apartment, received the deep bows and reverential curtseys of the people filing past them, the men in full uniform, the women in white

29 AN 03 195 f. 83; Burney, *Diary and Letters*, VII, 41, Monsieur to Madame d'Arblay, 30 August 1814; William Roots, *Paris in 1814*, Newcastle, 1909, p. 102, entry for 13 September 1814.

30 H. Vigier, *Davout maréchal d'empire*, 2 vols., 1898, II, 195, Davout to Louis XVIII, 9 August 1814; Baron Thiébault, *Mémoires*, 5 vols., 1893–5, V, 231; Léon Pelissier (ed.), *Le Portefeuille de la Comtesse d'Albany*. 1902, p. 204, Madame de Souza to Comtesse d'Albany, 8 August 1814; Jaucourt, *Correspondance*, p. 62, Jaucourt to Talleyrand, 1 November 1814.

dresses with long court trains and lappets. One innovation was that duchesses could now enter the *salle du trône* before anyone else, a measure which gave the duchesses of the Empire precedence over many noble royalist ladies. Madame de Chasteney records: 'I do not think I have ever heard anything like the outcry which was raised on this occasion.'[31]

The popularity of the court helped create the strange amalgam of Versailles, the emigration, the Empire and the provincial nobility which ruled France under the restoration. The court receptions also brought into evidence what Pasquier, a politician who served so many governments that he was called *l'inévitable*, called 'insurmountable incompatibilities'. There were too many people after the same political, social and financial rewards and the court was where they met. One minister thought the state apartments of the Tuileries were the best place to judge public opinion: people's faces revealed their hatred and resentment of each other. The favour shown to the British and to former emigrés caused disgust. Maréchal Ney is said to have complained of the unpleasantness shown to his wife at court, although she later claimed that she had always been well treated by the King and the royal family.[32] On the other hand some members of the Napoleonic elite, such as General Rapp and Queen Hortense (now known as the Duchesse de Saint-Leu) were pleased by their welcome at the court of Louis XVIII. However, the salon of the Duchesse de Saint-Leu remained a Napoleonic stronghold.[33]

The rush to court in 1814 also heightened royalists' desire for military position or promotion. In the dream world of the Empire, the Emperor had reintroduced the *habit habillé* in 1811 for wear at the grandest court entertainments. However, it was ridiculously unfashionable in the real world of the restoration. As the Marquise de Sémonville wrote, 'with our present customs it immediately makes the wearer ridiculous'.

[31] AN 198 AP 12, 8, La Fare to Mademoiselle de Choisy, 20 December 1814; E. D. Pasquier, *Histoire de mon temps*, 6 vols., 1893–5, IV, 2; *Chastenay*, II, 360.

[32] Pasquier, *Histoire*, III, 3; AN 40 AP 10, Beugnot to Louis XVIII, 26 November 1814; British Museum Additional Manuscripts, Dumouriez Papers 31231 f. 169, anon. to Dumouriez, 30 October 1814; *Archives parlementaires*, 2nd series, XV, 365, *Déposition* du Marquis de Vaulchier, 4 December 1815; cf. BN NAF 11771, 9 vo., *Journal de Madame de Chastenay*, 27 January 1815; AN 300 AP II 20, Maréchale Ney to Louis XVIII, 1816, copy.

[33] General Rapp, *Mémoires*, 1896, pp. 357–8; Masson, *Napoléon et sa famille*, X, 179–80, Duchesse de Saint-Leu to Alexander I, 4 October 1814.

No civilian uniforms were designed for wear at court. As it had been during the emigration, military uniform was the only alternative. Just as dances increase the demand for new dresses, so the court receptions increased demand for military uniforms, and so for high military ranks, in order to have something suitable to wear. Between April and December 1814 62 new *généraux de division* and 80 *maréchaux de camp* were appointed.[34] By March 1815 almost all the civil household had been given military rank and so were able to wear military uniform. The award of such positions to court officials like Duras, d'Escars and Dreux-Brézé, with no military ability, naturally irritated Napoleonic officers like Castellane and Flahault.[35]

The court of Louis XVIII was a mixture of those of Louis XVI, of the emigration and of the Empire. The outer structure, the palaces, and much of the social life of the court remained Napoleonic. The inner court, and the court's accessibility to the public, were a revival of the traditions of the court of Louis XVI. Of the King's 36 senior court officials (including *capitaines des gardes* and heads of other guards units, who were considered court officials) 22 were pre-1792 court officials or their heirs.

However this did not mean they had not served subsequent regimes. The Duc de Mortemart, *capitaine des cent-suisses* as heir of his cousin the Duc de Brissac, had served in the Napoleonic army. In the *chambre* 25 per cent of the pre-1792 officials and servants reappointed in 1814 had served the republic or the Empire, like Dumouthier, *huissier* of Marie-Antoinette, Josephine and finally Louis XVIII.[36]

Of the other senior court officials in 1814 nine received their positions as rewards for their role in the counter-revolution. Among them were a hero of the wars of the Vendée, the Marquis de La Rochejaquelein, captain of the Grenadiers à cheval, and a favourite of the King Comte Charles de Damas, captain of the Chevau-légers, de la garde. Marshals Berthier and Marmont, captains of companies of *gardes du corps*, and the Comte de Nansouty, captain of the first company of Mousquetaires

[34] AN 03 487 doss. Longueil, Madame de Sémonville to Lauriston, 19 January 1821; Eugène Titeux, *Le Général Dupont*, 3 vols., Puteaux-sur-Seine, III, 585.
[35] AN 03 72, *Ordonnances et Règlements du Roi*, Baron d'Egvilly to Condé, 11 March 1815; AHMG XAD 3, *Rapport au Ministre*, 20 February 1815; *Castellane*, I 260, 5 August 1814.
[36] AN 03 352, *Etat des anciens services des divers officiers de la Chambre du Roi*, 1818; AN 03 355 doss. Silvestre, *État des services*, 1 January 1815.

de la garde, were chosen to represent the Empire at the court of Louis XVIII.

The restoration court therefore confirms the truth of Balzac's remark, 'In every period the throne and the court have been surrounded by favourite families without any resemblance either in name or character to those of other reigns.'[37] Under Louis XVIII the grandest court families of the eighteenth century, the Rohan, the Lorraine and the elder branch of the Noailles, no longer occupied high court office, and the Blacas, Damas and Croÿ families, and many figures from the Empire, were newcomers. The restoration court was more military, more concerned with loyalty and less interested in birth than the court of Louis XVI.

One of its weaknesses was that the revival of the pre-1792 *chambre* meant that there were fewer posts for members of the elite than in the household of the Emperor. This was an anachronism. Napoleon I had accustomed opinion to a large and elitist household and 1814 could have been the take-off point for a rival royal version. For the events of the revolution, the emigration and the Empire had strengthened most nobles' attachment to monarchy and desire for court office. From the evidence of their *cahiers* in 1789, Guy Chaussinand-Nogaret states that 'the king occupies a negligible place in noble preoccupations'. By 1814, however, most nobles, like Mathieu de Montmorency, had been shocked into royalism. For the Comte de Kerolais in the novel *Christophe Sauval ou la société sous la restauration* (published 1845) by de Bonnechose (librarian of the palace of Meudon during the restoration), 'The successes of the revolutionaries soon increased this feeling [for royal authority] to enthusiasm . . . from then on there were no limits to his devotion to the royal cause.' The irreverence shown in the salon of Madame de Brionne had few imitators in the nineteenth century.

The French nobility's new-found royalism was caused by ambitions as well as emotions. The government now had more direct power and more jobs in the army or the administration to offer; and nobles needed them more because of their losses during the revolution. This explains why Barante, a Napoleonic prefect, wrote of the *servilité d'antichambre*

---

[37] Honoré de Balzac *Le Cabinet des antiques*, 2 vols., 1839, I, 141–2.

into which the nobility had fallen by 1814.[38] Court office would have been a cheap and effective way of satisfying it.

The classes which had risen to prominence since 1789 also wanted court office. For them the court was no longer an inaccessible paradise. Before the revolution there had been immense (although diminishing) differences of manners and clothes between the court and the rest of the elite. Madame de Pompadour, a bourgeoise of Paris, had to learn the language and manners of the court before appearing there: and she never fully mastered them. Court manners were characterised by politeness, lack of pretension and total confidence: Lévis praised them in a speech in 1817 as 'that social manner which consists of talking of everyday things with nobility and of important ones with simplicity'. In a more intimate work he wrote that banality or blandness was almost universal at court.[39]

Since 1789 there had, paradoxically, been a spread of court manners, perhaps because so many non-nobles now enjoyed the confidence derived from power and authority. The elite was more courtly than before; and foreign travellers remarked on 'the extreme politeness and civility of everybody, even the lowest person' in France. Actresses could play aristocratic parts more convincingly in France than in England, where differences of accent and manner were so great. Maréchal Bernadotte, son of a provincial lawyer, is described as having court manners, and these were one reason for his success on the throne of Sweden.[40] The Prefect of the Seine could praise four members of the Corps municipal of Paris for their excellent manners which made them suitable for court office. Decazes, a non-noble from Libourne, had the smooth manners of a courtier, perhaps because of his years in the service of King Louis of Holland and Madame Mère. It was generally agreed that restoration court officials (except Dreux-Brézé) were polite and lacked the 'forced', exaggerated tone of the Empire. It was provincial ultra royalists with little experience of the world of power and pleasure in Paris, such as

[38] Guy Chaussinand-Nogaret, *La Noblesse française au XVIIIe siècle*, 1975, p. 206; Comte de Barante, *Souvenirs*, 8 vols., 1890–1907, II, 40.
[39] Nancy Mitford, *Madame de Pompadour*, 1970 edn., pp. 44–6; A. Caillot, *Mémoires pour servir à l'histoire des moeurs et usages des français*, 2 vols., 1827, I, 193; *Réponse de M. le duc de Lévis à M. Roger successeur de M. Suard*, 1817, p. 9; Lévis, *Pensées et maximes*, 1825, p. 196.
[40] Elizabeth Suddaby and P. J. Yarrow (eds.), *Lady Morgan in France*, Newcastle, 1971, p. 68; Surgeon James, *Journal*, 1964, p. 74; Gabriel Girod de l'Ain, *Bernadotte*, 1968, p. 347.

the ministers Corbière and Guernon-Ranville, who were noted as having 'worse than bourgeois manners'.[41]

There were no longer barriers of manners, taste or costume to prevent the new elite holding court office. With the spread of the *frac* differences of costume within the elite had disappeared as well. Bankers like Perregaux and Péreire, sons of Third Estate deputies like General Lamarque and Hutteau d'Origny, applied for court office. Non-noble as well as noble court officials of the Empire, as has been pointed out, hoped to continue under Louis XVIII. Madame de Staël felt that it would have been wise to make Napoleonic generals chamberlains, although she admitted their vanity was insatiable. Vitrolles, the provisional Secrétaire d'Etat, wrote a skit in the *Journal des débats* in May in which he estimated the demands for places of page at 3,775; but no *maison des pages* was set up until 1820.[42]

The hunt for office, status and money had replaced the idealism of the revolution, as Napoleon's creation of a court and aristocracy demonstrated. Many people, on both left and right, now felt that vanity was at the origin of 'most French feelings and even opinions'. Stendhal agreed and after the Hundred Days the Duchesse de Duras wrote to Madame de Staël of 'these vanities which still create all the problems'. A large and splendid court would have satisfied many of 'these vanities'. Indeed the conseil-général des manufactures, the body representing French industry, told the Duchesse d'Angoulême in May 1814, 'You know, Madame, the French people more than any other likes to find its models at the court of its Kings.' But she had simple tastes and preferred good works to entertaining. As many people complained, her household was less impressive than the Empress's.[43]

Unlike his elder brother, Louis XVIII knew the importance of vanity

[41] AN 03 364, Comte de Chabrol to M. de Serre, 19 November 1820; anon., *La Politesse qui régnait à l'ancienne Cour de France comparée au ton de la Cour de Buonaparte*, 1814, pp. 11–12; *Barante*, II, 236n.; Baron d'Haussez, *Mémoires*, 2 vols., 1896, II, 109, 152.

[42] AN 349 AP 1, *Liste des Personnes qui sollicitent l'honneur d'être chambellans de S. M. l'Empereur et Roi*, entries for Lamarque and Perregaux; AN 03 460, *Demandes de places dans la maison du roi* for Péreire 1821; AN 03 364, *Nominations collectives*, Baron d'Hutteau d'Origny to Charles X, 29 November 1829; *Journal des débats*, 29 May 1814, p. 2; Staël, *Considérations* III, 95, 111–12.

[43] AN BB30 257, *Papiers saisis chez le Duc de Richelieu*, f. 65, plan by M. de Cormenin for a reform of the Conseil d'état sent by de Serre to Richelieu, 7 August 1820; Comte d'Haussonville, *Femmes d'autrefois, hommes d'aujourd'hui*, 1912, p. 202, Duchesse de Duras to Madame de Staël, 1 September 1815; *Moniteur*, 31 May 1814, p. 600.

and of a splendid court. In 1785 he had written to Louis XVI that vanity was 'a real political weapon'. In 1814 he declared to his ministers, who were preparing an economy drive in every government department, 'The only expense which cannot be diminished is the civil list... there must be splendour, outward show, for *capimur oculis*.'[44] Nevertheless, in 1814 the King did not use his household as a political instrument. He did not want to change the habits, and courtiers, of a lifetime.

The organisation of the heralds shows what could have been done. Of the total of 26 appointed in 1814 8 had served in the army, and 4 as heralds, under the Empire. Five had been prominent royalists and 9 had been pre-1792 heralds or their relations. The intention was, as the Marquis de Vernon a pre-1792 *écuyer* in charge of the *écuries* wrote, 'to conciliate all interests... and you will see that old and new services rendered to the Prince and the State are lost in an equal balance'.[45] Such a desire for conciliation was evident in the government, the army and the social life of the court but not in the choice of court officials.

This was indeed one of the major mistakes of the first restoration. Hatred of the court increased. 'The King is just and good but his entourage is implacable', wrote Flahault's mother and many agreed. Beugnot, *directeur-général de la police*, told Louis XVIII that some court officials were opposed to the *charte*. Names were never mentioned and this hatred may reflect the vigour of the anti-court literary tradition (see p. 155) as much as reality. Despite his freezing manner, Blacas tried hard to be conciliatory. Madame de Staël, one of the few genuine liberals of the day, admired him enough to write a pamphlet defending his political moderation.[46]

Other court officials also tried to be conciliatory. One sign of the social character of the restoration court was the enormous evening receptions given by the *premier gentilhomme* and the *premier maître d'hôtel* at the instigation and expense of the King. It was part of their functions to *faire les honneurs de la cour* (as the Polignacs had done under Louis XVI), and they entertained on alternate Sundays so as not to clash.

[44] AN c 187, Monsieur to Louis XVI, 24 February 1785; BN NAF 24062 ff. 263, 276, *Procès-verbaux du conseil du roi*, 20, 24 June 1814.
[45] AN o3 533 106–7, *Ordonnance* of 12 January 1815; AN o3 426, Vernon to Blacas, 17 December 1814.
[46] Pelissier, *Le Portefeuille*, p. 227, Madame de Souza to Comtesse d'Albany, 11 November 1814; Norman King, 'Libéralisme et légitimité', *Europe*, January–February 1987, pp. 75–8.

In 1814–15 the Duchesse de Duras, who was exceptionally intelligent and broad-minded, entertained Bonapartists such as Maréchales Soult and Suchet and writers like Villemain, Cuvier and Chateaubriand, the 'dear brother' she worshipped, as well as the court nobility. In contrast Duroc, who gave dinners for the court of Napoleon I, although very well mannered, according to Madame de Rémusat 'had no idea of social pleasures'.[47]

The Bourbons' court officials were generally loyal. But this did not mean they were blind; and, being at the centre of events, they had excellent opportunities for judging them. At the time of Louis XVIII's arrival in England in 1807 the Duc de Gramont had lamented the policy of 'inflicting pin-pricks and receiving hammer-blows' which in his opinion had characterised royal policy since 1789 and was the reason for its failures. The same criticism applies to many acts of the first restoration such as the choice of senior court officials, the revival of the *maison militaire*, and Louis XVIII's failure to wear the Légion d'honneur.

These factors, and many others, including the proximity of Elba to the French coast, led Napoleon to try his luck again in France. Moreover Napoleonic courtiers like Bassano, Davout and Flahault, who had suffered catastrophic losses of income, property and status, advised him to return. As he advanced on Paris in March, people went to court to show their loyalty to the King: 450 women one day, 578 the next.[48] Unlike Fontainebleau in April 1814, the Tuileries was packed with loyal courtiers, for royalism was stronger than Bonapartism within the elite. But Louis XVIII had no reliable armed force at his orders: the *gardes du corps* and the *maison militaire* were no match for the French army. On the night of 19/20 March he fled north with Blacas, Duras, the Prince de Poix, Maréchal Berthier and a few other faithful courtiers and servants (plate 14). Hue had already been sent ahead with the crown jewels.

On 20 March the remaining court officials and servants abandoned the palace. At first it remained under the guard of its architect Fontaine,

[47] AN 03 90, *Distributions, soirées de la Duchesse d'Escars*; AN 03 1902. 111, *Rapport au Marquis de Lauriston*, September 1821; Archives x, Duchesse d'Escars to Madame de Podenas, 5 September 1816; BN NAF 11771 f. 20, *Journal de Madame de Chastenay*, 12 January 1815; *Comtesse de Rémusat*, II, 244.
[48] AN 300 AP III 16, Duc d'Orléans to Comte de Beaujolais, 26 December 1807; Baron Gourgaud, *Journal*, 2 vols., 1896–7, I, 492; Sismondi, 'Lettres écrites', p. 333, letter of 9 March 1815.

who protected it from crowds bent on loot. In the afternoon Napoleonic court officials started to reappear, as eager to resume their duties as their royalist rivals had been in April 1814. That evening the Emperor returned to a delirious welcome from soldiers outside the palace, and courtiers at the top of the stairs: 'Everyone had come in their uniform to resume their functions as a right which belonged to them. You did not realise that another sovereign had inhabited the palace... it simply seemed that His Majesty was returning from a long journey', wrote his dedicated *premier valet de chambre* Marchand, who had followed him to Elba. Among the resurrected Napoleonic household one of the *huissiers* who had served Louis XVIII assured the Emperor that he had done so simply 'in order to serve your Majesty better'.[49]

The Bourbon and Napoleonic monarchies had different styles and purposes. But they also had much in common. They were both elitist, authoritarian regimes which believed in a court and aristocracy as weapons to increase their prestige. Their shared dislike of popular disturbances could even overcome their mutual rivalry. When he left Paris on 19 March, Monsieur (*colonel-général des Gardes nationales du royaume*) confided command of the Garde nationale de Paris to one of its most Bonapartist officers, Napoleon's devoted *grand chambellan* the Comte de Montesquiou (plate 17). Monsieur thought it was more important to maintain law and order in Paris than to disorganise the force entrusted with its preservation. In a similar way after the Emperor's return the royalist La Boulaye presented the employees of the *ministère de la maison* to the new *intendant-général*, the Bonapartist Comte de Montalivet. They were nearly all the same people as under the Empire and Montalivet took La Boulaye's advice about whom to employ.[50]

Court life flourished during the Hundred Days. The Emperor reappointed a full household, including Ségur, Montesquiou and Caulaincourt, and excluding Berthier, de Pradt and many others who had become royalist. Chamberlains reappeared, including Béarn, who was called 'one of the oldest and most faithful servants of Your Majesty'. He must have had a very 'open' marriage since his wife (daughter of Madame de Tourzel) was a lady-in-waiting of the Duchesse d'Angou-

---

[49] Fontaine, 21 March 1815; L. N. Marchand, *Mémoires*, 2 vols., 1952, I, 126, 135.
[50] Information about Montesquiou kindly communicated by Comte G. de La Bouillerie; *La Boulaye*, pp. 280–1.

lême while he was a chamberlain of Napoleon I. La Bédoyère, who had led the first regiment to join the Emperor during his march on Paris, became an aide-de-camp. One of his colleagues, Flahault, was sent to Vienna to persuade the Empress Marie-Louise to return. He never saw her and after he came back was put in charge of all matters concerning military personnel, to the fury of Maréchal Davout, the minister of war.[51]

Just as Louis XVIII had been impressed by the state of the palaces, so Napoleon wanted to know every detail of the King's daily life. Perhaps influenced by accounts of the Bourbons, he also tried to change his manners. Instead of the overbearing rudeness he had often shown before 1814, he now treated courtiers with unaccustomed kindness. His *levers* were crowded. Even enemies such as General Souham, who had led the defection of Marmont's troops in April 1814, could not resist attending. The Emperor also invited people to dinner to convince them in conversation that he had become a constitutional monarch.[52]

However his love of power and pride in his rank could not be suppressed. He insisted on wearing his *petit costume* at the proclamation of the new constitution on 1 June instead of the uniform of the Garde nationale de Paris. His use of a chamberlain to transmit messages to the Chamber of Representatives was as tactless as a similar use of Dreux-Brézé 26 years earlier. It caused 'the most violent murmurs… At last a member declared a chamberlain a very unfit channel of official correspondence between the Emperor and the representatives of the people.' According to the English Whig Hobhouse it was decisive in convincing them that he wanted an autocratic courtly monarchy and so in turning them against him.[53] After Waterloo, his court officials again took the initiative by advising him first to abdicate, then to throw himself on the mercy of England.[54] As he moved from the Elysée to Malmaison, Rambouillet, and Rochefort, his court shrank around him. In contrast

---

[51] AN 349 AP 1, *Liste des personnes qui sollicitent l'honneur d'être chambellans de S. M. l'Empereur et Roi*, 1815; Françoise de Bernardy, *Son of Talleyrand*, 1956, p. 131.

[52] *Mémoires sur Carnot par son fils*, 2 vols., 1863, II, 444–5; Napoleon I, *Correspondance*, XXXI, 103; Fontaine, 6 April 1815.

[53] *Moniteur*, 6 June 1815, p. 638; J. C. Hobhouse, *The Substance of Some Letters… during the Last Reign of the Emperor Napoleon*, 2nd edn, 2 vols., 1817, I, 405–11, 440, letters of 2, 7 June 1815.

[54] Baron Gourgaud, *Journal*, 2 vols., 1896–7, II, 553, diary for 20 June 1815; *Caulaincourt*, I, 198.

officials and politicians had been flocking to Louis XVIII's court in Ghent since April. On 8 July the King re-entered Paris in triumph. On 15 July the Emperor, partly on the advice of his few remaining courtiers, Bertrand, Gourgaud, *premier officier d'ordonnance* and Las Cases, a chamberlain, handed himself over to Captain Maitland of the *Bellerophon*.[55] On 17 October he landed at St Helena.

[55] Henry Lachouque, *The Last Days of Napoleon's Empire*, 1966, pp. 182, 229.

1 Monvoisin, *Confrontation of Mirabeau and the Marquis de Dreux-Brézé, 23 June 1789* (Rafael
Valls Fine Paintings)

Mirabeau, in the black costume of deputies of the Third Estate, is telling the *grand maître des
cérémonies* that they will only leave 'by the force of bayonets'. This famous confrontation led
to the creation of the National Assembly and the triumph of the revolutionaries. However, Dreux-
Brézé is a symbol of the survival as well as the defeat of the court. He continued to serve as
the chief organiser of court ceremonies until 1792 and from 1814 to 1825, when he was succeeded
by his son. This picture was painted for the museum of French history organised by Louis-Philippe
at Versailles.

2 Hubert Robert, *The royal family at mass in the Tuileries*, 1792 (Photo Bulloz)

Left to right: Madame Elizabeth, the Dauphin, the Queen, the King and Madame Royale, with courtiers and (right) an officer of the Garde nationale, hear mass in a room of the state apartments. It was too dangerous for them to attend the chapel in the north of the palace. This picture is traditionally held to represent their last mass in the Tuileries.

3 Hickel, *The Princesse de Lamballe* (Liechtenstein collection, Vaduz)
A cousin of Louis XVI, the Princesse de Lamballe, as *surintendante de la maison de la Reine*, was in charge of Marie-Antoinette's enormous household. Her salon was one of the centres of the court. She was a loyal friend who returned to France to resume her duties in 1791. She suffered a terrible death during the September massacres in 1792.

4 Roslin, *Thierry de Ville d'Avray*, 1790 (Thierry de Ville d'Avray collection)
Thierry de Ville d'Avray was a *premier valet de chambre*, head of the *garde-meuble* and first
mayor of Versailles. He loved Louis XVI, whom he called 'an angel', and disliked *grands seigneurs*,
especially the Noailles family. He was murdered during the September massacres.

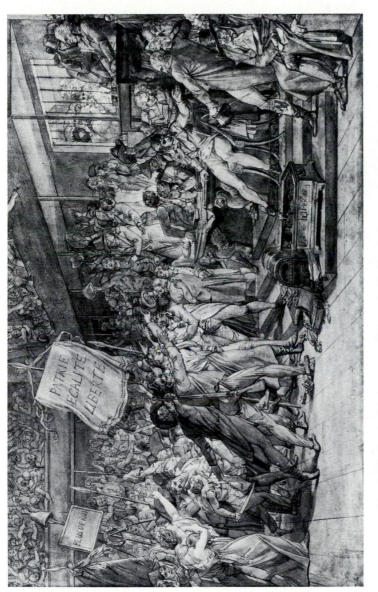

5 Gérard, *The Tenth of August, 1792* (Cabinet des Dessins du Louvre, photo réunion des musées nationaux)

After they left the Tuileries, the royal family was kept for three days in the building of the Legislative Assembly. The King and Queen can be seen in the box normally reserved for journalists. A few courtiers and servants attended them but were sent away when the royal family was taken to the prison of the Temple. This savage, Jacobin drawing, commissioned by the Assembly, originally depicted the King eating dinner while battle raged at the Tuileries. During the restoration Gérard erased the dinner, became *premier peintre du Roi* and painted the picture of the coronation of Charles X which is the frontispiece of this book.

6 Hubert Robert, *The farewell of their family to the Maréchal and Maréchale de Mouchy*, 1794
(Mouchy collection)
The guards in the prison of Saint-Lazare have been bribed to look away. The next day the Maréchal
and Maréchale, formerly governor of the palace of Versailles and *dame d'honneur* of the Queen
(who called her *madame étiquette*), were guillotined. However, their children survived to serve
at the courts of Napoleon I and Louis XVIII.

7 Danloux, *Jean-Baptiste Cléry*, 1798 (réunion des musées nationaux)
Cléry was a *valet de chambre* who was appointed by the commune of Paris to attend the royal
family in the Temple. His account of Louis XVI's last weeks is a masterpiece of royalist propaganda.
He is wearing the *croix de Saint Louis*, normally awarded for military service, which Louis XVIII
gave him for his service to the royal family in the prisons of the republic.

8 Thomas Girtin, *The Tuileries palace*, 1802 (author's collection)

The Tuileries palace, burnt during the commune in 1871, was the principal residence of the court of France in winter. It was linked to the Louvre by the long gallery along the Seine which became a museum of painting in 1793.

9 Louis Ducis, *Panoramic view of Saint-Cloud during the visit of the King of the Two Sicilies in 1830* (Musée de l'Ile de France. Photo Lauros-Giraudon)

Saint-Cloud, only a few miles from Paris, was destroyed in the Franco-Prussian War in 1871. It was smaller than Versailles and was the principal summer residence of the court in 1788 and 1790, and after 1802. Francis I of the Two Sicilies, father of the Duchesse de Berri, visited France a few weeks before the July revolution which led to the expulsion of the Bourbons and the dissolution of the court.

10 Stool or *pliant* (Château de Fontainebleau)
Reserved for wives of dukes, marshals and ambassadors, this stool was made for the *salon des jeux* of Marie-Antoinette at Compiègne in 1786. It was subsequently used by the Directors at the Luxembourg and then, having been recovered, was transferred to the Tuileries and finally to the *salle de trône* of the Emperor at Fontainebleau, where it still is. It symbolises the taste for rank and splendour which persisted in France despite changes of regime.

11 Benjamin Zix, *Wedding procession of Napoleon I and Marie-Louise*, 2 April 1810 (Weinstein collection) Ségur, the *grand maître des cérémonies*, holding his baton of office, leads the procession through the long gallery of the Louvre, which is lined with looted pictures and cheering spectators. The Napoleonic court was the most splendid in Europe, and the centre of power and promotion in the Empire. The Emperor is in the *petit costume* which he wore on formal occasions.

12 Gros, *The Emperor confides his wife and son to the Garde nationale, 23 January 1814* (réunion des musées nationaux) The scene takes place in the large central room of the Tuileries, the *salle des maréchaux*, which is lined with marshals' portraits. Madame de Montesquiou is holding the King of Rome. The next day the Emperor left to lead resistance to the invading armies. Despite its cheers and oaths, the Garde nationale was not prepared to fight for the Empire and helped ease the transition to the restoration.

13 Melling, *Hartwell House*, 1817 (Cabinet des Dessins du Louvre, photo réunion des musées nationaux)

After his return to France Louis XVIII sent his *dessinateur du cabinet*, Melling, to draw scenes of his life in exile. Louis XVIII lived with his court at Hartwell in Buckinghamshire from 1809 to 1814. This drawing may represent his departure in triumph for France on 20 April 1814.

14 Gros, *Departure of Louis XVIII from the Tuileries, 19 March 1815* (réunion des musées nationaux)

The King leaves the Tuileries a day before the Emperor returns. Over his left shoulder are his favourite Blacas, *ministre de la maison*, Duras *premier gentilhomme* in waiting and Maréchal Macdonald, a Napoleonic marshal who remained loyal to the King. Two footmen

15 Isabey, *The lying-in-state of Louis XVIII in the Tuileries*, 1824 (Musée Carnavalet)
In death as in life the court surrounded the King with splendour and deference. The lying-in-
state was open to the public and thousands of people filed through the palace to see it.
The drawing shows the *salle du trône* at its most sumptuous, after its redecoration under
the restoration.

16 Gérard, *Isabey and his daughter*, 1798 (réunion des musées nationaux)
Isabey was the most prolific court artist of the period, and produced flattering images of
both the Bonapartes and the Bourbons. *Dessinateur ordinaire du cabinet, des cérémonies et
des relations extérieures* under the Empire, he was sacked for Bonapartism in 1815 but reinstated
as *dessinateur ordinaire des spectacles de la cour* in 1828. Both Empresses and the Duchesse
de Berri liked him personally.

17 Fauconnier, *Bust of the Comte de
  Montesquiou*, 1812 (private collection)
Montesquiou came from a family which,
like the Talleyrand, considered itself older
than the Bourbons. He had served at the
court of Versailles but in 1809 replaced
Talleyrand as *grand chambellan*. He
remained loyal to the Emperor until the
end of the Hundred Days.

18 Gérard, *The Duchesse de Montabello and her
  children*, 1818 (Bibliothèque Nationale)
The Duchesse de Montebello, widow of Maréchal
Lannes and daughter of a *valet de garde-robe* of Louis
XVI, was *dame d'honneur* and an intimate friend
of the Empress Marie-Louise. She acquired great
influence over her mistress, which she used to drive
the Emperor and Empress apart.

19 Augustin, *The Comtesse de Montalivet*, date unknown (private collection)
Madame de Montalivet was an illegitimate daughter of Louis XV who became a lady-in-waiting
of the Empress Josephine. Her husband was a minister and, during the Hundred Days, *intendant-
général de la couronne* of Napoleon I. Their son was *intendant-général de la liste civile* of Louis-
Philippe. Many other families also served at different courts with equal success.

20 Bosio, *The Marquis de Lauriston*, *c.* 1823 (Los Angeles County Museum of Art, gift of Mrs Robert Mandel)

Lauriston flourished at court under the restoration even more than under the Empire. An aide-de-camp of his former school-fellow Napoleon I, he became *capitaine des mousquetaires gris* of Louis XVIII in 1815, *ministre de la maison* in 1820 and *grand veneur* in 1824. His wife was a lady-in-waiting first of the Empress, then of the Duchesse de Berri. This bust, by the *premier sculpteur du Roi*, was placed in the *salle des maréchaux* in the Tuileries.

21 Ingres, *Comte Amédée de Pastoret*, 1826 (courtesy of the Art Institute of Chicago)
Pastoret was one of the young, non-noble, ex-Napoleonic officials appointed *gentilshommes de la chambre* in the reform of 1820. His manners at first shocked Louis XVIII, and in this portrait he is shown in the uniform of a *conseiller d'état*, not a court official. However, he remained a prominent legitimist after 1830, until he became a senator in 1853.

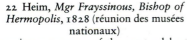

22 Heim, *Mgr Frayssinous, Bishop of Hermopolis*, 1828 (réunion des musées nationaux)

Frayssinous was one of the most celebrated preachers of his day. He was a favourite of Louis XVIII and became *premier aumônier* in 1822, and minister of ecclesiastical affairs and public instruction from 1824 to 1828. He was tutor to the Duc de Bordeaux in exile.

23 Boilly, *The Duc de Lévis*, 1822 (author's collection)

Described by the Duchesse de Maillé as the dirtiest and ugliest man in France, Lévis was also a knowledgeable and perceptive observer of the court until his death in 1830, just before the July revolution. He is wearing the order of the Saint-Esprit, the grandest French royal order, which every courtier coveted.

24 Ary Scheffer, *Maréchal Mouton, Comte de Lobau*, 1836 (Hervé Poulain)
Mouton was one of the favourite aides-de-camp of the Emperor, who said *mon mouton est un lion* and arranged Mouton's marriage to a Belgian aristocrat, Madamoiselle d'Arberg, daughter of a lady-in-waiting of the Empress Josephine. During the restoration he was out of favour. In 1830 he helped lead the July revolution and subsequently commanded the Garde nationale de Paris.

25 Horace Vernet, *Charles X at a review*, 1824 (réunion des musées nationaux)
The King is accompanied by the Dauphin, the Ducs d'Orléans and de Bourbon, Marshals Macdonald and Oudinot Major-Generals of the Garde royale and the Ducs de Maillé and de Fitzjames,
premiers aides-de-camp du Roi. In reality Vernet preferred Napoleonic subjects, such as the
Emperor's farewell to the imperial guard, which he was painting at the same time.

26 E. Wattier, *The throne-room in the Tuileries, 29 July 1830*, 1830 (Musée Carnavalet)
During the revolution of 1830 the Tuileries was invaded by a crowd for the first time since 1793. People took turns to sit on the throne until a dead revolutionary was put there. It was the end of one of the most glorious periods

CHAPTER 6

Reform

Voulant donner à notre maison civile une organisation qui la mette complète-
ment en rapport avec l'état politique de notre royaume, voulant faire disparaître
la confusion que le temps a introduite dans l'ordre hiérarchique des diverses
charges et emplois, et donner à la fois plus d'éclat à notre cour et plus de
régularité au service de notre maison, en appelant un plus grand nombre de
nos sujets auprès de notre personne.

Ordonnance of Louis XVIII, 1 November 1820

After the Hundred Days the court, like every other government department, was purged. Among those dismissed for Bonapartism were Isabey
the *dessinateur du cabinet*, the 4 *huissiers* who had returned to the
Napoleonic court, and 108 employees of the *écuries*.[1] One was called
Louvel. Born, like many servants of the court, in Versailles, he was
a fanatical Bonapartist who had joined the Emperor's stables on Elba
and followed him to Paris and Rochefort. After his dismissal he worked
for a tradesman attached to the royal stables, but brooded on the crimes
of the Bourbons.

The man in charge of the purge was the Comte de Pradel, self-effacing
and efficient, who had acquired what were known as 'English manners'
during his years in England with Louis XVIII.[2] As *directeur-général
de la maison* he replaced Blacas, who had been sacrificed by Louis XVIII
after Waterloo as a scapegoat for the mistakes of the first restoration.
Blacas became French ambassador in Naples, and later Rome, but continued to direct the *garde-robe* from abroad.

In June 1816 the court celebrated the marriage which Blacas had

[1] Françoise Waquet, *Les Fêtes royales sous la restauration*, 1980, p. 19n.; AN o3 533 f. 206,
Duras to Louis XVIII, 12 September 1815; AN o3 414, *Etat nominatif des employés aux Ecuries
du Roi ... rayés ... à compter du 1 aout 1815.*
[2] J. Lucas-Dubreton, *Louvel le régicide*, 2nd edn, 1923, pp. 35, 46–9; *La Boulaye*, p. 325.

117

arranged between the Duc de Berri and Marie-Caroline of Naples with
a round of entertainments. The traditional ceremonial was modified
and the marriage, unlike the Emperor's in 1810, took place in the cathedral of Paris, not the palace chapel. Some of the decorations used
were inherited from the Empire: their colour was simply changed from
Napoleonic green to royal blue. In a gesture to the Napoleonic aristocracy, the princess's *dame d'honneur* was the wife of Maréchal Oudinot.
Born Mademoiselle de Coucy, she was apparently sweet natured and
sensible and made no enemies at court. All the other ladies-in-waiting,
however, were royalists already connected with the court although, as
with the King's senior court officials, this did not exclude service in
the Empire. Comtesse Just de Noailles, for example, one of the best-
dressed women in Paris, had also been a lady-in-waiting of the Empresses
Marie-Louise and Josephine.[3]

The *chevalier d'honneur* of the Duchesse de Berri was Louis XVIII's
old friend, the indestructible Duc de Lévis (plate 23). He had been overjoyed by the restoration and wrote, with the honesty which makes him
one of the best observers of his world, 'after 25 years of rule by despicable
wretches who despise us, one is after all rather pleased to be back at
the top, in the position from which nothing should have toppled us'.[4]
He had wanted to be a minister or an ambassador but was happy to
have a court position. He often had audiences with the King and spent
evenings with the princess, who called him Gogo. He also spoke in
the Chamber of Peers and the Académie française. Money and good
manners, two particularly important topics during the restoration, were
his favourite subjects.

In September 1816 the King dissolved the ultra-royalist *chambre
introuvable*. The ministry headed by the Duc de Richelieu, *président
du conseil* and minister of foreign affairs, and Decazes, minister of police
and the King's favourite, introduced a series of liberal measures, such
as the electoral law of 1817 favouring the inhabitants of the towns.
Most court officials were horrified. Although there were exceptions such
as the Prince de Poix and the Duc de Gramont, Richelieu complained
that 'those who lunch with the King and dine off his favours' voted

---

[3] *Castellane*, II, 201, entry for 10 November 1827.
[4] Archives du Comte Charles de Nicolay, Duc to Duchesse de Lévis, Arras, 23 August 1815.

against his government in the Chamber of Peers. In 1818 the Ducs d'Havré, d'Avaray and d'Aumont, who as *capitaine des gardes*, *maître de la garde-robe* and *premier gentilhomme* in waiting respectively had accompanied the King on his afternoon drive, rushed to the Chamber of Peers to vote against the government the moment it was over. Officials of the *maison de Monsieur*, in particular the Duc de Fitzjames, were also notorious for their opposition to the King's government.[5]

Contemporaries found this shocking. It implied that the King was not whole-hearted in support of his government. In the other great constitutional monarchy, England, the ministry insisted on senior court officials voting in support of the government. By 1820 it had also established the right to select them, despite the opposition of George IV, and Queen Victoria's audacious rearguard action during the Bedchamber Crisis in 1839. The court had become an instrument in the hands of the government.[6]

Metternich was also appalled at the rift between the court and the government. He told the French ambassador that 'the court was our disease, and a very bad disease'. The King should form a court on 'a completely new basis', and his own officials should serve the princes. The powerful and reactionary *premiers gentilshommes* should be replaced by 100 chamberlains, as was the case in Austria (and had been at the court of Napoleon I): 'he regards this remedy as sovereign'. The Emperor Francis, who had disobedient brothers of his own, was even more insistent.

The Marquis de Bonnay, who knew the King intimately, having been his private secretary in 1802, also urged Richelieu to persuade the King not to 'treat well those who are treating him badly'. He should use the *entrées*, a disapproving silence, words, requests for a pinch of snuff and the promise of the order of the Saint-Esprit as political weapons,

[5] Duc de Richelieu, *Lettres ... au Marquis d'Osmond*, 1939, pp. 72, 165, letters of 7 November 1816, 9 March 1818; A. Polovtsov (ed.), *Correspondance diplomatique des ambassadeurs et ministres de Russie en France et de France en Russie avec leurs gouvernements de 1814 à 1830*, 3 vols., 1902–7, II, 565, Pozzo di Borgo to Nesselrode, 20 January 1818.
[6] Duke of Wellington, *Supplementary Despatches*, 15 vols., 1858–72, V, 513, Wellington to the Lords of the Household, 28 February 1829; for the attitude of George IV, see A. Aspinall, *The Letters of George IV*, 3 vols., Cambridge, 1938, II, 449, George IV to Lord Liverpool, 25 July 1821.

to force his court officials to follow his ministers' policies.[7] Louis XVIII did give his court officials political lectures and occasionally prolonged his drives to prevent them voting against the government. But that was as far as he would go: he had too much experience of political disagreements to believe that they could be ordered to disappear. Even if he had dismissed disobedient court officials it would not have made much difference. The ultra-royalist opposition was based in the chambers, not the court, under the leadership of independent politicians like Villèle and Chateaubriand. Above all, as he often told Decazes, he wanted to keep his court out of politics and under his own control: 'I want an impassable barrier between the household and the ministry.'

Another reason why the government wanted to reform the court was its desire to win over a coterie of rich and discontented Napoleonic nobles, many of them former court officials. They were more hostile to the restoration than in 1814–15 and rarely went to court. As Stendhal wrote of Ségur, being out of office they had become liberal – despite years in the service of Napoleon I. Bondy and Rambuteau, chamberlains of Napoleon, never went to court and opposed the government after 1815. In 1820 at a ball given by a former aide-de-camp of the Emperor, Duc Charles de Plaisance, Castellane noted that 'the former court of the Emperor formed the core of the party'.[8]

The excluded bourgeois were another problem. In 1820 the famous scientist and liberal Baron Cuvier wrote to Decazes that the 'injured vanity' of the rich and the parvenus excluded from court office was more dangerous to the regime than any 'real grievances'. Other liberals who attacked the court as anachronistic and reactionary were Guizot, Benjamin Constant and de Pradt.[9] Even the ultra-royalist La Boulaye thought that the restoration, like the sun, should shine for everyone

[7] BVC FR 73 f. 118, Bonnay to Richelieu, 4 November 1816; ff. 120–1, Caraman to Richelieu, 25 November 1816.

[8] Ernest Daudet, *Louis XVIII et le Duc Decazes*, 1899, pp. 454–6; Roger Langeron, *Decazes ministre du Roi*, 1960, p. 141, Louis XVIII to Decazes, September 1817; Stendhal, *Napoléon*, I, 218; *Castellane*, I, 387, diary for 15 January 1820.

[9] Bibliothèque de l'Institut Mss 3,295 Fonds Cuvier, *Mémoire secret sur la politique intérieure de l'état*, January 1820, f. 9; François Guizot, *Du Gouvernement de la France depuis la restauration et du ministère actuel*, 1820, p. 178; Duc Victor de Broglie, *Souvenirs*, 4 vols., 1886, II, 93, *Journal de la Duchesse de Broglie*, 1 October 1819; Abbé de Pradt, *Petit Catéchisme constitutionnel à l'usage des français*, 1820, pp. 151–2, 154.

and helped organise a *maison des pages* with pages from 'both sides' in 1820.[10]

On 14 February 1820 Louvel, the former groom in the Emperor's stables, finally assassinated the Duc de Berri, whom he had been stalking for months. In the face of a surge of ultra-royalist outrage, and of pressure from within the royal family, Decazes had to resign. Liberal riots that June in Paris shook the confidence of the new royalist government headed by Richelieu. Hostility among the elite was confirmed by a conspiracy in August which involved La Fayette, Laffitte and several Napoleonic officers. The government decided to act.

In the seventeenth century the reform of the *maison du Roi* had been one of the few measures which had daunted Richelieu's great ancestor the Cardinal. He wrote in his *Testament politique* that too many vested interests were at stake, and Louis XIII was too fond of his courtiers, for it to be possible.[11]

His liberal descendant, however, was braver and undertook the only complete reorganisation in its history. Richelieu was too frank and independent, and too fond of Tsar Alexander I, to be an intimate of the royal family: indeed Monsieur disliked him. However, he had inherited a *charge* of *premier gentilhomme* (which he never exercised) and had been made *grand veneur* in 1819. Being part of the court, having known it from the inside all his life, he knew how to deal with it.

As in the reign of Louis XVI the leading figures behind the reform of the court were moderate royalists, such as Richelieu himself, Mounier the *intendant des bâtiments*, de Serre the minister of justice and Pasquier the foreign minister. Serre wanted to add 'splendour, brilliance, pleasure even' to the court and to end 'the almost total exclusion of new families from the *maison du Roi*'. Richelieu wanted to 'open this career to to all social successes, without any exception'. An influential liberal, de Cormenin, wrote to de Serre that the court should be 'a means of strength and influence', to 'attach rich and powerful families' to the regime.[12]

The difficulty was to persuade the King, whose attachment to the

---

[10] *La Boulaye*, p. 314.
[11] Cardinal de Richelieu, *Testament politique*, 1947, p. 280.
[12] Comte L. M. Molé, *Le Comte Molé ... sa vie, ses mémoires*, 6 vols., 1922–30, IV, 367–70; AN BB30 257 60, *Papiers saisis chez le duc de Richelieu*, Serre to Richelieu, 7 August 1820, enclosing Cormenin's plan; AN 40 AP 19 Richelieu to Beugnot, 11 November 1820.

traditional *maison du Roi* was well known. As Richelieu wrote, 'it is the holy ark on which one hardly dares lay hands'. Nevertheless Louis XVIII knew that 1820 was a crisis for the restoration: for the first time since 1817 the court did not go to Saint-Cloud in the summer. In the end Richelieu was able to write, with only a touch of sarcasm, 'the King ... has agreed to these changes, which rather disturb his habits, with the best grace in the world'.[13] An ordonnance reforming the entire *maison du Roi* was issued on 1 November 1820. However the King was still sufficiently independent to resist the government's efforts to make him appoint aides-de-camp. They would hardly have increased the prestige of an invalid who had never seen military action.[14]

One achievement of the reforming ordonnance of 1 November 1820 was to eliminate inconsistencies and anachronisms in the *maison du Roi*. The heralds were finally attached to the service to which they logically belonged, the ceremonies. The most ridiculous and useless positions, such as *pousse-fauteuil* and *capitaine de l'equipage des mulets* were abolished, as Pradel had suggested they should be in 1815. Anachronistic titles were changed: the *bouche* became the *hôtel*, the *premier tranchant* and *premier pannetier* the *chambellans de l'hôtel* and the *menus-plaisirs* the *fêtes et spectacles*.[15]

An attempt was also made to reduce the number of servants. The *garde-robe* was dissolved (Blacas was compensated with a post of *premier gentilhomme*). The *gentilshommes servant* in the *hôtel* and some servants in that service and the *chambre* were dismissed. However, the court's tendency to increase, and the King's desire to have a large number of servants, were so strong that this reduction was purely temporary. The King maintained his personal servants although they were not mentioned by the ordonnance.[16]

Although the *maison du Roi* was not permanently reduced in 1820, it was streamlined in the sense that, in place of the haphazard accretion

[13] Comte de Serre, *Correspondance*, 6 vols., 1876–7, IV, 75, Richelieu to Serre, 16 August 1820; AN 40 AP 19, Richelieu to Beugnot, 11 November 1820.
[14] AN 03 530, *Ordonnance* of 1 November 1820; National Library of Scotland, Edinburgh, Manuscripts 6202 f. 565, Stuart de Rothesay Papers, Stuart to Castlereagh, 27 November 1820.
[15] AN 03 227, Pradel to the *premier gentilhomme de service*, 13 November 1815.
[16] AN 03 540 f. 516, *Rapport au roi* 26 December 1820; cf. AN 03 227, Doudeauville to Aumont, 28 October 1825, complaining that the number of *huissiers* exceeds the limit prescribed by the *ordonnance*.

of officials before 1820, the ordonnance endowed each service with a regular hierarchy of *grands officiers*, *premiers officiers* and, for the first time, *officiers de la maison* and *du service*. This hierarchy was extended throughout the 1820s to include all officials depending on the ministry of the *maison du Roi*, such as those running the museums and forests of the crown.

These ranks were especially popular because they now conferred a splendid uniform. In 1827 Rossini, who had been brought to Paris and made *premier compositeur du Roi*, became an *officier du service de 2e classe* for the sake of the uniform.[17] For one of the most important aspects of the reorganisation of 1820 was that the court officials of Louis XVIII finally received uniforms, which were consciously modelled on those of the court of Napoleon I. The colour for each service was the same: red for the *gouvernments*, blue for the *écuries*, green for the *vénerie*, violet for the *cérémonies*: the higher the official the more gold embroidery on his uniform. Only the *chambre*, dark blue instead of scarlet, was different. Trousers and boots could be worn in the day during the week, but in the evening knee-breeches and silk stockings were obligatory. This increase in the visual splendour of the court was extremely important for an age which judged people, even more than today, by their clothes. It was the only aspect of the reorganisation noted by the Piedmontese ambassador: he wrote that 'nothing will be omitted to eclipse by the richness and elegance of the costumes the luxury with which the previous government had affected to surround itself'.[18]

The most important aspect of the reorganisation, however, was the creation of 32 salaried *gentilshommes de la chambre*, 12 *écuyers cavalcadours* (there had been only 5 before), 32 pages and an indefinite number of unsalaried *gentilshommes honoraires de la chambre*. Hitherto restricted to the outer structure of the court, Napoleonic influence now reached its heart, the *service de la chambre*. For, despite the difference in nomenclature, the *gentilshommes de la chambre du Roi* were based on the *chambellans de S.M. l'Empereur et Roi*.

---

[17] AN 03 540 ff. 459–60, *Rapport au roi*, 1 December 1820; AN 03 552 f. 176, *Ordonnance* of 12 March 1827.

[18] AN 03 885, 101, *Règlement arrête par le Roi concernant l'habillement*, 10 December 1820; Archivio di Stato Turin, Lettere Ministri Francia (henceforward referred to as AST LMF), Mazzo 246, Pralormo to Comte de Saint-Marsan, 9 December 1820.

All these positions were specifically designed to satisfy what Pasquier called 'so many *amours-propres* which are dying of thirst'. They were essentially companions or escorts, rather than servants, of the King and their duties were restricted to receiving people coming to court. They could receive the King's orders directly, not through a superior. As one wife assured her husband, 'the position is very fine, in waiting on the King, at the same time as and like the *premiers gentilshommes*'.[19] The expansion of the court was intended to win the support as well as to satisfy the vanity of the elite. Just as Napoleon I had hoped to win the royalist nobility, so in 1820 the government of Louis XVIII hoped to gain the Napoleonic elite and the bourgeoisie, through the court.

It was a reasonable calculation. In late 1820 and 1821 alone there were 288 applications for the post of *gentilhomme de la chambre*, 60 for that of *écuyer* (which was restricted to good horsemen) and 193 for that of page. Many Napoleonic court officials applied, including the Comte de Turenne, the Emperor's rich and devoted *maître de la garde-robe*, who still had the Emperor's clothes and jewels in his custody. Stressing that he was 'a man of honour who has a faithful heart', he used his loyalty to the Emperor as an (unsuccessful) argument for obtaining a post with the King. By 1830 there had been 779 applications for the post of page and 867 for that of *gentilhomme de la chambre*.[20] In comparison there had been only 247 applications for the post of chamberlain during the Empire.[21]

Clearly an expansion of the court fulfilled a need in the elite. But would it open the court to new families? Many people feared, and Pasquier believed, that the recommendations and influence of the princes and the high court officials were so powerful that the court in fact remained an exclusively noble and royalist institution. However, Louis XVIII refused to appoint the son of the Duc de Castries and the grandson of the Duc d'Avaray *gentilshommes de la chambre* (it is a sign of the

---

[19] Serre, *Correspondance*, IV, 5, Pasquier to Serre, 1 August 1820; AN 03 540 f. 559, 541 f. 167, *Rapport au roi*, 29 December 1820, *Ordonnance*, 22 April 1821, describe the *gentils-hommes'* functions; Archives x, Madame to Monsieur de Podenas, 5 November 1820.

[20] AN 03 373, Turenne to Louis XVIII, 2 January 1821; AN 03 355–64, 676, 373, 2243, 459, 630, 706, *Demandes de places (gentilshommes de la chambre)*; AN 03 460, *demandes de places d'écuyers travail terminé le 10 septembre 1821*; AN 03 480, *Listes Générales des demandes de places de pages, 1820–30*.

[21] AN 349 AP 1, *Liste des Personnes qui sollicitent l'honneur d'être chambellans de Sa Majesté l'Empereur et Roi, 1809–15; ibid.*, 5, 19 requests for office as chamberlain.

King's desire to rally the Napoleonic elite that both these elderly royalist Dukes stressed their descendants' service in the *Napoleonic* army in their letters of application). The ultra-royalist Madame de Podenas complained that 'the old families cannot be accused of having exercised too much influence when you think that one [the court's expression for the King] has refused the Duc d'Aumont for his nephew, M. d'Escars for his son-in-law and the Ducs de La Chatre and de Luxembourg for their nephews'.[22]

In fact, of the 107 new court officials appointed in 1820–1, 22.5 per cent were non-noble, 39 per cent came from the *noblesse non-présentée* and 38.5 per cent from the *noblesse présentée*. Excluding the pages, who were too young to have had the opportunity, 60 per cent had served the Empire. Moreover, many of the new court officials came from especially humble or hostile backgrounds. Three new *gentilshommes de la chambre*, Colonels Druault, Mermet and Coutard, were sons respectively of a shop-keeper, a tailor and a peasant. Whereas the Académie française still defined *gentilhomme* as 'someone who is noble by race', at court the word was simply a title. One liberal lady, Madame de Coigny, sneered that Louis XVIII had surpassed Molière, since the latter had only created one *bourgeois gentilhomme* 'whereas H.M. has just made 12'.[23]

In addition many new court officials had been enemies of the restoration. Ten of the Emperor's court officials received court office in 1820–1. Comte Rapp, a Protestant aide-de-camp of the Emperor who had fought in the Hundred Days – three major sins in ultra-royalist eyes – was appointed one of the four *premiers chambellans maîtres de la garde-robe*. He became a favourite of the King as they shared a taste for dirty jokes. General Reille, who had fought at Waterloo, became *gentilhomme de la chambre* of the King who had drunk to Wellington's victory.

The role of the reorganised household, and Louis XVIII, as agents of reconciliation was demonstrated by a famous incident in 1821, when

---

[22] Pasquier, *Histoire*, IV, 468; AN o3 373 doss. Sourdis, Duc d'Avaray to Louis XVIII, n.d.; AN o3 373 doss. Castries, Duc de Castries to Louis XVIII, n.d.; Archives x, Madame to Monsieur de Podenas, 18 April 1821.

[23] Vicomte Révérend, *Titres, anoblissements et pairies de la restauration*, 6 vols., 1901–6, II, 407, V, 111; H. L. de Riancey, *Le Comte de Coutard*, 1857, p. 421; *Dictionnaire de l'Académie française*, 2 vols., 1825, I, 647; AN 234 AP, Papiers Mounier 2, *Lettres interceptées*, Madame de Coigny to Lady Holland, 3 January 1821.

news of Napoleon's death on St Helena reached Paris. To the end the Emperor had been surrounded by faithful courtiers, Bertrand (who as *grand maréchal du palais* signed his death certificate), his chamberlain Montholon and his *premier valet de chambre* Marchand. The news had little impact in France, except on some of his courtiers. Rapp, who was in waiting at the Tuileries, was accosted by Fitzjames. The outspoken ultra-royalist said that, since Rapp's former master was dead, no doubt he was going to wear mourning. Rapp replied that he wore mourning in his heart and that he would never forget a man to whom he owed his entire success. An hour later, when he was in the King's presence, Louis XVIII said 'I am aware of the impertinence to which you were subject and of the reply you made. I congratulate you on it, it was the right way to take up the challenge.' Rapp replied: 'Sire, the author of my success will be the object of my eternal gratitude, and this success is all the more precious to me in that, without it, I would not have the honour to approach Your Majesty.' The story raced round Paris, redounding to their credit.[24]

The *maison du Roi* was transformed. Reforms which had been advocated since 1790 had finally been accomplished. It could no longer be accused of being a preserve of the *ancien régime* or the counter-revolution. It had lost its most anachronistic aspects and was less domestic and more elitist than before. Nevertheless, since the princes' households were left untouched, one-third of the court remained the same.

The *entrées* to the palace were also modernised and expanded. The *entrée* to the *salon bleu* was extended to all officers in the army and the Garde nationale de Paris, which was more generous than the practice of the Empire. It was also given to magistrates and mayors, *sous-préfets* and Paris *curés*, none of whom, except the mayors, had had the *entrée* under the Empire.[25]

The next room, the *salle de la paix*, was opened to officials of the *cours des comptes* and *de cassation*, the *premiers présidents* and *procureurs-généraux* of *cours royales* throughout the country, the presidents of the Lutheran, Calvinist and Jewish consistories and colonels and lieutenant-colonels of the Garde royale and the Garde nationale de Paris.

[24] J. P. Viennet, *Journal*, 1955, p. 59, entry for 6 July 1821.
[25] AN 03 541 f. 151, *Rapport au Roi*, 16 April 1821; AN 03 530, *Règlement sur les Entrées dans le Palais du Roi*, 1 December 1820; AN 03 530, *Rapports au Roi 27*, 31 December 1820.

Peers, archbishops, *Chevaliers du Saint-Esprit* and the most senior judges, officers of the Garde royale, *maison militaire* and Garde nationale de Paris and court officials received the *entrée* to the *salle du trône*. The *entrée* to the *grand cabinet* had already, by a special favour of Louis XVIII, been given to marshals.[26] In 1820 it was extended to ministers, cardinals, a few court officials and guard officers, the Chancellor, the *grand référendaire de la chambre des pairs* the Marquis de Sémonville, and the President of the Chamber of Deputies. In addition there were what was known as *entrées de faveur*, lists of people with access to the *grand cabinet* which were the last relic of the *entrées de la chambre* and *du cabinet* of before 1792. They were drawn up every three months and included dukes, valets, the most senior court officials and ministers.[27]

The extension of the *entrées* in 1820–1 confirmed the process which had begun in 1814. The court was now restricted to people with official positions in the service of the King. The separate category of *hommes présentés* was from 1819 only admitted 'into the rooms to which their rank or their distinctions assign them'. No presentations of men on Mondays are recorded in the *Moniteur* after 1819 and no separate Monday receptions for men after the accession of Charles X.[28]

Official and military rank was now the only means by which men, whatever their background, could obtain access to court receptions. This was one reason why the position of *gentilhomme honoraire de la chambre* was so popular. It gave its holder the *entrée* to the *salle du trône* and a splendid uniform. To take only two examples, the Comte de Caumont-La Force, brother and son of *ducs et pairs*, and a member of one of the oldest noble families of France, applied for this position since 'No longer having the costume of a Deputy or a Colonel of the Garde nationale I can no longer present myself in the *château*' (as the Tuileries was called during the restoration). The Marquis de Biencourt, a member of the old *noblesse présentée*, requested it since 'he has not been able to obtain a high rank which would enable him to pay his

[26] AN 03 530, *Règlement sur les Entrées dans le Palais du roi*; AN 03 195 f. 34, Duras to Comte Belliard, 18 June 1819.
[27] AN 03 546 f. 178 *Rapport au Roi*, 8 April 1824; AN 03 529, *Rapport au Roi* 23 October 1824; AN 03 506, *Demandes au premier gentilhomme de la chambre*.
[28] AN 03 199, *Registre des présentations*; AN 03 195 ff. 31–2, *Décision du premier gentilhomme*, 20 March 1819.

court suitably to the King. Deprived of this favour, which he enjoyed before the revolution ...'[29] Like the *maison du Roi*, the *entrées* had been transformed, in character even more than in composition. Official rank, not social class, was now the basis of the court of France.

[29] AN 03 357 doss. Caumont, Comte de Caumont-La Force to La Bouillerie 5 February 1829; AN 03 356 doss. Biencourt, Biencourt to ?, 15 January 1828 to?; cf. AN 03 359 doss. Guébriant, Comte de Guébriant to Charles X, 27 April 1827.

CHAPTER 7

The promised land

Elle est entrée dans sa terre promise.

> The court, according to *Biographie des dames de la cour et du Faubourg Saint-Germain*, par un valet de chambre congédié, 1826

The decade following the reorganisation of 1820–1 was a golden age for the court of France. It was equal in energy and optimism, and superior in realism, to the first decade of the reign of François Ier or of the personal rule of Louis XIV. Having lost its most controversial aspects, the court functioned relatively smoothly. An important part of the reorganisation had been the appointment, after a gap of five years, of a *ministre de la maison*, the Marquis de Lauriston. Like Alexandre de Girardin he knew how to turn changes of regime to his own advantage. A former aide-de-camp of Napoleon, he had never forgiven the Emperor for choosing Caulaincourt rather than himself as *grand écuyer* in 1804.[1] In 1815 Lauriston, as royalist as he was once Bonapartist, became *capitaine-lieutenant* of the first company of Mousquetaires, and then served in the Garde royale.

The minister was able to exercise more authority than Pradel, whose term of office, according to Fontaine, had been 'a reign of waste and weakness'. The days when court officials could claim that their offices dated from 'the origin of the monarchy' were over. It was now clear that they dated from an ordonnance of 1820. The blow to their pride and prestige was painful. The aged Duc d'Avaray, *maître de la garde-robe*, wrote a long letter to Richelieu complaining of 'the degradation of my charge'. The Duc d'Escars contemplated going abroad.[2]

---

[1] *Méneval*, I, 344.

[2] *Fontaine*, I, 597, entry for 13 November 1820; AN 03 72, Grand Maître, *Notice sur la charge de Grand Maître de France* by Agasse, June 1818; AN 03 352 Chambre, Personnel 1818–24, d'Avaray to Richelieu, 26 December 1820; Archives x, Duchesse d'Escars to Madame de Podenas, 26 June 1821.

After 1820 the King succeeded in keeping the *ministère de la maison* under his control: Lauriston did not resign in 1821, like Richelieu and the other ministers, when they were replaced by ultra-royalists headed by Villèle.[3] In 1824 Lauriston was replaced by the Duc de Doudeauville, a *grand seigneur* and father of Monsieur's influential aide-de-camp, Sosthènes de La Rochefoucauld, who was a friend of the King's favourite, Madame du Cayla. Doudeauville fought many battles with senior court officials over control of their departments. The Duc de Polignac, *premier écuyer* after 1824 (a position he had held in the *maison de Monsieur*), was particularly troublesome and independent. In 1827, to Doudeauville's fury, he reorganised the riding school at Versailles on his own initiative. Like the *grand aumônier* and the *premiers gentils-hommes*, he occasionally appointed junior officials without consulting the minister.[4]

However in 1827, when Doudeauville resigned in protest at the abolition of the Garde nationale de Paris, Charles X replaced him by a tough former Napoleonic official, the Comte de La Bouillerie. La Bouillerie was an example of the continuity of the court bureaucracy under different regimes and proof that there was no incompatability between fervent royalism and previous service of the Empire. His brother married a niece of Laporte, Louis XVI's *intendant de la liste civile*, and he was *trésorier-général du domaine extraordinaire* under the Empire and an ultra-royalist deputy after 1815. He was more successful than his predecessors in keeping the *chefs de service* under control. He prevented their appointing new court officials, and was prepared to be icily insulting to the Duc de Polignac, suggesting that he did not read the letters he signed.[5]

Despite struggles over servants and junior officials, the King and the minister or *intendant-général* retained control over senior appointments, especially the *gentilshommes de la chambre*, *écuyers cavalcadours* and

[3] BVC FR 96 f. 194, *Mémoire du duc de Richelieu à sa sortie du ministère*, 3 January 1822.
[4] AN 03 551 f. 164, *Rapport au Roi*, 24 September 1826; AN 03 227, Doudeauville to d'Aumont, 12 November 1825; AN 03 426, 389, Polignac to Doudeauville, 21 February 1827, Doudeauville to Polignac, 1 March 1827.
[5] AN 03 523, *Nominations 1814 à 1830*, La Bouillerie to Dreux-Brézé, 25 July 1829; AN 03 557 f. 34, *Rapport au Roi*, 21 July 1829; AN 03 871, *Logements*, draft of La Bouillerie to Polignac, 8 January 1828.

pages. A determined court official, such as the bankrupt but influential Duc d'Aumont, succeeded in having six nephews and grandsons and two of his mistress's sons appointed pages: two of them later received permanent posts at court.[6] Otherwise the recommendations of court officials and even of members of the royal family were too infrequent and too unsuccessful to affect appointments enormously. For example only 4 of the 9 protégés of Mathieu de Montmorency and 6 of the 19 of the Duc d'Angoulême became court officials.[7]

The crucial factor in deciding court appointments was that, like other ministers, Lauriston, Doudeauville and La Bouillerie worked alone with the King. They drew up lists of applicants which they then discussed directly with the King during their regular private audiences. They had opportunities to put over their ideas, or obey the King's, which no court officials and few members of the royal family shared (see chapter 8). Court officials knew this very well. The Marquise de Dreux-Brézé wrote to Richelieu, who was replacing Lauriston until his arrival in Paris, that failure for her request for a place of *gentilhomme honoraire de la chambre* was certain 'if the *président du conseil* does not make it [her demand] stand out among the crowd by saying something in its favour'. Other senior court officials asked the minister to 'fix', 'finish' or 'support' their applications for court offices. The applications were clearly unlikely to succeed on their own.[8] The power retained by the King and the minister meant that new court offices were not overwhelmed by other court officials and their families. In 1830 only 32 per cent of senior court officials were close relations of other or previous senior court officials, compared to 54 per cent in 1815. The reorganisation of 1820–1 had succeeded in opening the court to new families.

The choice of pages, however, went against this trend. In 1789 the *maison des pages* had been composed above all of the provincial nobility.

[6] AN 03 475, *État des pages de la chambre* for de Champs de Blot; and doss. E. and G. de Sainte-Aldegonde; AN 03 476 doss. J. d'Aumont, AN 03 477 doss. E. de Sainte-Aldegonde and de Marguerittes; AN 03 478 doss. M. d'Aumont.
[7] AN 03 356–64, 371, *Demandes de places de gentilshommes de la chambre, passim.*
[8] AN 03 373 doss. Monteynard Madame de Dreux-Brézé to Richelieu, 12 November 1820; AN 03 489 doss. Pisançon Marquis de Chabrillant to La Bouillerie, 20 August 1827; AN 03 371 doss. Machault d'Arnouville, Duc Charles de Damas to Doudeauville, 25 June 1826; AN 03 479 doss. Mortemart, Duchesse de Mortemart to La Bouillerie, 28 August 1829.

Only 18 per cent had come from the *noblesse présentée*. But between 1820 and 1830 the proportion was 38 per cent. This reflects not only the greater deference of the *noblesse présentée* for the monarchy (before 1789 the post of page had been considered slightly demeaning), but also its inability to pass exams. Gérard de Rohan-Chabot, dismissed from Saint-Cyr for failure in exams, passed through the *maison des pages* in 1825 simply in order to acquire the rank of *sous-lieutenant*.[9] Places of page were in such demand that the number rose from 36 in 1820 to 60 by 1830.

However the minister of war complained of the 'lack of ability of the pages'.[10] The Ecole polytechnique and Saint-Cyr had higher standards and were smarter than the pages' school. In 1825 and 1829 Doudeauville and La Bouillerie brought about some improvement, raising entrance requirements and delaying the admission of incapable pages.[11]

Despite its bad reputation, the pages' school did, Sémonville wrote to Charles X, fulfil its main purpose: 'in general the pages admitted into regiments have brought with them more ardent zeal than the pupils of the other schools, with less knowledge'.[12] Sémonville was a brilliant, supple politician who had served every regime since 1789 and knew more about monarchies and revolutions than most of his contemporaries. Here he went to the heart of the court. Emotions such as 'zeal' and vanity were its driving-force. Admission to the royal palaces and service in the royal households were an emotional, personal complement to the rational, institutional side of the restoration represented by the charter and the two chambers.

The government's choice of *gentilshommes de la chambre* shows its use of the court to satisfy the emotions of loyalty and vanity. By 1830, 309 had been appointed. Probably because the regime was now relatively self-confident, they were not chosen from members of the opposition or the Empire aristocracy. Except in 1820–1 the court was not used as an instrument of government. For example the *grande aumônerie* was not employed to control the church, as it had been, to a certain extent, under the Empire. In a furious jurisdictional dispute between the *grand aumônier* and the Archbishop of Paris the King and the govern-

---

[9] AN 03 477, 112, Ministre de la Guerre to Doudeauville, 15 July 1825.
[10] AN 03 469, *Rapport au ministre*, November 1824.
[11] AN 03 480, draft of *Note pour le roi* by La Bouillerie, June 1829.
[12] AN 03 470, 262, Sémonville to Doudeauville, 20 June 1826.

ment in the end supported the latter. After 1826 the *grand aumônier* the Prince de Croÿ spent more time in his diocese of Rouen than at court. Maréchal Moncey, Duc de Conegliano, the senior Napoleonic marshal, wrote that it was 'the most ardent of his wishes' for his son-in-law and heir to become a *gentilhomme honoraire de la chambre* of Charles X, but his wish was not granted.[13]

Nor were the *gentilshommes de la chambre* chosen for their wealth, as many of Napoleon's chamberlains had been. The grant of 60,000 francs in 1821 to help them with the cost of their uniform implies that they were not rich. Candidates with 150,000 or 180,000 francs a year, like the Marquis de Biencourt and the Comte de Mandat, were unsuccessful.[14]

Birth was more important. The *noblesse présentée* provided 38 per cent, 48 per cent were from the *noblesse non-présentée* and only 14 per cent were non-noble. However, this was rather due to the importance of nobles in every area of public life – the administration, the army and local government – than to their birth alone. When 75 per cent of the richest notables in France in 1820 were noble, the proportion at court was unlikely to be less. Many nobles from ancient ducal families, such as the Comtes de Caumont-La Force, de Crillon, de Broglie, and de Clermont-Tonnerre, were refused the post. Among non-nobles appointed were a banker, two stock-brokers, Baron Rabusson, who was a colonel in the Garde royale and Cadudal, brother of the royalist conspirator executed in 1804. Doudeauville felt that under Napoleon 'historic nobility' was 'more respected, more feted than it has been since, under Louis XVIII as well as under Charles X'.[15] The Emperor was an autocrat who valued historic nobility for itself (partly because so many nobles opposed him). Louis XVIII and Charles X were parliamentary monarchs whose rule was accepted by the immense majority of

[13] See R. Limouzin-Lamothe, *Monseigneur de Quelen, archevêque de Paris*, 2 vols., 1955–7, I, 182–205; AN 03 358 doss. Conegliano, Maréchal Moncey to Charles X, 5 June 1829.
[14] AN 03 541 f. 46, *Rapport au Roi*, 27 January 1821; AN 03 356 doss. Biencourt, Biencourt to Doudeauville, April 1825; AN 03 361 doss. Mandat de Grancey, Marquise de la Magdeleine to La Bouillerie 2 January 1829.
[15] AN 03 369, *Demandes de places de gentilshommes de la chambre*, 1828–30, *passim*; Madame Soutade-Roger, 'Les Notables sous la restauration', *Revue d'histoire économique et sociale*, XXXVIII, 1960, p. 104; S. de La Rochefoucauld, I, 213; cf. the Duchesse de Maufrigneuse in Balzac, *Le Cabinet des antiques*, II, 73: *Nous étions plus puissants sous Napoléon.*

of the nobility. Neither King needed to pay much attention to the nobility. They had other problems on their hands.

The basis of selection for court appointments was service. France finally had a ruling class based on service of the King and court positions were used to reward it, as is shown by a comparison of the different factors mentioned in official lists of candidates for the positions of chamberlain and *gentilhomme de la chambre* (see appendix, p. 200). Since emigration and acts of royalism were also considered services to the monarchy, the primacy of service is clear. In contrast the Empire was more interested in wealth and age, qualities which made a notable. Of the total of 309 *gentilshommes titulaires* and *honoraires* appointed, 150 were in the army, 58 in the administration, 25 were deputies, 9 were peers and 7 were officers in the Garde nationale de Paris. Thus the court was used, as Cormenin hoped as 'an instrument of strength and influence'.[16] But this was restricted to encouraging, rewarding or compensating people already in the King's service. For example four former officers of the Garde nationale de Paris were appointed by Martignac in 1828 to compensate them for its abolition under Villèle in 1827. In the crisis of the reign of Charles X, in 1829–30, some ultra-royalists were appointed to encourage voters to vote for the new *gentilhomme de la chambre*.[17]

By 1830, with 300 *gentilshommes de la chambre* and a total of 2,219 court officials and servants, Charles X had the largest and most elitist household of any Bourbon king. Court office was so popular that Comte Beugnot, non-noble, a former deputy in the Legislative Assembly and Napoleonic official, wrote in 1830 that 'The Tuileries could not contain all those who desire the post of *gentilhomme*.'[18] He was not exaggerating.

At the same time the Tuileries could hardly contain everyone attending the Sunday receptions. In 1827 a die-hard Bonapartist like Stendhal wrote that he was one of those who had not 'entered the first floor of the Tuileries since 1814'. But there were few others. Most Bonapart-

---

[16] AN BB30 257 f. 60, note by Cormenin, 7 August 1820.

[17] AN O3 554 f. 157, *Ordonnance* of 11 April 1828; AN O3 364 doss. Vérac, the Prince de Polignac to La Bouillerie, 11 April 1830; cf. AN O3 356 doss. Baudon, five *députés du nord* to Charles X, 6 July 1830; AN O3 358 doss. Contades, La Bourdonnaye Minister of the Interior, to La Bouillerie 13 September 1829, recommending two candidates.

[18] AN 40 AP 16, *La prérogative du roi*, 16 February 1830.

ists had returned by the time of the Emperor's death in 1821. In 1825 what was left of the hard core, Generals Foy, Exelmans and de Lobau, went to the New Year reception of Charles X.[19]

The court was popular. In 1821, recording his memories of his presentation at Versailles, Chateaubriand wrote, 'Today we rush to the palace even more eagerly than before.' Attendance figures were impressive. The same year 675 men and 421 women went to the first reception held by the Duchesse de Berri since her husband's death, which is probably about the maximum number of people regularly attending the court. Between two and three hundred went on an average day. Castellane, an officer not especially fond of the restoration, could write in 1827: 'As it was Sunday I went to the *château*', as if he went every week. By 1830 the *grand cabinet* and the *salle du trône* could hardly contain the people who made use of their *entrées* on Sundays.[20]

Going to court often became such an addictive habit that it was a weapon in the hands of the government. If it did not want to dismiss its enemies from office, it could ban them from court. Talleyrand in 1817, the Duc de Fitzjames in 1818 and the Cardinal de Clermont-Tonnerre in 1828 were some of those informed by the *premier gentil-homme* that they were temporarily forbidden to go to court because they had attacked the King's government.[21] The Baronne de Feuchères, formerly Sophie Dawes, one of the most accomplished prostitutes in London, was mistress of the aged Duc de Bourbon, the last of the Condés. In 1824 she was banned from the court receptions following the collapse of her marriage to one of the duke's aides-de-camp. When she was readmitted in 1830 through the intercession of the pious Duchesse d'Orléans (with help from Talleyrand), it was seen as such a favour that it was enough to decide her doting lover to leave the bulk of his fortune, including Chantilly, to the Orléans's youngest son, the Duc d'Aumale.

[19] Stendhal, *Armance*, 3 vols., 1827, I, II; AN 03 364 doss. Verteillac, Verteillac to Mathieu de Montmorency, 8 October 1824; General Lamarque *Mémoires et souvenirs*, 3 vols., 1835–6, II, 178, diary for 3 January 1825.

[20] Chateaubriand, *Mémoires d'outre-tombe*, I, 174; ABR, *Journal de la Duchesse de Berri*, 2 April 1821; *Castellane*, II, 160 entry for 17 February 1827; Comte de Montbel, *Souvenirs*, p. 256; AN 03 227, Aumont to Garde des Sceaux, 27 May 1829.

[21] *Moniteur*, 3 March 1817, p. 225; Polovtsov, *Correspondance*, II, 566, Pozzo di Borgo to Nesselrode, 20 January 1818; AN 359 AP 65, *Correspondance du Cardinal de Clermont-Tonnerre, archevêche de Toulouse 1823–30*, Duc Charles de Damas to Clermont-Tonnerre, 15 October 1828.

The round of court receptions kept the monarchy in contact with the public as well as the elite, since members of the public were admitted to the chapel and the *salle des maréchaux*. Again, by the end of the reign of Charles X, the Tuileries was becoming too small. After 1829 the public had to have tickets for admission to the *salle des maréchaux* 'in order to cope with the crowds every Sunday'.[22]

The entertainments at court increased in splendour and number after 1820, and also acted as a link between the monarchy and the people. The *premier gentilhomme* and *premier maître d'hôtel* continued to entertain for the King. Guests were delighted to go. The Duchesse d'Escars, a virulent ultra-royalist, was witty and charming and very good at entertaining what she called 'the grandest society in Europe', ministers, ambassadors and courtiers. The rooms were hung with silk or cashmere shawls and crowded with busts and pictures of royalty, and often with real princes as well. The great counter-revolutionary writer de Maistre wrote to her, 'Nowhere is there more life than *chez vous*.' Maria Edgeworth, a relation of Louis XVI's last confessor as well as a famous novelist, was popular in restoration Paris. She loved going to the Duchesse d'Escars's 'routs' for 200 people in the attic of the Tuileries. She wrote that the Duchesse d'Escars was 'perfectly well bred while others with all the striving and struggling and riches and titles can never attain this indescribable, uncommunicable charm'.[23]

The Duchesse de Duras continued to have one of the most fashionable salons in Paris. It was as important for the restoration court as the Duchesse de Bassano's had been for the Empire and the Duchesse de Polignac's for the court of Louis XVI. Villemain, a famous liberal writer, remembered that her salon was 'naturally monarchical, but with very marked nuances of English constitutionalism and French liberalism'. She was an exceptionally intelligent and broad-minded woman who regretted royalists' 'follies' during the first restoration and their use of Catholicism during the second. Her novels *Ourika* and *Edouard* deal with the eternal issues, race, class and impotence. Her remark to

[22] Marie-Amélie, *Journal*, 1981, pp. 358, 383, 387, entries for 3 July 1827, 30 August 1829, 15 January 1830; AHMG xae 11 (Papers of the Garde Royale) Baron de Gressot, *aide-major-général* of the Garde Royale to Comte Bordessoulle, 7 November 1829.

[23] Archives x, Duchesse d'Escars to Madame de Podenas, 24 June 1819; Comte Joseph de Maistre, *Lettres et opuscules inédits*, 2 vols., 1851, I, 512, to Duchesse d'Escars, 28 May 1819; Christine Colvin, *Maria Edgeworth in France and Switzerland*, Oxford, 1979, pp. 113, 122, letters of 3, 14 May 1820 to Mrs Edgeworth.

Charles X, defending the rising of Greece against the Ottoman Empire, illustrates her combination of royalism and liberalism. She said: 'After all, Sire, Greece today is the Vendée of Christianity.'[24]

1822 was her year of glory. Her husband was in waiting. Her salon was attended by Villèle, Talleyrand, Humboldt, James de Rothschild and almost anyone well known. She tried to convert Cuvier and Chaptal to royalism and to advance Chateaubriand's political career. He was an able political operator and a writer of genius and would have gone far in any case. But no one else could write 'I will see Villèle on Sunday and will speak to him at length about you.' She helped him become first an ambassador, then foreign minister. She fed him with the latest political news and reminded him to flatter the King and remain friendly with Villèle.[25]

The court now dominated upper-class social life in Paris, as Balzac remembered when he created characters like the Olympian and influential Ducs de Lenoncourt and de Chaulieu in the *Comédie humaine*. When he gave his first ball, in 1821, James de Rothschild allowed Comtesse Just de Noailles, *dame d'atours* of the Duchesse de Berri, to choose the guests: everyone at court, men and women, wanted to go. No other court in Europe would have been so tolerant. At Vienna the high nobility, the equivalent of the Noailles, was so isolated from other sections of the elite that it did not even make jokes about them. Among the guests were one of the most fashionable couples at court, the Duc and Duchesse de Guiche. She was beautiful and elegant. He was handsome and, as *premier écuyer* of the Duc d'Angoulême, ensured that his master's horses and carriages were the smartest in Paris.[26]

The social dominance of the court increased with the emergence of the Duchesse de Berri from mourning for her murdered husband. Every court derives its characteristics from the royal family it serves. The

[24] D'Haussonville, *Femmes d'autrefois*, p. 198, Duchesse de Duras to Madame de Staël, 16 June 1815; *Villemain*, I, 465.

[25] Abbé Pailhes, *La Duchesse de Duras et Chateaubriand*, 1910, p. 418, Duchesse de Duras to Chateaubriand, June 1822; Comte d'Antioche, 'Le Dernier Hiver d'un Règne', *Revue d'histoire diplomatique*, 1903, pp. 134–5, diary of Comte Raczynski for 20, 22 January 1824; A. Bardoux, *La Duchesse de Duras*, 1898, pp. 302, 327, Duchesse de Duras to Chateaubriand, 28 April 1822, 27 May 1823.

[26] AN 234 AP (Mounier papers) 2, police report of 3 March 1821; Antioche, 'Le Dernier Hiver' p. 140, diary of Comte Raczynski, 18 March 1821; Captain Gronow, *Reminiscences and Recollections*, 3 vols., 1900, II, 41–2; E. Chapus *Les Chasses de Charles X. Souvenirs de l'ancienne cour*, 1837, p. 11.

official, international, staid and domestic character of the restoration court was in part a reflection of the characters of Louis XVIII, Monsieur and the Duchesse d'Angoulême. After the traumas they had been through, they wanted a quiet life. The Duchesse de Berri was completely different. She was young, believed that 'The French must be amused' and loved dancing. Therefore she gave frequent balls either in her own name or (to avoid having to invite the official world) in that of the *gouvernante des enfants de France*, the brilliant, witty and liberal Madame de Gontaut.

Frivolity returned to the court of France for the first time since 1789. In 1823 it was reported that 'Balls are starting, above all at court. The Duchesse de Berri loves them, and is inexhaustible.'[27] As many as 600 people came. The rare official entertainments by the King inspired a famous remark by Talleyrand: 'Life would be bearable if there were no amusements.' However the Duchesse de Berri's parties were fun. Certain balls, the Bal Turc in 1828, or the Bal Marie Stuart in 1829, were unforgettable. Castellane recorded one as 'a model ball', Rodolphe Apponyi, a young Austrian diplomat, described another as 'delicious ... the Duchesse de Berry was in extraordinarily high spirits'.[28]

Like the composition of the court, the entertainments at court were not completely exclusive. Since guests had to have been presented, the people presented at court provide a guide to the guest list. Of the 421 French people presented between 1816 and 1822, 37 per cent came from the *noblesse présentée*, 45 per cent from the *noblesse non-présentée* and 18 per cent were non-noble: compared to the Empire slightly fewer non-nobles and more members of the *noblesse non-présentée* were presented (see appendix, p. 201). But to be presented at court all that was needed was the support of two people who had already been presented and to be of high official rank or noble birth. During the first restoration even these requirements were relaxed.

The presence of non-nobles among those presented shows that Cuvier was incorrect when he wrote to Decazes that 'only those who have

[27] Duchesse de Gontaut, *Mémoires*, 1893, p. 266; Pelissier, *Le Portefeuille*, p. 628, Madame de Laborde to Comtesse d'Albany, 20 December 1823. In 1828, for example, the Duchesse de Berri gave two balls, Madame de Gontaut three, and there were two children's balls. AN 03 138, Brossard to La Bouillerie, 6, 9, 13, 27 January 1828, 1, 3, 19 February 1828.
[28] G. Lacour-Gayet, *Talleyrand*, 4 vols., 1928–34, III, 165; *Castellane*, II, 226, diary, 22 January 1828; Comte Rodolphe Apponyi, *Journal*, 3 vols., 1913–14, I, 50–1, diary, March 1827.

lost by the revolution have received the honours of the court'. Of the 61 women who took advantage of their right to sit on a stool or *tabouret* at the celebration of the *fête du Roi* in 1817, 10 were *maréchales* and 3 *duchesses* of the Empire, and 2 were wives of revolutionary soldiers who had become marshals since 1814.[29] People from revolutionary backgrounds could become assimilated to the restoration court. The Duchesse d'Escars enjoyed complaining about the reforms of 1820–1 and the 'odious' dinner over which she now had to preside. But she became a friend of Maréchal Victor, and General Rapp came to see her every morning. Maréchal Oudinot and his wife and children were part of court society, favourites of Charles X and the Duchesse de Berri and close friends of the Duc de Mortemart and the Comte de La Ferronays.[30]

Most of the Duchesse de Berri's guests were noble. But of the ten men who danced with her at her ball in 1824, two were sons of Maréchals Mortier and Soult. The only quality required of the three officers from each cavalry regiment of the Garde royale regularly invited to her balls was that they should be good dancers. As Apponyi wrote, 'To be a successful courtier at the court of France you must above all have good legs.'[31]

The court was flexible enough to accommodate non-nobles. The Duc de Duras for example appeared to be the quintessence of the aristocratic, royalist court official, with an unusual capacity for living in the past. Madame de Boigne's remark that he was 'more of a Duke than the late M. de Saint-Simon' is confirmed by Duras's assertion in 1822 of ancient perogatives of the *premiers gentilshommes* 'such as that of passing the shirt of His Majesty, which personal motives have let fall into disuse. It is decided in this regard that the usages of the King's *lever*, suspended during the reign of His Majesty, are nevertheless maintained in principle' (they were never revived). In 1829, only a few months after the death of his first wife, he showed a disregard for social origins

[29] Institut Ancien et Nouveau Fonds 3295, Cuvier, *Mémoire secret sur la politique intérieure de l'état*, January 1820, f. 9; AN 03 195 f. 20vo., *Fête du Roi*, 1817.

[30] Archives x, Duchesse d'Escars to Madame de Podenas, 7, 11, 18 July 1821; Maréchale Oudinot, *Récits de guerre et de foyer*, 1894, pp. 385, 472.

[31] ABR, *Journal de la Duchesse de Berri*, 26 January 1824; AHMG xae 11, 9, Marquis de Choiseul to Comte Partounneau, 20 January 1829; *Apponyi*, I, 234, diary, 27 February 1830.

by marrying, as his second wife, Madame Dias-Santos, born Knusli, the Swiss widow of a Portuguese banker. The royal family signed the contract (as it did for any senior official who asked). Her attractions were her money and the relief, after his first duchess, of having a wife less intelligent than himself.[32]

The court was too close to the political and social realities of the age, and valued money, success and official rank too highly, to be completely exclusive, either socially or politically. Liberal deputies such as Casimir Perier and Benjamin Constant were invited to the King's evening card-parties or *jeux* during the reign of Charles X. As Balzac pointed out, before 1830 it was the Faubourg Saint-Germain, not the court, which was the bastion of noble exclusiveness. It was a sign of the influence of the restoration court that in 1828 the Duc de Guiche founded the Cercle de l'Union, one of the first Paris clubs, with other court officials, Comte Sébastiani, a general of the Empire, and the liberal Amiral de Rigny. By the standards of a book written in 1875 criteria of admission were 'fairly free' *before* 1830.[33]

The court also acted as a 'link between the people and the throne', as Lévis hoped (see p. 3), through its role as a disseminator of news and gossip. It did not stand in silent isolation in the middle of Paris. Indeed, since the royal family did not require their services all day long, many court officials had little to do but sit in their apartments, or the royal antechambers, and talk. The Baron de Damas, an aide-de-camp of the Duc d'Angoulême who later became *gouverneur* to the Duc de Bordeaux, remembered the 'continual humming' of the Tuileries where 'so many useless people tried to make themselves important with real or false news'. Even the austere and august Duchesse d'Angoulême had 'a very keen ear and one always listening'. It was courtiers who spread the news of the sudden return of Blacas in 1817 or of Charles X's frequent hunting trips in 1825, which led him to be nicknamed Robin Hood. Sosthènes de La Rochefoucauld complained, 'All the news comes

[32] Boigne, *Mémoires*, I, 260; AN 03 871, drafts of the *procès-verbaux de la commission pour la fixation des rangs*, seance of 16 January 1822; *Castellane*, II, 286–7, diary for 5 April 1829.
[33] AN 03 138, Brossard to La Bouillerie 24 March 1828; *Castellane*, II, 162, diary 27 February 1827; Balzac, *Le Cabinet des antiques*, II, 73; Charles Yriarte, *Les Cercles de Paris*, 1875, pp. 10, 21.

from the *château*.'[34] Mathieu de Montmorency wrote to Madame Récamier, on a Monday, 'M. de Chateaubriand told me yesterday morning
at the Tuileries that he had received some news from Rome the day
before.' In Balzac's *La Duchesse de Langeais* the Duchess's relations
take her to a Monday evening reception at court as the best place to
deny rumours about her latest love affair.[35] With the Chambers and
the *bourse* (stock market), the court was one of the main centres of
news in Paris.

Another area in which the court acted as a 'link between the people
and the throne' was in politics. Before 1820 it had been, on the whole,
reactionary, but thereafter a transformation took place. The new solidity
of the restoration, the triumph of the Duc d'Angoulême and his army
in Spain in 1823 and France's slow adaptation to parliamentary life
meant that court officials stopped feeling frightened or insecure. They
began to realise that the *charte* gave the court and the peers as well
as the crown a favourable field of action. The court was delighted by
the acclamations which greeted the accession of Charles X and the splendid ceremonies which followed. Lévis wrote, correctly, 'never has the
crown passed more peacefully from one head to another'. Dreux-Brézé
boasted that the funeral given to Louis XVIII impressed foreigners even
more than ceremonies at St Peter's Rome.[36]

Court officials felt that they had entered the promised land and they
now became more moderate. Villèle was a major contributor to the
evolution of this change in attitude. He was the most effective conserva-
tive minister of the restoration, but he never liked the court. He wrote
in his memoirs that, at the accession of Charles X, he would have liked
to abolish 'a Court so large, so expensive, so fertile in pretensions,
so greatly in contradiction with the customs of the day, so potentially
compromising to the King and his august family, above all in a country

[34] Baron de Damas, *Mémoires*, 2 vols., 1923, I, 259; BAVP Lévis, 7 March 1824; Polovtsov
Correspondance, II, 165, Pozzo di Borgo to Nesselrode, 10 May 1817; *S. de La Rochefoucauld*,
IX, 127, La Rochefoucauld to Charles X, 17 June 1825.
[35] BN NAF, Fonds Récamier 14071 f. 301, Correspondance de Mathieu de Montmorency, letter
to Madame Récamier, 15 March 1824; cf. AN 359 AP, Clermont-Tonnerre papers f. 100,
Marquis to Marquise de Clermont-Tonnerre, 18 May 1823, relating the latest news from
Spain which he has heard at the *château*; Honoré de Balzac, *La Duchesse de Langeais*, Galli-
mard, 1958, p. 140, 146.
[36] BAVP Lévis, 23 September 1824; AN 03 527, *Relation de la Pompe Funèbre du Roi Louis
XVIII*, f. 197.

like our own and with the kindness natural to the princes of the house of France'. The dislike was mutual: Lévis sneered that 'he began rather low'.

In addition to the resentment of a provincial noble from Toulouse, Villèle felt the bitterness of a prime minister who has been stabbed in the back by his own supporters. Many court officials, led by the Duras, were infuriated by his brusque dismissal of Chateaubriand in 1824. In June 1824 it was court officials in the Chamber of Peers, such as Blacas, Duras, Gramont and Mortemart, who decided the rejection of Villèle's law on government stocks, a blow from which his ministry never entirely recovered. Court officials were now closer to the opinion of Parisian bankers and *rentiers* than of the ultra-royalist government.[37]

Some court officials now tried to act as links between the monarchy and the public on a political level. In 1824 the Duc de Fitzjames, less extreme than in the past, resumed friendly relations with his brother-in-law Comte Bertrand, the former *grand maréchal du palais* of Napoleon I. He ensured that senior army officers took part in Charles X's triumphal *entrée* into Paris and protested violently against the retirement of former Napoleonic officers later that year.[38] Fitzjames was also a link with writers: he suggested to a popular playwright, Mazères, the idea for a play preaching the union of the Faubourg Saint-Germain and the Chaussée d'Antin (a liberal or Bonapartist quarter). After 1830 Fitzjames was one of Balzac's main sources of information about the nobility (another was one of his early mistresses, Madame de Jarjayes's daughter, Madame de Berny) and helped convert him to legitimism.[39] The life of the young Marquis de Dreux-Brézé, who succeeded his pompous father as *grand maître des cérémonies* in 1825, provides an example of the evolution of the court into a modern, constitutional ruling class. He had served in the army before 1814 and then in the Garde royale. Like many court officials, he was enchanted to be a member of the Chamber of Peers and was a leading speaker there until his death in 1846.

---

[37] Comte de Villèle, *Mémoires et correspondance*, 5 vols., 1888–96, v, 125; BAVP Lévis, June, October 1824; AN 359 AP 84 f. 63, notes by Clermont-Tonnerre, 7 June 1824; Archives x, Duchesse d'Escars to Madame de Podenas, 5, 7, 19 June 1824.

[38] Duchesse de Maillé, *Souvenirs*, 1984, p. 108; AN 359 AP 84 f. 64, note of Clermont-Tonnerre, 17 October 1824; Pasquier, *Histoire*, vi, 15.

[39] E. Mazères, *Comédies et souvenirs*, 3 vols., 1858, I, 224; André Maurois, *Prometheus ou la vie de Balzac*, pp. 77, 196.

Careers were another way in which the court provided a link between the monarchy and the rest of the population. Very few individuals spent all their time at court: the *capitaines des gardes* and *écuyers cavalcadours* for example only served three months in the year, the *premiers gentils-hommes* one year in four. Even when they were in waiting they were not completely absorbed by their duties. Although the dinners provided by the Duc d'Escars were superb, court officials did not use their right to dine at his table more than necessary. Numbers fell in the 1820s; clearly distractions outside the court were more attractive.[40]

Being part of the restoration court was a means to an end as well as an end in itself. Court office increased officials' appetite for worldly success. Many felt that, in exchange for acting as the personal servants of the royal family, they deserved to have brilliant careers in the army, the administration or the church. Thus when the princes were 'remarkably amiable' to the Duchesse d'Escars, she immediately wondered how to exploit their mood; and her life at court was poisoned by her husband's failure to obtain a peerage, a loan, the reversion of his position as *premier maître d'hôtel* and the Saint-Esprit. By 1821, although she had a luxurious apartment in the Tuileries and a brilliant position as an official hostess for the King, she was overwhelmed by 'sadness and disgust'. As traditional moralists had always said, court life did not lead to happiness.[41]

Politics were all-important during the restoration. They could decide an individual's choice of residence, spouse and friends and could even make court officials disobey the King. It is not therefore surprising that many court officials wanted a political career, either as peers or ministers. The Chamber of Peers was extremely powerful under the restoration and Duras's plans for the summer of 1825 were regulated by the sessions of the Chamber, not the movements of the court. When he became *premier aumônier* of the Duchesse d'Angoulême in 1815, La Fare wrote that 'The Roman purple, the posts and dignities of church and state mean nothing to me.' But this is simply an example of what the Duchesse d'Escars called 'the marvellous dissimulation of courts'. La Fare had

---

[40] The number fell from 442 in January 1821 to between 280 and 250 after January 1827; AN 03 116, *Etat des Tables et du Nombre des Couverts*, 1814–30.
[41] Archives x, Duchesse d'Escars to Madame de Podenas, 25 July 1817, to Comte de Nadaillac, 21 July 1821.

already been told that this place will stop nothing in the future'; and he did indeed become an archbishop, a peer, a cardinal and a minister of state, honours which the *premier aumônier* of Monsieur, Monseigneur de Latil, also received.[42]

Court officials' political ambitions gave the restoration court a uniquely political, constitutional flavour. Richelieu for example always put his political career before his court offices. Of the 58 *ministres secrétaires d'état* of the restoration 11 had been court officials before their nomination: Blacas, Richelieu, Lauriston, Mathieu de Montmorency, Frayssinous, Damas, Feutrier, Polignac, Bourmont, Haussez and Mortemart. They did not necessarily owe their appointments to their court office. Damas, for example, was out of favour with his master, the Duc d'Angoulême, when he became minister of war in 1823. But many owed the fact that they were considered potential ministers to their position at court. Without it Blacas, Richelieu, Polignac, Feutrier and Damas would have been unknown.

Many court officials also had interests in the army. Many *gentilshommes de la chambre*, such as Reille and Bourmont, were serving officers and preferred to wear their military rather than their court uniforms in the Tuileries, thereby confusing the *huissiers* who had to decide who had the right to enter different rooms.[43] However, under the restoration the court was not the passport to a brilliant career that it had been under the Empire. Of the 30 *gentilshommes de la chambre* and *écuyers cavalcadours* appointed in 1820–1, 14 were still in the same rank in 1830, while 3 others had lost important military commands. Two ministers, Corbière and Clermont-Tonnerre, record how easy it was to refuse Louis XVIII's recommendations in favour of court officials and their families.[44] A young man such as Charles de Rémusat, a future politician whose father had secured him a ceremonial job in 1814, saw it as a drawback and resigned it as soon as possible.[45]

[42] Pailhes, *La Duchesse de Duras*, p. 460, Duchesse de Duras to Rosalie de Constant, 15 May 1825; AN 198 AP 12, 8 La Fare to Mlle de Choisy, 24 January 1815, 20 December 1814.

[43] AN 03 558 f. 90, *Ordonnance* of 5 February 1830.

[44] Comte de Corbière, 'Souvenirs d'un ministre de Louis XVIII', *Revue des deux mondes*, 1 April 1966, p. 367; AN 359 AP 82 f. 436, memoirs of Clermont-Tonnerre. However, Saint-Chamans felt that he owed his command of a brigade in the Garde royale to talking to the minister of war during his service at court (Comte de Saint-Chamans, *Mémoires*, 1896, p. 393). Everything depended on individual circumstances.

[45] Charles de Rémusat, *Correspondance pendant les premières années de la restauration*, 6 vols., 1883–6, 1, 366, Charles to Madame de Rémusat, 21 April 1816.

Court office was a reward for the middle-aged and the old rather than a career for the young. However there were two exceptions. As befitted a social and domestic institution, court office could help to arrange a marriage. In 1825 the Comte de Brehan could secure an heiress worth 100,000 francs a year if he was appointed *gentilhomme honoraire de la chambre*: 'all the family asks is a place at court'.[46] The fact that he was a *gentilhomme de la chambre* cannot have hindered the marriage of the Comte de Rochechouart to one of the richest heiresses of the day, Mademoiselle Ouvrard, an army contractor's daughter.

The aides-de-camp of Monsieur were the second exception. His household was smaller and more intimate than the massive, impersonal *maison du Roi*. There were many opportunities to get to know him and he was a major force in politics and the army. Of Monsieur's 15 French aides-de-camp in 1815 (he also had 4 Swiss aides as *colonel-général des Suisses*), Bruges became *grand chancelier de la Légion d'honneur*, Rivière, Jules de Polignac and Trogoff ambassadors, Wall military commander of Paris, and Digeon commander of the second division of the Garde royale and interim minister of war in 1823. La Rochefoucauld became *directeur-général des beaux-arts* in 1824 and Bouillé, against the advice of the entire council of ministers, governor of Martinique in 1826. Among the Duc d'Angoulême's aides-de-camp Bordessoulle and Champagny had brilliant military careers. In Balzac's *La Rabouilleuse* the unscrupulous ex-Napoleonic officer Philippe Bridau strives to become an aide-de-camp of the Dauphin, a post which he regards as automatically leading to a peerage and the rank of lieutenant-general (as it did in the case of Bordessoulle); and he had many imitators in real life.[47]

Another way in which the court acted as a link between the throne and the people was in its indifference to morality or clericalism. The *aumônerie* was not an especially active department, and many

[46] AN 03 357 doss. Brehan, Marquise de Brehan to Doudeauville, 22 October 1825; cf. AN 03 357 doss. Chambrun La Ferronays to La Bouillerie, 23 November 1828, AN 03 364 doss. Tocqueville (the author's brother) Comte de Tocqueville to La Bouillerie, n.d.
[47] AN 359 AP 84 f. 66, notes by Clermont-Tonnerre, 1826; Honoré de Balzac, *La Rabouilleuse* (Société d'Éditions Littéraires et Artistiques, 1901), pp. 253–5; cf. BN NAF 6549 f. 203vo., *Archives de la Famille de Narbonne-Lara*, ? to Comte Louis de Narbonne-Lara, 4 May 1817, urging him to join *les gardes de Mr, les aides de camp et officiers d'ordonnance* to *relever l'éclat de notre nom*.

aumôniers resigned in order to take up more demanding posts elsewhere. Court officials talked and joked through Sunday mass at the Tuileries, even during the reign of Charles X.[48] The governor of the school of pages expelled one *aumônier*, declaring 'I want no more priests in my house.' Fitzjames was famous for his mistresses, Madame de Gontaut and the Duc de La Chatre lived apart from their spouses, Lauriston died in bed with a dancer (she thought his dying groans were cries of pleasure); and the Comte de Lucinge became an aide-de-camp of the Duc de Bordeaux in 1825 because he had married one of the Duc de Berri's illegitimate daughters.[49] Even Blacas, with his 'long sad face, his haughty manner and diplomatic airs', enjoyed telling dirty stories.

After the reforms of 1820, public opinion accepted the court. Richelieu boasted that the royal hunts in the forests around Paris hardly aroused a murmur in the newspapers. Nor did the size of the royal households. The Duc de Bordeaux had 9 senior court officials, 10 Swiss aides-de-camp as *colonel-général des Suisses* and 86 teachers and servants, a colossal total for a child of 10, and more than the 45 deemed sufficient for the Dauphin in 1789. But the favourable financial position of the court (see chapter 9) removed it from public controversy and enabled it to be as extravagant as it wished.

The size of the court of France meant that Paris was now a court city. The buildings connected with the court, the palace and *quartier* of the Tuileries, the Elysée, the *hôtels* of the court officials in the Faubourgs Saint-Germain and Saint-Honoré, the guards barracks, the royal factories of Gobelins and Savonnerie, the five royal theatres with their boxes reserved for court officials, occupied a large area of the city. In addition an enormous number of shops were allowed to add the magic words *du Roi*, *du Dauphin* and so on to their names. Complete figures do not exist, but in 1816 there were 56 shops displaying the

---

[48] See for example AN 03 1, *Rapport au Roi*, 24 September 1821, AN 03 65, *Rapport au Roi*, 2 August 1828 for *aumôniers* resigning; Cardinal Lambruschini, *La Mia Nunziatura di Francia*, Bologna, 1934, p. 41n.; cf. anon., *Letters written from France and the Netherlands in the Summer of 1817*, Liverpool, 1817, p. 49.

[49] AN 03 18, Pages du Roi, *note confidentielle sur la maison des pages demandée par Son Excellence le Ministre de la Maison* by Abbé Perrin, 8 November 1824; Baronne du Montet, *Souvenirs*, 1914, p. 337; *Castellane*, II, 346, diary, 7 May 1830; *Baron de Damas*, II, 51; AN 279 AP 11, Maréchal Macdonald to Duchesse de Massa, 17 June 1828; AN 359 AP 84 f. 65, notes by Clermont-Tonnerre, 9 May 1825.

title *des Menus-Plaisirs du Roi*; and that is simply one department of one of the royal households.[50]

Just as there was no special court culture distinct from the aristocratic culture of the day, so an individual court style did not exist under the restoration. Since Napoleon I had ordered so much, there was little need to build or redecorate. The same artists, Gérard, Isabey, Fontaine, were employed. If there was a distinguishing feature it was relative simplicity, which was cultivated as a contrast to the strain and exaggeration of the Empire. The Duchesse d'Angoulême compared the royal family to goats tethered at pasture (see p. 151). The Duchesse de Berri described herself as 'having a chat' (*faire la causette*) with her ladies.[51] In a similar way the villa built by Louis XVIII at Saint-Ouen for Madame du Cayla and the guards barracks constructed at Saint-Cloud under Charles X are plain, unpretentious buildings which make no attempt to impress. Rossini's opera *Il Viaggio a Reims*, commissioned to celebrate the coronation of Charles X at Reims, is about fashion and love. Servants have important parts. The music is cosmopolitan, exhuberant and light. It is difficult to imagine such a simple work being commissioned for the coronation of Napoleon I. Indeed the works which were performed on the occasion (although not strictly comparable since they are not operas), Le Sueur's *Coronation March* and Paisiello's *Coronation Mass* and *Te Deum*, are pompous and strident.

Although it did not have a special style, the court did resume its traditional role as a model for the other courts of Europe. The process had begun under the Empire. Napoleon's family installed courts modelled on their brother's in Lucca, Naples, Amsterdam, Cassel and Madrid. The size, splendour and formality of the Napoleonic court, the result of the Emperor's insecurity and personal preferences, helped to inspire a return to grandeur in other European courts, including the court of England. The glaring colours and rigid lines of the Empire

[50] AN 03 505, administration 1821, Richelieu to Lauriston, 24 February 1821; AN 03 244, *Etat nominatif des artistes, des entrepreneurs, des marchands, des fournisseurs attachés par brevets à l'administration des menus plaisirs du roi.*
[51] ABR, *Journal de la Duchesse de Berri*, 19 February 1822.

style showed a desire to overawe which appealed to many other monarchs. Alexander I of Russia received a full acount of the work of the Emperor's court architects Percier and Fontaine every month from 1808 to 1812. When he arrived at the Tuileries in 1814 he told Fontaine that he knew it so well that he did not need to be shown around. Other monarchs, such as the Kings of Bavaria and Württemberg and the future King Leopold of the Belgians, really did know it well since they had all rushed to pay court to the Emperor there, when he was the lord of Europe.

Schinkel in Berlin, von Klenze in Munich and Grandjean de Montigny in Rio de Janeiro helped to spread the Empire style to the courts of Prussia, Bavaria and Brazil. In 1814 Isabey stayed with Metternich in Vienna, drew the participants in the Congress and arranged the decorations for some of the parties. The Empire style continued to win victories after the defeat of the Empire.

Like Napoleon I the Bourbons maintained an enormous court and an elaborate social life, when other dynasties had retreated into privacy. Their court rightly had the reputation of being 'the most brilliant ... in Europe'. In comparison its main rival, the Austrian court, seemed to Mathieu de Montmorency 'of the greatest simplicity'.[52] Therefore the restoration court was subject to the supposed sincerest form of admiration, imitation. In England in 1820, after the abolition of the hoop, female court dress was modelled on that of France. The King of Bavaria sent his pages to tour the pages' school at Versailles, the King of Naples copied the court mourning, the King of Sardinia the receptions and the Tsar of Russia the *menus-plaisirs* of the court of France.[53] Its influence even stretched across the Atlantic. Gilded *tabourets* were ordered from a court furniture-maker in Paris for the White House.

[52] AN 439 AP 1, Prince Alexander Kourakine to Fontaine, 20 December 1810, Schinkel to Fontaine 20 October 1826; Fontaine, 4 April 1814; Dorothy Gies McGuigan, *Metternich and the Duchess*, New York, 1975, p. 287; A. Caillot, *Mémoires pour servir à l'histoire des moeurs et usages des Français*, 2 vols., 1827, I, 17; BN NAF 14098 f. 61, Mathieu de Montmorency to his wife, 7 September 1822.
[53] Mrs Warenne Blake, *An Irish Beauty of the Regency*, 1911, p. 344, letter of 15 June 1820; AN 03 470, 280, letter from the Comte de Belle-Isle, 17 September 1825; AN 03 223, Affaires Etrangères, 1826–8, Prince de Castelcicala to Baron de Damas, 12 May 1826; Antonio Manno (ed.), *Lettere inedite di Carlo-Alberto Principe di Carignano, al suo Scudiere Carlo di Robilant*, Turin, 1883, p. 35, letter of 31 December 1826; Waquet, *Les Fêtes royales*, p. 15.

In 1828 an envoy from Brazil made a special survey of the organisation and etiquette of the court of Charles X for the Emperor Pedro I.[54] The court of France was again the most splendid and influential in Europe.

[54] H. Huth, 'The White House Furniture at the time of Monroe', *Gazette des beaux-arts*, XXIX, January 1946, p. 32; AN 03 886, 169, Vicomte de Pedrabranca to La Bouillerie, 6 February 1828, La Bouillerie to Pedrabranca, 28 February 1828.

CHAPTER 8

❧ ❦

Kings and courtiers

Je l'ai toujours vue faible sur les autres et je l'ai toujours sentie nulle sur moi.

Comte d'Artois to Monsieur de Barentin, January 1799, on courtiers' influence

The *raison d'être* of the restoration court was to enhance the monarch's authority. Every aspect of, for example, the court receptions emphasised the power and prestige of the King. In the chapel the *gardes du corps* presented arms when he entered, knelt down and stood up, and at the *Domine Salvum Fac Regem*. For members of the royal family the court receptions were political not social occasions, when they received homage from silent and deferential subjects, wearing the king's uniform, in one of his splendid palaces. The monarch's conversation was restricted to an enquiry about the courtier's health or movements, or an expression of welcome. It was a sign of favour rather than a means of communication.[1] In order to emphasise dynastic continuity, both the King of Rome and the Duc de Bordeaux 'received' in their cradles. The Comtesse de Montesquiou carried deference so far that she wrote that the King of Rome, aged two months, received his uncle the King of Westphalia 'perfectly'.[2]

These receptions were extremely important to the Bourbons. Their frequency and the number of people attending gave an impression of stability and popularity to the monarchy. Ministers and their wives

---

[1] AN o3 519, *Consignes générales des gardes du corps*, f. 9; see for example M. F. P. G. Maine de Biran, *Journal*, 3 vols., Neuchâtel, 1954–7, II, 3, diary for 1 January 1817; *Viennet*, p. 90, diary for 23 February 1829, *Castellane*, II, 57, diary for 9 January 1825 for royal conversation at receptions.

[2] BN NAF 14356, Madame de Montesquiou to Napoleon I, 29 May 1811; Archives X, Duchesse d'Escars to Madame de Podenas, 4 August 1822.

had a duty to go every week and everyone presented less frequently.[3] Members of the royal family were also expected to attend. The Duchess d'Angoulême told her sister-in-law the Duchesse de Berri, who was lingering in her luxurious château at Rosny on the Seine, that she must return to the Tuileries. In a characteristically simple metaphor for the obligations of royalty, she wrote: 'where the goat is tethered, there it must graze'. Charles X scolded the Duc d'Orléans if he absented himself for a week.[4]

The receptions held for the New Year, the anniversary of the King's return to Paris (3 May for Louis XVIII, 12 April for Charles X) and the *fête du Roi* (25 August for Louis XVIII, 5 November for Charles X) were particularly important. People like Talleyrand or the Duchesse de Rohan came to Paris from the country especially for the occasion.[5] Deputations from the most important institutions in the kingdom, such as the two chambers, the law-courts, the Académie française and the army, organised by the *grand maître des cérémonies*, presented their congratulations to the King in the throne-room, making three reverences as they advanced to the centre and leaving backwards. The number of institutions sending deputations increased throughout the restoration.[6]

This routine of receptions may have encouraged the royal family to exaggerate the strength and stability of the regime – although the contrast between the crowded court of the first restoration and the Hundred Days should have been a warning. Holding court was so important to them that they disliked leaving the Tuileries and Saint-Cloud, which were easily accessible for members of the elite. Louis XVIII was even reluctant to leave the Tuileries; and his insistence on holding receptions

---

[3] Daudet, *Louis XVIII*, p. 333, *cahiers de la Duchesse Decazes*; Serre, *Correspondance*, IV, 347, Richelieu to Serre, 13 October 1821; Duchesse de Mouchy, *Vie de la Vicomtesse de Noailles*, 1852, p. 52.

[4] Vicomte de Reiset, *La Duchesse de Berri*, 1905, p. 345, Duchesse d'Angoulême to Duchesse de Berri, undated letter; A. Cuvillier-Fleury, *Journal*, 2 vols., 1900–3, I, 271, entry for 26 April 1830.

[5] Archives x, Duchesse de Dino to Duchesse d'Escars, 13 September 1828; AN 40 AP 17, Talleyrand to Beugnot 20 ?September 1829; AN 03 479 doss. Gontaut-Biron Duchesse de Rohan to Doudeauville, 13 November 1826.

[6] AN 03 525, *Note remise à M. le Baron de Berthois Aide de Camp de Sa Majesté sur les honneurs rendus sous le dernier gouvernement aux Autorités Civiles et Militaires dans le Palais du Roi*; *Moniteur, passim* for which institutions sent deputations.

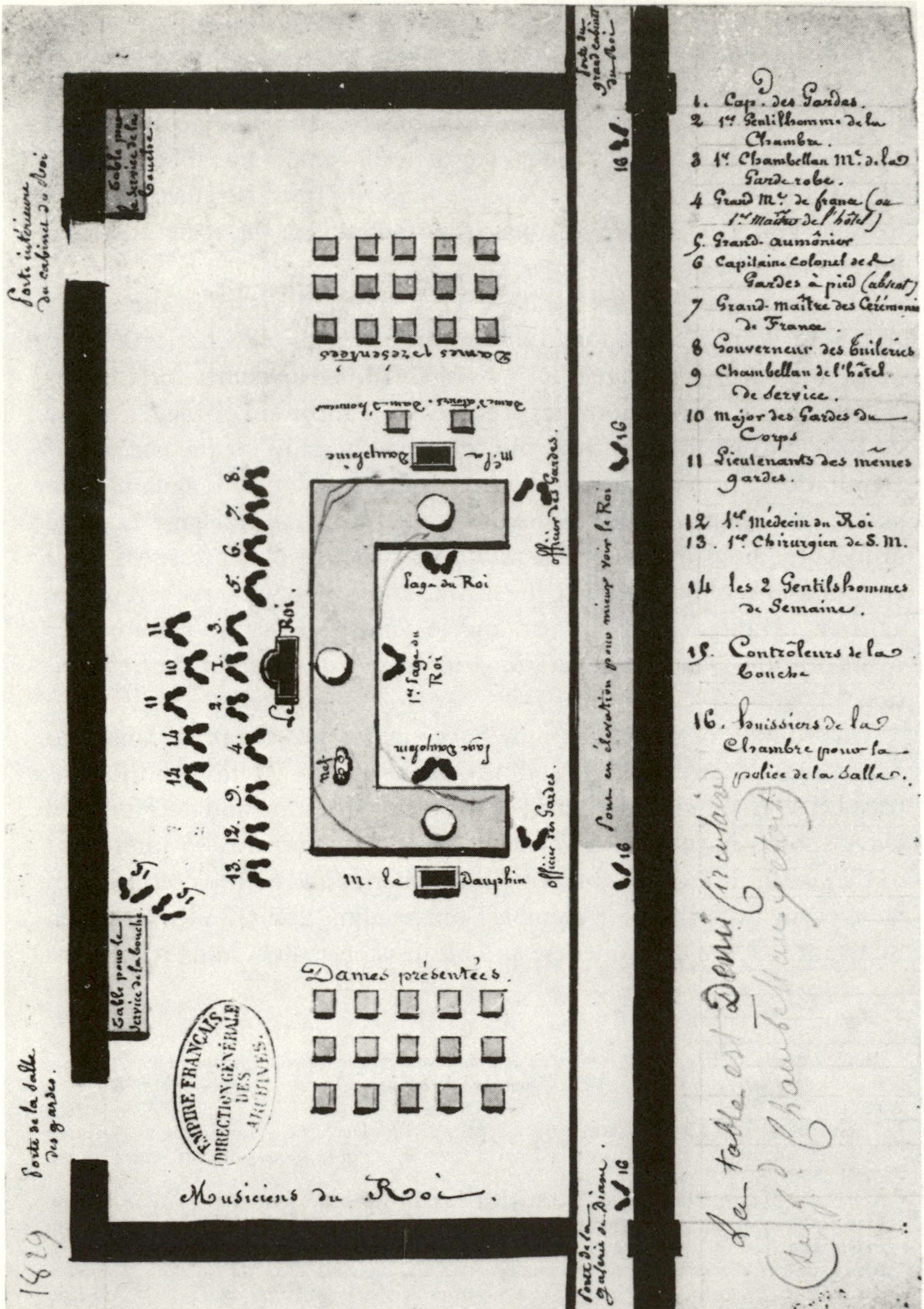

Plan showing the seating and placement arrangement in a royal dining hall.

Legend (right side):

1. Cap.ne des Gardes.
2. 1er Gentilhomme de la Chambre.
3. 1er Chambellan Mre de la Garde robe.
4. Grand Mre de France (ou 1er Maître de l'hôtel)
5. Grand aumônier.
6. Capitaine colonel des Gardes à pied (absent)
7. Grand-Maître des Cérémonies de France.
8. Gouverneur des Tuileries.
9. Chambellan de l'hôtel de service.
10. Major des Gardes du Corps.
11. Lieutenants des mêmes gardes.
12. 1er Médecin du Roi.
13. 1er Chirurgien de S. M.
14. les 2 Gentilshommes de Semaine.
15. Contrôleurs de la Bouche.
16. huissiers de la Chambre pour la police de la Salle.

Bottom right note:
La table est Demi Circulaire
(Chef Chambellan y sont)

Labels on plan:
Porte intérieure du cabinet du Roi.
Table pour le service de la Couche.
Table pour le Grand Cabinet du Roi.
16
16
16
16
Dames 12 présentées
Dame d'atour, Dame d'honneur
M. le Dauphine
Page du Roi
1er Page du Roi
Sous Dauphine
Le Roi
officier des Gardes
officier des Gardes
Pont en élévation pour monter pour le Roi
M. le Dauphin
13. 12. 9. 4. 2. 1. 3. 5. 6. 7. 8.
11. 10. 11
14. 15. 11
5
Table pour le service de la Couche.
Dames présentées
EMPIRE FRANÇAIS
DIRECTION GÉNÉRALE DES ARCHIVES
Musiciens du Roi
Sortie de la Salle des gardes.
1629
Porte de la Galerie de Diane.
16

until the last week of his life, despite the advice of his family and his ministers, hastened his death.

The lure of the court had another important consequence. One of the most important features of the years 1814–15 was the aggressive royalism of certain provinces, particularly in the south and south-west. But members of the royal family could never bring themselves to reside in the provinces, even in royalist Bordeaux where they had inherited a large and splendid palace, next to the cathedral, from Napoleon. The Duc and Duchesse d'Angoulême stayed there with their households in March 1815 and during the duke's campaign in Spain in 1823. Thereafter, however, the magnet of the court kept the royal family in the Ile de France (even though it held such appalling memories for the Duchesse d'Angoulême). It is not surprising that already by 1823 Bordeaux was less royalist than in 1815.

Chambord is the largest château in the valley of the Loire and had been owned by the king at the time of the revolution. It was relatively accessible and was part of the history of the French monarchy. Napoleon gave it to Maréchal Berthier but in 1821 it was bought from his heirs for the Duc de Bordeaux by national subscription. Nevertheless the gift was not accepted until 1829. The reason for the delay was court officials' feeling that it was too small and too distant for convenience.[7]

On the other hand members of the royal family, particularly the Duchesse de Berri, did make frequent tours in the 1820s. Charles X himself went to a military camp in Saint-Omer in 1827 and Lunéville in 1828. On these occasions they entertained or received more widely than Napoleon I. In 1828 *curés*, junior officials and members of the Conseils-généraux de commerce were added to the categories of officials allowed to pay court to the monarch on his *voyages*, which had been

4 Plan of the *grand couvert* for the *fête du Roi* in the *galerie de Diane*, 1829 (Archives Nationales O3 525)
The King's musicians play and the ladies of the court look on as Charles X, the Dauphin and the Dauphine dine. Members of the public file past *huissiers* (16) on a gangway specially raised to let them 'see the King better'. This plan shows that the *premier gentilhomme*, *capitaine des gardes* and *maître de la garde-robe* were the court officials nearest the King.

---

7 BAVP Lévis, 23 September 1824; Bibliothèque Historique de la Ville de Paris, Manuscrits v 1022; K. de Bontault to M. Berthier, 11 April 1829; Alfred Nettement, *Mémoires de la Duchesse de Berri*, 3 vols., 1836–7, II, 88–9.

established in 1804.[8] An entry in the diary of the Duchesse de Berri
is typical of her whirlwind passages through provincial towns: 'As soon
as I arrived I received the authorities and the ladies.' She usually dined
with the authorities and, at the inevitable official ball, danced with the
mayor, the commander of the garrison and an officer of the Garde
nationale.[9]

The Duchesse de Berri also spent many summers at Dieppe, which
she made fashionable, as her sister-in-law did Vichy.[10] Like the royal
family, senior court officials now spent long periods in the provinces.
To take only a few examples, Maréchale Oudinot spent most summers
with her family in Lorraine and Duras often went to his château at
Ussé on the Loire. The Ducs d'Havré and d'Avaray spent the winter
of 1822 in the latter's château near Orléans while the Duchesse d'Escars
was staying nearby with Maréchal Victor.[11] Moreover, a large number
of provincial nobles were now officials of the court (43 per cent in
1830) and had access to its receptions and entertainments. It was felt
that as a result of the creation of *gentilshommes de la chambre* the
King had 'admitted his subjects from the provinces to the joy of being
attached to his person and of forming part of his court'. During the
restoration the chasm between the court and the provinces was narrower
than before 1789.

The size and splendour of the court helped to give an image of stability
to the restoration, to increase the prestige of the King and to satisfy
the vanity of some of his subjects. However, one drawback traditionally
associated with a large and elitist court was that it might dominate
the King and the royal family and turn them into instruments of their
own courtiers. Villèle wrote that the court made him fear 'compromises
for the King and his august family, above all in a country like ours
and with the kindness (*bonté*) natural to the princes of the House of
France'. The key word is *bonté*, which Villèle used here to mean weak-

[8] AHMG XAD 12, *Instructions du ministre de l'intérieur aux préfets*, 9 August 1828.
[9] ABR, *Journal de mon voyage au Mont d'Or*, Nevers, 30 August 1821; cf. *Journal*, 1824–7,
     entry for Rouen, 22 July 1827, Bordeaux, 11, 15 July 1827.
[10] P. J. Feret, *Histoire des bains de Dieppe*, 1855, pp. 74, 162; A. Mallat, *Histoire contemporaine
     de Vichy*, Vichy, 1921, p. 271.
[11] Oudinot, *Récits de Guerre*, pp. 476–7; Pailhes, *La Duchesse de Duras*, pp. 351, 448, Duchesse
     de Duras to Rosalie de Constant, 5 May 1817, 24 July 1824; Archives X, Duchesse d'Escars
     to Madame de Podenas, 12 November 1822.

ness, as contemporaries frequently did.[12] General Lamarque attacked the number of the King's aides-de-camp in the Chamber of Deputies in 1829 and denounced the 'surprises made on his generous *bonté* by the obsessions of the court (hear, hear!)'.[13]

Such attacks owed as much to the anti-court literary tradition, or to personal envy and disappointment, as to reality. Since the early middle ages it had been fashionable to denounce courts, particularly the court of France, as repositories of every vice. Since so many people were together near the source of power and preferment and excitement for so long, the court did indeed distort human nature. As has been explained in the previous chapter, service at court did lead to heightened expectations of worldly success and an unusual desire to hear, or invent, news.

Nevertheless most attacks on the court were primarily variations in a literary tradition, rather than precise, informed denunciations. The onslaughts of La Bruyère and Montesquieu – 'a corrupt monarchy is not a state, it is a court' – were frequently quoted to support attacks on the restoration court, although both were long dead. Paul-Louis Courier, a celebrated liberal pamphleteer, boasted that his criticisms were based on accounts of the courts of François I and Louis XIV and that he knew nothing about the court of Louis XVIII.[14] Extravagant as the restoration court was, it could hardly justify Courier's claim 'all our money goes there, all of it, down to the last penny'. Denunciations of courtiers were also predictable and self-fulfilling. Even for court officials the word *courtisan* had come to mean someone smooth, unreliable and wicked. Thus Baron d'Aubier, a *gentilhomme ordinaire* of Louis XVI and Louis XVIII, in his account of 10 August 1792, wrote 'the courtier forgets his master ... the faithful servant defends the memory of his prince'.[15]

[12] AN 03 360 doss. Hauteroche Comte d'Hulst to Charles X, n.d.; *Villèle*, v, 125; cf. Maréchal Marmont, *Mémoires*, 9 vols., 1857, VII, 85, VIII, 341 for attacks on the King's *bonté*.
[13] *Moniteur*, 28 June 1829, p. 1128.
[14] Hippolyte Mauduit, *Souvenirs d'une garde à Saint-Cloud en 1829*, 1835, pp. 12–13; Paul-Louis Courier, *Oeuvres complètes*, 2 vols., 1828, I, 227, *Procès de Paul-Louis Courier*, August 1821; idem, *Simple discours*, 1821, pp. 13–14, 19–20; even if his attitude was partly adopted as a defence against prosecution, his attacks on Madame de Pompadour and Madame de Maintenon seem slightly out of place in 1821.
[15] Courier, *Oeuvres complètes*, I, 57; Baron d'Aubier, *Observations sur les mémoires de Madame Campan*, 1823, p. 1; cf. Madame de Gontaut, *Mémoires*, p. 326 for another use of the word *courtisan* by a court official in a pejorative sense.

Villèle's attack belongs to this tradition. He ignored the forces protecting the royal family from its courtiers. For the royal family kept its court under control through respect and routine. The respect felt at court for the royal family was greater than before 1789. All (even, after the murder of her husband, the Duchesse de Berri) shared the glamour of misfortune as well as the prestige of belonging to what the Bourbons and their supporters regarded as the oldest and grandest dynasty in Europe. Court officials felt that 'No glory has been lacking to the ancient race of our kings and perhaps the distinction of great misfortune has given it a more august and more sacred character.'[16]

Royalism had become a religion. Indeed more outward respect was shown the royal family at court after 1814 than before 1792. The court was based on the principle that, as Dreux-Brézé wrote when arranging for Louis-Philippe's mother to receive more honours at her funeral than previous *princesses du sang*, 'now more than ever it is indispensable to mark the extreme distance which separates every prince or princess of the royal house from every other family'. Courtiers – for example Maréchal Ney off to capture Bonaparte in 1815 – now kissed the King's hand, a form of deference unknown at Versailles.[17]

The King was the object of reverential respect at court. His food was escorted by *gardes du corps* from the kitchen to the dining-room. Every apprentice in the stables wrote a composition in his honour on the day of his *fête*.[18] The furniture in his apartments emphasised his rank. Only the King had an armchair. Members of the royal family were allowed cross-legged stools (*pliants*), the most senior court officials, and wives of dukes, marshals and ambassadors straight-legged stools (*tabourets*) and the rest of the court benches. For many, not only at court, the king was still the representative of God on earth.[19]

[16] E. Mennechet (*secrétaire de la chambre*), *Lettres sur la restauration*, 2 vols., 1832, I, 360, letter of 20 June 1816; cf. for the same feelings expressed in a sermon at court, Abbé Dupanloup, *Vie de Monseigneur Borderies*, 1905, p. 228–9.

[17] AN 03 527, *Relation des obsèques de la Duchesse Douairière d'Orleans*, f. 11, 23 June 1821; *Archives parlementaires*, 2nd series, xv, 363, *Déposition du Duc de Duras*, 4 December 1815; S. de La Rochefoucauld, IX, 120, note of July 1825; cf. Earl of Chesterfield, *Letters to His Son*, 6th edn, 4 vols., 1775, I, 271, letter of 7 August 1747, 'in France nobody bows at all to the King nor kisses his hand'.

[18] AHMG xad 12, *Ordre du jour du capitaine des gardes de service*, 23 December 1815; AN 03 414, *Ordre du Marquis de Vernon*, 31 August 1815.

[19] AN 03 1878, 8, *Rapport* by Monsieur Longroy to Thierry de Ville d'Avray, 23 October 1815; *Baron de Damas*, I, 336, Duc d'Angoulême to Baron de Damas, 9 January 1819.

There were immense and important differences between the King and the rest of the royal family. In 1824 Monsieur's personality appeared to change and the structure of his life was transformed when he ascended the throne as Charles X. He left the Pavillon de Marsan for the King's apartments in the central section of the Tuileries and was no longer served by the *maison de Monsieur* but by the *maison du Roi* (although room was found in it for his most important officials, Fitzjames, Maillé, Rivière and a *premier valet de chambre*, Baron Bourlet de Saint-Aubin). After the first reception of the reign an officer of the Gardes du corps wrote: 'we were all struck with the same feeling when we saw this Prince, whom we have seen until now the most submissive of subjects' speak of his 'protection' to the *premier président* of the Cour de cassation. By 1825, according to Beugnot, 'the court officials ... all, without exception, no longer find in Charles X what used to enchant them in Monsieur, his confidence and his familiarity'. They blamed Villèle; but the real reason was Charles X's exalted concept of the behaviour appropriate to the King of France.[20]

In addition to the awe felt for the King as an abstract principle, the personal qualities of Louis XVIII and Charles X inspired respect. Unlike Louis XVI they had the authority of age over their court officials: in 1814 the King was 59 and Monsieur 57 compared to their courtiers' average age of 51. For most courtiers Charles X had 'the same empire over hearts that his brother could have over minds'. Yet many court officials, such as Charles de Damas, loved Louis XVIII, whom he had served for half a century. For a doting *écuyer cavalcadour* Louis XVIII was 'the embodiment of royal grandeur ... One was never tempted to forget that he was King.'[21]

Charles X, one of the most charming men of his age, was adored at court. He was a kind man and more than anyone made the Duchesse de Berri's first years of widowhood bearable. The Duchesse d'Escars wrote 'never was a creature more in the image of god'. Sosthènes de

---

[20] Archives x, Officer to Duchesse d'Escars 19 September 1824; AN 40 AP 16, *Coup d'oeil sur les affaires du moment, pâques 1825,* by Beugnot; cf. S. *de La Rochefoucauld,* IX, 85, La Rochefoucauld to Charles X, 5 March 1825.
[21] *Villèle,* v, 119; Comte de Neuilly, *Souvenirs,* 1865, p. 384.

La Rochefoucauld believed that he 'possessed on his own more grace than all the kings of France'.[22]

The respect accorded the royal family arose in large part from the fact that the courtiers were primarily servants. They all, except the *gentils-hommes de la chambre* appointed after 1820, had a domestic function such as looking after the King's food, clothes or horses. One reason why the Bourbons were so fond of employing members of the traditional court nobility in their households was that, as Napoleon realised, they made such good servants. They were experts on the pleasures of life and court service was in their blood. The Duc d'Escars was a great gourmet, the Duc de Guiche an expert on horses, the *premiers gentils-hommes* had excellent manners. Louis XVIII's comment on the Duc de Gramont could be applied to many other court officials: 'he has been created and put in the world for the post he occupies'.[23]

The royal family in fact treated its courtiers as servants. The Duchesse d'Angoulême described herself as 'dismissing' her ladies as if they were chambermaids. Charles X ordered a *premier gentilhomme* not to overeat or go out, as if he were a child, and praised Blacas as 'this excellent servant of our family'. The degree of independent authority permitted to the *chefs de service* over their departments was because they were senior servants and, like butlers and housekeepers in private households, needed such authority in order to do a good job.

The royal family lived in a different world from their courtiers, however grand or favoured. An Englishwoman saw the royal family looking in at the *premier maître d'hôtel*'s dinner for a newly arrived ambassador 'just as we should at a Tenants' dinner, they were laughing and appeared much amused'.[24] The gap between the royal family and its courtiers was comparable to that between a landowner and his tenants. It was because they thought of their courtiers as servants that they were so reluctant to change them with each change of ministry. It would interfere

[22] Archives x, Duchesse d'Escars to Madame de Podenas, 17 October 1827; *S. de La Rochefou-cauld*, IX, 41, letter to Charles X, 10 December 1824.

[23] Tulard, *Napoléon à Sainte-Hélène*, p. 458, diary of Gourgaud, 16 December 1817; Langeron, *Decazes*, p. 140, Louis XVIII to Decazes, 11 August 1817.

[24] Duchesse d'Angoulême, 'Souvenirs de 1815', *Le Correspondant*, CCXXX, 25 August 1913, pp. 670–1; AN 03 138, Brossard to La Bouillerie, 22 May 1828; ABR, Album Verde Charles X to Duchesse de Berri, 12 May 1831; *The Letter Bag of Lady Elizabeth Spencer-Stanhope*, 2 vols., 1913, II, 85, Mrs Spencer-Stanhope to Mrs John Spencer-Stanhope, 27 December 1824.

with their own comfort and the smooth running of their households.

The courtiers were proud to be the Bourbons' servants. In 1820, when Monsieur rushed from the Tuileries to the Duc de Berri's death-bed, his *premier gentilhomme* Maillé had the 'sublime idea' of jumping up behind the carriage with the footmen, an act of self-absement which aroused much approving comment.[25] D'Escars, Rivière and Dreux-Brézé were so dedicated that they could not give up the court, and died in office. Their love for their jobs meant that the restoration court was alive in a way in which the strained and formal court of Napoleon I was not. When he was made a *capitaine des gardes* of Monsieur, Rivière wrote to a cousin: 'I could not obtain a more agreeable or honourable position nor one which made me happier in every way.' He seemed not to mind that he was constantly at his master's orders and had hardly a moment to see his own family.

When she became a lady-in-waiting of the Duchesse de Berri, Madame de Podenas wrote to her husband: 'Fall on your knees, my dear Felix, what we have so desired has happened, I am appointed to the Duchesse de Berri ['s household].' Her mother, the acid Duchesse d'Escars, was 'drunk with joy'. However, Madame de Podenas also found she was treated as a servant. After three-and-a-half months of what she called 'the greatest intimacy' with the Duchesse de Berri, she was left behind when the duchesse went to spend the evening with the King at Saint-Cloud, without a word or even a look of farewell. She had forgotten to bring the right clothes. She realised that 'royal friendship' was quite different from other varieties.[26]

Courtiers were so proud of their jobs that even the most easy-going were determined to defend every inch of their traditional prerogatives, which were referred to in countless disputes as *les droits de ma charge*. If a courtier did not defend them, he felt humiliated. The *capitaines des gardes* wrote to Louis XVIII 'we owe it to our predecessors in our *charges*, we owe it to our successors, to transmit to them the sacred depot we hold by the King's favour as fine, as pure as we received it'. Such feelings were to be found at every level of the court, from

[25] J. B. A. Hapdé, *Relation historique, heure par heure, des evènements funèbres ... du 13 fevrier 1820*, 4th edn, 1820, pp. 13–14n.; cf. *La Quotidienne*, 20 February 1820, p. 2.
[26] Vicomte de Naylies, *Mémoires du Duc de Rivière*, 1829, pp. 169–70, Rivière to Marquis de Maupas; Archives x, Duchesse d'Escars to Madame de Podenas, 25 April 1822, Madame to Monsieur de Podenas, 25 May 1825, 4 October 1828.

Talleyrand, the *grand chambellan*, down.[27] The only duties he considered sacred were his court duties, remarked the Marquis de Montcalm, and Talleyrand attended court throughout the restoration. In the middle of the July revolution a *huissier* performing some of the duties of a *valet* let Duras know that it was out of necessity, in order to defend himself from the charge of 'usurpation'.[28]

The main reason why the royal family let whole families colonise the court was because it made them better servants. Since the contemporary British solution of bachelor courtiers was not available (everyone married under the restoration), the Bourbons tried to satisfy courtiers' family commitments within the framework of the court, in order to encourage attachment to the court. Such considerations, as well as nepotism, explain why more than 50 per cent of members of families like the Montsoreau, Gontaut, Damas and Polignac were court officials (see appendix, p. 210). A family's ties outside the court lessened its commitment to the Bourbons and the time available for the performance of court duties. When she went into exile in 1815 and 1830, the Duchesse d'Angoulême would not take women who had families in France.[29]

While they were in waiting, court officials were so busy being servants that they hardly had the opportunity, or desire, or courage to act as politicians and try to manipulate their masters. In addition routine ensured that they had few opportunities to talk to the King. Both Kings were old men preoccupied with politics and official duties. They were, Clermont-Tonnerre wrote, 'on a theatre whose curtain never falls'. Charles X told Lévis that whereas royalty had been a sinecure in the eighteenth century, it now needed 'talents' and 'firmness'. Both brothers used court etiquette to defend their time and preserve their energy. A *garde du corps* wrote that 'everything is regulated at court with perfect routine. What happens one day happens the next, and thereby routine is a very powerful goddess'.[30] It was not easy to surprise the King.

[27] AN 03 194, *Ordonnances et règlements de 1820 à 1823*, Talleyrand to Lauriston 16 April 1821; AN 101 AP (Archives de la Maison de Gramont, consulted by kind permission of the Duc de Gramont), D2, 8, *capitaines des gardes* to Louis XVIII, n.d.

[28] *Maillé*, p. 139; Edmond Marc, *Mes Journées de juillet*, 1930, p. 153.

[29] D'Angoulême, 'Souvenirs de 1815', pp. 670–1; *Apponyi*, I, 295, 7 August 1830.

[30] AN 359 AP 84 f. 75, notes of Clermont-Tonnerre, 17 November 1828; BAVP Lévis, 21 January 1824; Théodore Anne, *Mémoires, souvenirs et anecdotes sur l'intérieur du palais du Charles X*, 2 vols., 1831, I, 92.

The fixed points in Louis XVIII's day were mass in his bedroom, lunch at half past ten with his senior court officials, drives, dinner at six, the *ordre* or giving the password at nine, which could be attended by everyone with the *entrées du cabinet* and audiences. Charles X replaced drives with hunting and shooting, heard mass in the chapel rather than his bedroom and lunched alone. After the *ordre* he spent the evening in the apartment of the Dauphine or the Duchesse de Berri.

The rules surrounding the King's life were rarely broken. For example in Paris he always dined with the royal family, except when he invited the *princes du sang* or members of foreign royal families. The only people not of royal blood to dine with the King at the Tuileries during the restoration were Lord Moira (a friend in exile), Wellington, Metternich and Canning.[31]

At the *ordre* and the *déjeuner* the King might have conversations with his courtiers (he never talked with ordinary servants). But, just as royal friendship was different from other varieties, so royal conversation was an art of its own. The King was always surrounded by an awe-struck silence (even at the court theatre there was no clapping in his presence). He began the conversation, and used words to convey favour rather than to communicate. The subjects of conversation were deliberately frivolous: travel, literature, anecdotes (often extremely *risqué*), the past and food. There was no informality. Even members of the royal family, the Duc and Duchesse de Berri, were forbidden to *tutoyer* each other in Louis XVIII's presence.[32]

Although it dominated everyone's thoughts, politics was never mentioned. Even in the relatively relaxed circumstances of exile in Ghent during the Hundred Days, no court official dared, for a long time, inform the King of Blacas's unpopularity.[33] The only occasion when the King talked freely with people was during private audiences, which were obtained by writing to the *premier gentilhomme*. The advantage of this system for the royal family was its formality. When she was waiting

[31] AN 03 116, *Etat des Tables et du Nombre des Couverts*, 1814–30; *Anne*, I, 95, 118; Prince Richard Metternich (ed.), *Mémoires et documents du Prince de Metternich*, 8 vols., 1880–4, IV, 172, Metternich to Francis I, 11 April 1825; Aspinall, *George IV*, III, 174, Canning to George IV, 20 October 1826.
[32] *Anne*, II, 132–4; Comte de Saint-Chamans, *Mémoires* 1896; pp. 390–3, diary for 16, 17, 22 January 1822; ABR Album Verde Duc to Duchesse de Berri, 14 June 1816.
[33] Jaucourt, *Correspondance*, p. 291, letter to Talleyrand, 24 April 1815.

to see Charles X in 1825, Madame de Podenas found the *salle du trône* crowded with deputies, courtiers and generals also waiting for an audience in the *grand cabinet*. 'The whole household of H.M. saw me and teased me about my audience ... the whole of Paris knows about my request and that makes success a thousand times more necessary.'[34] Clearly only a matter of extreme importance would lead to a request for an audience; and the King was ready in advance to meet requests with 'I will see' (in the case of Louis XVIII) or 'I do not say yes, but I do not say no' (in the case of Charles X).[35]

The formality of the audience system, the splendour of the palaces and the prestige of the King meant that even senior court officials were overawed when they were alone with him. When Dreux-Brézé asked Louis XVIII for the *entrée* to the *salle du trône* for his wife, 'what the King said to me deprived me of all force and reduced me to silence'. Richelieu wrote that he did not have the 'courage' to persuade Louis XVIII to change a name on a list of *gentilshommes de la chambre*.[36] Court officials were so frightened of Louis XVIII that they went through his favourite, Madame du Cayla. Between July 1823 and February 1824 the Ducs d'Avaray, d'Havré and de Castries, who had all known Louis XVIII since before the revolution, wrote to her to ask for favours, such as the command of a military division, or the Saint-Esprit. Only the first was successful.[37]

Charles X was scarcely less alarming. Madame de Podenas was a woman of the world, familiar with the royal family since 1814. Nevertheless the prospect of an audience with him made her feel sick with apprehension and tremble like a leaf.[38] Duc Charles de Damas and the Duc d'Aumont, elderly, self-assured court officials who saw the king every day they were in waiting, dared not ask him for money and positions in person, and requested La Bouillerie to do it for them.[39] Ministers

[34] Archives x, Madame to Monsieur de Podenas, 4 May 1825.

[35] AN 03 147, 143, Nantouillet to Pradel, 8 July 1819; Archives x, Duchesse d'Escars to Madame de Podenas, 10 April 1821; AN 03 491 doss. Wignacourt, Comte de Wignacourt to La Bouillerie, 29 July 1830; AN 03 469 doss. Montlivault, Comte de Montlivault to La Bouillerie, 1829.

[36] AN 03 518, *Droits et prérogatives du Grand Maître des Cérémonies*, Dreux-Brézé to Louis XVIII, n.d.; BVC FR 83 f. 57, Richelieu to Madame de Montcalm, May 1821.

[37] BN NAF 4760, *Registre de correspondance de Madame du Cayla*, entries for 20 September, 12, 24 December 1823, 8 January 1824.

[38] Comte de Mérode, *Souvenirs*, 2 vols., 1864, II, 138; Archives x, Madame to Monsieur de Podenas, 4 May 1825.

[39] AN 03 351, 151, Duc Charles de Damas to La Bouillerie, 13 May 1828.

were more important, and had better access to the King than any court officials. It was ministers whom the King received in audience most frequently and they could see him alone in the evening between eight and nine o'clock without prior arrangement. Sémonville, *grand référendaire de la chambre des pairs*, who received the privilege in 1828, appreciated it because it enabled him to 'guide' the conversation without Charles X having time 'to prepare his reply'.[40]

Despite their insistence on formality, both Kings felt the need for a degree of relaxation. Louis XVIII liked and respected his court officials. But he found it necessary to compensate for what he called 'the dullness of his court and the want of all Society', and for his lack of sympathy with his own family. So he took favourites: Blacas, Decazes, Madame de Mirbel and Madame du Cayla. They took the place of the children he had never had and occupied some of his evenings.

Charles X preferred to spend the evening with his daughters-in-law. The Duchesse d'Angoulême's *soirées* were stiff, although she tried to be welcoming. They were restricted to court officials and guards officers in waiting and cards were the main entertainment. The Duchesse de Berri invited more people, including ministers, deputies and officers of the Garde nationale. One liberal deputy found Charles X easy to talk to at such evenings and recorded that 'nothing was simpler than these *soirées*, free of all ceremony and splendour; all distinctions of rank and all etiquette were banished'.[41]

Lévis also found these *soirées* very relaxed. From his account it is clear that, for the royal family, their courtiers were not only servants but also pets, to be scratched, pinched (like Napoleon, Charles X pinched courtiers' ears) and teased. The Berris made Lévis, an elderly duke, climb trees in the Elysée garden; Charles X stroked his thighs. Even the Duchesse d'Angoulême, 'so imposing and with such a proud character', toyed with the epaulettes of Charles X, d'Havré and Lévis. Lévis also recorded some startling specimens of royal conversation. Before he became King, Monsieur could be quite frank. Discussing the death

---

[40] AN 359 AP 82, Clermont-Tonnerre, *Mémoires*, f. 72; cf. Corbière, 'Souvenirs', p. 369; AN 115 AP 6, Sémonville's account of July 1830, referring to 1828.
[41] National Library of Scotland, Edinburgh, Stuart de Rothesay Papers, 6202 f. 339, Stuart to Castlereagh, 9 November 1820 (private); ABR, *Journal de la Duchesse de Berri*, passim, for example 26 April 1821; Comte de Pontécoulant, *Souvenirs historiques et parlementaires*, 4 vols., 1861–93, IV, 156–7.

of Prince Eugene, Napoleon's step-son, in 1824, Lévis congratulated
Monsieur, saying that it was one less obstacle to stability. He replied
'the child [that is, the Duc de Reichstadt] would have been better'.
Lévis laughed that 'your appetite grows with eating' and recalled that
in 1814 Talleyrand had said that someone should ensure that Napoleon's son acquired 'a fine voice' (in other words that he was castrated).[42]
Despite such informality, these *soirées* did not provide an
opportunity to exert influence, nor were they a place to make a career
like the *lever* and *coucher* of the Emperor or the salon of the Duchesse
de Polignac. They never aroused the anger or even the interest of opposition newspapers.

This view of the court's lack of influence is not conventional, as the
denunciations of Villèle and others make clear. One reason why the
court's influence was exaggerated was the desire to find a scapegoat
for decisions which royalism or dishonesty prevented from attributing
to the King. Villèle, for example, did not want to believe that Charles
X himself thought he should resign. In 1814–15 many Frenchmen used
'the court' as a scapegoat for their dissatisfaction with the first restoration.

The Bourbons' courtly mask was another reason. By royal standards
they were human, realistic and unpretentious. They were not deceived
by the atmosphere of loyalty and deference generated by the court.
Louis XVIII called his devoted *capitaine des gardes* d'Havré 'a lackey'
and compared the Duchesse d'Angoulême to Goneril and Regan. However, Louis XVIII rarely revealed his inner feelings. Like Charles X he
cultivated a façade of politeness and familiarity with his court which
was startlingly different from the condescension and rudeness of the
Bonapartes, the silences of Louis XVI, and the unrelaxed aloofness of
other royal houses. In 1814 Beugnot wrote to Louis XVIII: 'People
seem to enjoy comparing the affability, the touching kindness [*bonté*]
of this house with the repellent hardness, the farouche air of the Bonapartes.'[43] When Louis XVIII was annoyed, he would content himself
with a silent stare, rather than the torrent of invective characteristic
of Napoleon.

[42] BAVP Lévis, diary entries for early 1824, 5 March and October 1824.
[43] Langeron, *Decazes*, p. 213, Louis XVIII to Decazes 1818; Daudet, *Louis XVIII et le Duc
Decazes*, p. 433, Louis XVIII to Decazes, 18 February 1820; AN 40 AP 8 f. 38vo., *Rapport
of 27–8 May 1814.

The difference between the manners of Louis XVIII and those of Napoleon I is illustrated by their treatment of Talleyrand. Talleyrand served at both monarchs' courts as *grand chambellan*. He was appointed by Louis XVIII in September 1815 as compensation after he resigned as *président du conseil* and perhaps as an indirect but public reminder of his service in the same capacity under the Empire. Both Napoleon I and Louis XVIII disliked and distrusted him. When Talleyrand attacked the government, the King's means of putting down his *grand chambellan* was less direct than the Emperor's. Napoleon I insulted him in front of other people, several times. Louis XVIII simply banned him from court for a month. In 1823 Talleyrand was accused of complicity in the death of the Duc d'Enghien by the Duc de Rovigo: Rovigo in his turn was banned from court. Yet Villèle's letter to Talleyrand, written under the King's dictation, although polite, was a masterpiece of concealed disdain: 'His Majesty had desired that the past should remain forgotten; he only excepts the services rendered to France and his person … the high rank which you still possess at Court, Prince, is certain proof that the imputations which wound and distress you have made no impression on the mind of His Majesty.'

The imputations had not been denied; and, although Talleyrand remained *grand chambellan*, he never held political office after 1815. For both him and Louis XVIII this was much more important than his position as *grand chambellan*.

Charles X also maintained a courtly mask. As his ministers complained, he appeared too kind and charming to inspire fear.[44] It was an age in which people were judged by their manners as much as their beliefs and such politeness led many people to exaggerate the malleability of the Bourbons. Moreover, in the emotional atmosphere of the restoration, after the hardships they had endured together, the King often used the language of friendship with his courtiers, which neither Louis XVI nor Napoleon had done. Louis XVIII felt that he had returned with 'friends' (such as Blacas, Gramont, and d'Havré) in 1814. Louis XVIII wrote to La Chatre 'let us finish our old age together' and addressed Charles de Damas as 'my dear Charles'. Among Charles X's many friends were Maillé, Fitzjames and Jules de Polignac. He addressed

[44] Molé, *Le Comte Molé*, III, 102; Lacour-Gayet, *Talleyrand*, III, 151, Villèle to Talleyrand, November 1823; AN 359 AP 84 f. 68, notes by Clermont-Tonnerre, 20 October 1827.

Rivière as *tu* and, in a rare act of condescension, delayed a hunting-trip to visit him on his death-bed.[45]

But this was (as Madame de Podenas found out) a special, royal form of friendship, the friendship of masters with their servants. In one of the remarks he added in 1825 to his brilliant, scourging *Pensées et maximes* Lévis wrote: 'The constraint to which princes are condemned by the elevation of their rank leads them naturally to familiarity with those whom a frequent and intimate service brings close to their persons. But despite appearances the heart enters not at all into this relaxation.'[46] This familiarity meant no more than the mask of friendship which another Bourbon, King Ferdinand II of the Two Sicilies, occasionally assumed, instead of that of 'the Severe Sovereign', when talking to the Prince of Salina in Lampedusa's *The Leopard*. In reality individual courtiers meant little to the Bourbons. The dead and the absent were soon forgotten. There were always people to take their place. The court and the dynasty had to go on.

Although they were in essence servants, nevertheless there were occasions when court officials tried to act as something else, as the Emperor's courtiers had shown in 1814–15. During the restoration courtiers felt they were part of the monarchy. They had suffered so much for the Bourbons. The Prince de Poix, Hue and many servants had witnessed the horrors of 10 August. Gramont, d'Havré, Blacas and others had wandered the length of Europe with the royal family during their years in exile. Fitzjames, Boisgelin, Mathieu de Montmorency, Rivière and the Polignacs had risked their lives conspiring against the Empire in France. Most of Monsieur's and Angoulême's aides-de-camp had joined them in early 1814 or during the Hundred Days, when it was still uncertain whether the Bourbons would remount the throne. All senior court officials had remained loyal during the Hundred Days and many had gone to Ghent.

They had risked lives and property for the monarchy. Yet after 1814, when they resumed their duties at court, they found that security was

---

[45] Chateaubriand, *Réflexions politiques*, 1814, pp. 40–1; AN 197 AP, Louis to La Chatre, 10 March 1816; Archives Départementales de la Côte d'Or Fonds Commarin, Louis to Charles de Damas, 27 June 1816; Vicomte de Naylies, *Mémoires du Duc de Rivière*, 1829, p. 179, Rivière to Marquis de Maupas, 16 September 1824; AN 03 128, Brossard to La Bouillerie 6, 11 April 1828.

[46] Lévis, *Pensées et maximes*, 1825 edn, 2 vols., I, 94.

still elusive. The royal government made frequent blunders. Many of the King's ministers, such as Blacas, Decazes, Villèle and Polignac, became extremely unpopular. The courtiers had suffered too much to be prepared to stand by and let the monarchy perish again. Therefore some of them overstepped the bounds of routine and respect and tried to influence the King.

An example of how far court officials could take matters is provided by the behaviour of Madame de Gontaut. Junior members of the ruling family had fewer defences against intrigue than the King since they were younger and less respected. After 1820 Madame de Gontaut spread rumours about the Duchesse de Berri and her *premier écuyer*, the Comte de Mesnard, and often tried to surprise them alone together. For a time the Duchesse de Berri's diary became a chronicle of despair. On 9 January 1822 she wrote: 'really I would prefer to lick the earth, provided I was left in peace'. Eventually her beloved father-in-law restored harmony in her household.

The feeling that they knew what was best for their master also affected some of the King's officials. In 1816 the audience the King granted Martin le Visionnaire, a peasant who claimed to have received warnings from heaven, may have represented an attempt by the *grand aumônier* and Sosthènes de La Rochefoucauld to make the King's policies more extreme. In 1817 Blacas suddenly arrived in Paris, in another attempt to turn the King against his liberal minister Decazes. Richelieu brought Blacas, who was still wearing a *frac*, to the King's *déjeuner* – probably the only time someone not in uniform sat down at Louis XVIII's table. Within a few minutes the news was all over Paris. However, the studied politeness with which the King treated his former favourite was a sign that he was simply a courtier, no longer a politician. Blacas returned to Rome a few days later, having had no effect on the King's policies. In 1823, when he was in waiting as *premier gentilhomme*, politicians' fears of a revival of his influence proved groundless. When he reappeared at court, Louis XVIII at first pretended not to recognise him.[47]

Many people believed that Charles X, so affable and charming, would fall into 'the hands of influences'. Whereas Louis XVIII had stayed at

[47] ABR, *Journal de la Duchesse de Berri*, January 1822, *passim*, especially entries for 9, 10 January; G. Lenôtre, *Martin le Visionnaire*, 1924, pp. 115–17; Daudet, *Louis XVIII*, pp. 181–96; S. de La Rochefoucauld, VIII, 338, 353, letters to Madame du Cayla, 1823.

most two months a year at Saint-Cloud, Charles X spent five or six,
and often went to Compiègne and Fontainebleau for a week's hunting.
One difference between the Empire and the Restoration is shown in
the different uses Emperor and King made of these country palaces.
When Napoleon visited them, he took his entire court, the *secrétairerie
d'état* and the ministers of foreign affairs of the French Empire and
the Kingdom of Italy. It was like a royal *voyage* before 1789, with
thousands of people on the move. He governed from Fontainebleau
and Compiègne, as Louis XVI had. In contrast Charles X lived very
simply on these *voyages*. He did not take his ministers and was only
accompanied by the Dauphin, the Dauphine and a few court officials.
He was a constitutional monarch not an autocrat. His *voyages* were
quite different from those of the *ancien régime*, during which new ministries had often been manufactured.[48]

No change in the ministry occurred until late 1827. Villèle still had
a majority in the Chamber of Deputies but was increasingly unpopular
in the country and the Chamber of Peers. Almost the entire court had
turned against him and many people believed that it was Fitzjames,
Jules de Polignac and above all the King's best friend Rivière, who
caused the fall of the ministry. He was *gouverneur* of the Duc de Bordeaux, and often had the opportunity to talk to the King in private
when he brought Bordeaux to see his doting grandfather. In retirement
Villèle blamed them bitterly.[49]

But the fallen minister was using the court as a scapegoat, as so
many others had done before, since it was almost impossible for a loyal
subject to admit that he disagreed with the King. In fact Charles X
was so angry with Rivière for attacking his ministers that Rivière was
briefly banned from the Tuileries. At the time the ministers knew who
their real enemy was: the liberal Dauphin who 'tormented' the King
to dismiss his unpopular ministers and told him that 'Villèle was com-

---

[48] S. de La Rochefoucauld, IX, 87–8, letter to Charles X, 5 March 1825; cf. *Castellane*, II, 224,
      diary for 29 January 1828, recording the return of Charles X from Compiègne, without having
      made an ultra-royalist ministry, 'as people feared'; John Hardman, 'Ministerial Politics from
      the Accession of Louis XVI to the First Assembly of Notables', unpublished D.Phil. thesis,
      University of Edinburgh, 1974, p. 142.
[49] See for example AST LMF 34 f. 126, de Vignet to La Tour, 20 January 1828; *Castellane*,
      II, 198–208, diary for November and December 1827; AN 359 AP 84 f. 75, notes of Clermont-
      Tonnerre, 27 August 1828.

promising the monarchy'.[50] In comparison court officials were much less important. As those who became ministers, such as Frayssinous (plate 22), admitted, they did not have influence while in waiting compared to that which they exercised in the council. Before he became a minister, Jules de Polignac wrote of 'an influence which neither I nor anyone else has had or will ever have'.[51]

The Dauphin, who toppled Villèle, was a much more forceful and impressive figure to the court than he appears to posterity. He was committed to the *charte* and had a reputation for disliking ultra-royalists and emigrés and preferring, in the words of the minister of war, Clermont-Tonnerre, 'men from a lower class', with revolutionary backgrounds. He had been successful in difficult undertakings such as his entry into Bordeaux while Napoleon was still on the throne on 12 March 1814 and his campaign in Spain in 1823. He hoped to bring glory to his reign by introducing constitutional monarchy into Spain, Naples and Piedmont and annexing Belgium to France.[52] Many politicians believed that the restoration would have lasted if Louis XVIII had been succeeded by 'Louis XIX' rather than Charles X. Despite their opposing ideas he was devoted to his father and (partly to prevent his becoming a focus of opposition), Charles X had given him a seat on the council, where he had immense influence.

The role of the court, the degree of its integration into French society and loyalty to the monarchy, are illustrated by its behaviour in the final crisis of the restoration. Charles X was not stupid. Within the limits of his right-wing ideas he could be flexible. Before 1824 he had used the Garde nationale, formerly a pillar of the revolution, as a power-base and supported freedom of the press.

As King he seemed to have accepted the *charte* whole-heartedly and to be in a strong position. In 1825, a few months after his accession, he told Lévis that the Dauphin wanted to see representative government introduced everywhere 'since it is succeeding with us here'. He wrote

[50] AN 03 359 doss. Feuillant Rivière to Feuillant, 27 November 1827; AN 359 AP 84 ff. 66, 69, notes of Clermont-Tonnerre, 11, 30 December 1827; cf. *Damas*, ii, 139, 'the worst of our enemies was the Dauphin'.

[51] J. Robin-Harmel, *Le Prince de Polignac*, 2 vols., Paris and Avignon, 1941–50, ii, 82 undated letter to Mathieu de Montmorency; cf. AN 359 AP 84 f. 64, Frayssinous to Clermont-Tonnerre, 31 December 1828; *Damas*, ii, 163–4.

[52] BAVP Lévis, February, 15 March 1824, 10 March 1825; AN 359 AP 84 f. 66, notes of Clermont-Tonnerre, 1825.

to the Duchesse de Berri from Saint-Cloud, after his coronation festivities were over: 'Despite the immense stupidity (*sottises*) of the newspapers we are very peaceful here and I believe that the same is true for all of France.' After the fall of Villèle he selected a relatively liberal ministry headed by Martignac, and signed laws expelling the Jesuits and closing seminaries.

But he could never entirely rid himself of what Leopold I of the Belgians, who knew him well, called 'certain absolute ideas', which owed as much to the Napoleonic Empire as to the *ancien régime*.[53] He believed in strong monarchy, and overestimated the threat presented by the liberal tide of 1826–30. In reality most liberals now accepted the Bourbons, and would have been happy to settle for observation of the charter and a share in the spoils of office. But in August 1829 Charles X reverted to one of his favourite ideas and appointed an ultra-royalist ministry composed of some of the most unpopular men in France. Since his carefree youth before the revolution, when he had spent so much time in the salon of the Duchesse de Polignac, he had liked the Polignac family. In 1799 he had wanted to place them in the Duchesse d'Angoulême's household. In 1804 he had sent Armand and Jules de Polignac to plot against Napoleon. Now he chose his aide-de-camp and ambassador in London, Jules de Polignac, to head the government.

Just as most of the court officials of Napoleon I had tried to prevent him destroying his own Empire in 1812–14, so most of Charles X's – Duras, Gramont, Maillé, Fitzjames and even Polignac's own brother the *premier écuyer* – were opposed to this fatal ministry. They preferred to see liberals such as Sébastiani and the former Napoleonic chamberlain Sainte-Aulaire in power rather than *l'incapable Jules*, who had no idea how to handle the chambers.[54] The King often scolded them: he told Maillé to assure the minister of the interior of his support: 'Maillé, do you hear, I want you to go this very day.'[55]

Like the country as a whole the court was satisfied with the status

53 BAVP Lévis, April 1825; ABR, Charles X to Duchesse de Berri, 27 August 1825; Queen Victoria, *Letters*, 3 vols., 1908, I, 53, Leopold to Princess Victoria, 18 November 1836.
54 Archives x, Luxembourg to Madame de Podenas, 18 September, 22 November 1829, Madame to Monsieur de Podenas, 18 November 1829, anon. to Duchesse d'Escars, 15 December 1829. Exceptions were Blacas and, surprisingly, Lévis. See *Villèle*, v, 379, Montbel to Villèle, August 1829.
55 AST LMF 35 f. 150, de Vignet to La Tour, 30 August 1829.

quo and did not want change. The most popular paper in France, the *Journal des débats*, praised court officials for trying to give truth 'access to the throne' and to 'push aside barriers which could separate the King from his people'.[56] The court was now playing the role advocated by Lévis and acting as a link between the throne and the people. It was official and conciliatory, neither completely royalist nor wholly exclusive.

But, since they had so little influence, there was little court officials could do. Moreover the Dauphin had swung round to his father's views. In March 1830 Charles X used the court to emphasise his support for his ministers. He received what he regarded as a disloyal deputation from the Chamber of Deputies with unusual ceremony, sitting on the throne, surrounded by his court and ministers. The president of the chamber, Royer-Collard, a royalist and a liberal, was overwhelmed. 'I have rarely seen a man more deeply moved', remembered Charles de Rémusat.[57] But he did not alter his opposition. When Charles X signed the fatal ordonnances of 26 July 1830 at Saint-Cloud, he kept them a secret from his court officials. No doubt he wanted to spare himself the protests which, in such a crisis, they would have felt obliged to make. On 27 July revolution broke out.

For a long time the court had thought that 'the people' were no longer a problem. They were indifferent to the court and acquiesced in the monarchy. A favourite saying in the Tuileries was that 'the people has handed in its resignation', as indeed they had since 1795. The court was more frightened of military conspiracies and liberal intrigues. The Duchesse de Duras wrote how amused she was by Liberals' belief that 'the people' loved the *charte*, when all they really cared about, in her opinion, was earning their daily bread.[58]

The anti-government riots in late 1827 had been a surprise. Like Nicholas II in 1917, Charles X believed that he could rely on his army

---

[56] *Journal des débats*, 10 November 1829, p. 1; cf. *Le Constitutionnel*, 21 May 1827, p. 4, which envies the constitutional Marquis de Boisgelin, a *maître de la garde-robe*, his illusory opportunities to tell Charles X the truth.
[57] AST LMF 39 f. 32, Comte de Brignoles to La Tour, 19 March 1830; Charles de Rémusat, *Mémoires*, 5 vols., 1958–67, II, 291.
[58] For popular indifference to the court, see A. Jal, *Le Peuple au sacre*, 1829, pp. 35–40, and Louis Lanfranchi, *Voyage à Paris*, 1830, pp. 263–4. For the court's attitude to the people, see Archives x, Duchesse d'Escars to Madame de Podenas, November 1827; Bardoux, *La Duchesse de Duras*, p. 262 Duchesse de Duras to Chateaubriand, 1822.

and, above all, his guard. In 1830 the Garde royale was a magnificent elite force of 30,000 men, linked to the regime by innumerable privileges of pay, uniform and royal attention, which had earned it the hostility of troops of the line. On 27 July, however, the response of the students and people of Paris to the ordonnances, their joy at the hoisting of the tricolour on Notre-Dame and their bravery in fighting the Garde royale were a shock. The printing trade was the biggest employer in Paris, and censorship was a threat to the livelihood of all involved. The court soon realised that they were in the middle of a revolution again. Nevertheless according to Sémonville Duras (who, as in 1791 and 1815, had a gift for being in waiting in times of crisis) only dared use his right to enter the King's bedroom on 28 July at 6 a.m. and urge concessions 'after long hesitations'. After the King withdrew the ordonnances a court official, Brissac's son-in-law the Duc de Mortemart, *capitaine-colonel des gardes à pied*, a liberal who had served in the army before 1814, was the last *président du conseil* of the restoration, briefly acceptable both to the King and the revolution.

In the ensuing débâcle it has been customary to lament the disloyalty of the court. The Comte de Mesnard wrote: 'What eagerness to be beside them [the royal family] in the Tuileries in embroidered uniforms! And how many of the three hundred gentlemen of the chamber came to Saint-Cloud and Rambouillet? *Not six!*'[59]

Yet this was more a ritual use of the court as scapegoat than a reflection of reality. The court was never summoned by Charles X. Those court officials in waiting remained loyal, including people with Napoleonic backgrounds such as Girardin and Talon. On 28 July, after two days' fighting in Paris, the galleries of Saint-Cloud were packed with courtiers and servants crying *Vive le Roi!* The pages came from their school in Versailles to offer their services.[60] Court officials who followed the King to Rambouillet were sent back to defend the cause of legitimacy in the Chamber of Peers: they made Charles X repeat the order three times before they would leave. Many court officials (and the Duchesse de Berri) felt that the royal family did not defend

[59] AN 115 AP, Papiers Montholon 6, Sémonville's account of the July revolution, written for Mounier in August 1830; Mortemart, 'Trois journées', *Le Correspondant*, CCCXXI, 10 December 1930, p. 647; Archives X, Mesnard to Duchesse d'Escars, 20 February 1837.
[60] AN 115 AP 6, account by Sémonville; Louis-Charles de Bonnechose, *Dernière Légende de la Vendée, Louis de Bonnechose, page de Charles X*, 1860, pp. 15–16.

the monarchy with sufficient determination. The Duc de Guiche was horrified that the Dauphin, as well as his father, abdicated without consulting the officials of his household who 'had no interest but his'.[61]

In the summer of 1830 most other court officials were on their estates in the country or fighting in Algeria. About 30 senior court officials and 200 servants, excluding *gardes du corps* and other soldiers, followed the King and the royal family to Cherbourg.[62] It was the only dignified royal exit from France in the nineteenth century.

Many court officials had worn the tricolour cockade in the last days at Rambouillet and had hoped that the restoration court and monarchy would continue with Orléans acting as regent for the Duc de Bordeaux. However, French society was now sufficiently stable, and court officials were sufficiently integrated in it, for them to take the peer's oath to Louis-Philippe, who was proclaimed King on 7 August. Among court officials who took the oath were Gramont, Duras, Fitzjames and even (under pressure from the ruthless Baronne de Feuchères) the Duc de Bourbon. But it was possible to take the oath and remain legitimist. In August 1830, for example, Fitzjames had the courage to proclaim in the Chamber of Peers 'my love and respect for my old master' at a time when Paris seethed with hate for Charles X. Very few court officials rallied to Louis-Philippe whole-heartedly. Mortemart was prepared to be French ambassador to Russia, but felt that his past at the court of Charles X made it impossible for him to act as a witness at the wedding of one of Louis-Philippe's daughters.[63]

In exile in Lulworth, Holyrood, Prague and Frohsdorf the royal family had as many court officials and servants as it wanted. Blacas, a paragon of loyalty, was in charge, and was succeeded by an aide-de-camp of the Dauphin, the Duc de Lévis, the wise, moderate son of the author of *Pensées et maximes*. Many court officials helped the Duchesse de Berri's conspiracies in 1832. Many more made the 'pilgrimage' to see the royal family in exile, although not particularly encouraged to do so. Indeed, as legitimist writers boasted, no court was ever formally constituted. The court was used as a scapegoat for the failure of the

---

[61] *Maillé*, p. 361; AN 101 AP E2 35, account by the Duc de Guiche, August 1830.
[62] *Anne*, II, 342–6; accommodation for 200 people was needed at Cherbourg, see AN 271 AP, Papiers Odilon Barrot 21, 3 Odilon Barrot to the *préfet maritime*, 10 August 1830.
[63] AN 101 AP E2 35, Guiche's account, August 1830; *Moniteur*, 12 August 1830, p. 884; *Castellane*, III, 82–3, 5 July 1833.

restoration, and the royal family reverted to its traditional preference for armies of servants rather than courtiers.[64] A rota of royalist nobles came from France to act as the Comte de Chambord's aides-de-camp and that was all.

Most court officials, non-noble as well as noble, remained loyal. General Vincent, an *écuyer cavalcadour* who had risen in the army under the republic and the empire, went to see the royal family in exile every year. Amédée de Pastoret, a non-noble *gentilhomme de la chambre*, was the chief representative of the Comte de Chambord in France. Frayssinous, the former *premier aumônier*, was Chambord's tutor. The daughter of Comte Curial, *chambellan* of Napoleon and *premier chambellan* of Louis XVIII and Charles X, was so royalist that she would only marry someone who was willing to conspire with the Duchesse de Berri.[65] In her massive castle of Brunnsee in Styria the Duchesse de Berri wrote the bitter word *transfuge* against only nine names in the copy of the *Calendrier de la Cour pour l'année 1830* which she had taken into exile: six *gentilshommes de la chambre*, an aide-de-camp of the Dauphin who became a foreign minister of Louis-Napoleon (the vicomte de La Hitte), an aide-de-camp of her son who became *chevalier d'honneur* of the Duchesse d'Orleans (the Duc de Coigny) and, inevitably, Talleyrand. It is not many out of more than 2,000.

---

[64] A. Nettement, *Henri de France*, 2 vols., 1846, II, 156, 294 is only one of many legitimist denials of the existence of a court in exile. One of Chambord's tutors wrote an especially vicious denunciation of the court: see Général Marquis d'Hautpoul, *Souvenirs*, 1902, pp. 66–7. In 1850 Chambord himself wrote to the Duc de Noailles that 'the Court can no longer be what it once was': Comte de Chambord, *Correspondance*, Geneva 1871, p. 109, letter of 22 December 1850.

[65] Sosthènes de La Rochefoucauld, *Pélérinage à Goritz*, 1839, pp. 314–23; *Castellane*, III, 325, diary for 27 December 1844; memoirs of the Marquise de Saint-Clou (née Curial), kindly communicated by M. Henri Curial.

CHAPTER 9

❧ ❧

Money

Il demande de la magnificence, de l'or.

Fontaine on Napoleon I, 23 March 1808

Money was not a problem at court. The civil list was always rich enough to pay for the court of France, although it was the most lavish in Europe. The number of different households required for members of the royal family and responsibility for payment of the guard were more important in determining the strength of the civil list than the cost of the court. Thus Louis XVI was, predictably, in the weakest financial position of any monarch in this period. He not only had to pay for his own household but also for those of his wife, children, sister and aunts. They were all considered his dependents, unlike his brothers Provence and Artois and their wives: their independent incomes had been fixed first by Louis XV in 1771 and 1773, then by the National Assembly in 1790. The National Assembly also decided that the civil list should pay for the King's guard and for all official pensions, and the King paid a subsidy to the Garde nationale de Paris. In addition he continued to pay members of disbanded units of the guard such as the Gardes françaises and Gardes du corps, who had not received new employment. Nevertheless, he had enough money spare to send one million *livres* to Bouillé, a month before the flight to Varennes, to prepare an 'armed camp' at Montmédy.[1]

In contrast Napoleon I was in a far stronger financial position. At first this might seem surprising since he had the same civil list as Louis XVI and prices had risen by as much as one-third since 1790. Moreover

---

[1] Girault de Coursac, *Enquête*, p. 229: the author feels that the fact that Bouillé did not spend it indicates that he expected the King's escape to fail; *idem*, 'La Liquidation des pensions et des charges de la maison du Roi', *Découverte*, XLVIII, p. 20.

salaries had to be higher because there were fewer financial privileges attached to service at court than there had been before 1789.

But the Emperor had fewer financial burdens than the King. His family, except for his mother and his sister Pauline, was a charge on the countries they ruled rather than the French civil list. Josephine's household, which cost approximately one-and-a-half million francs a year, was less expensive than Marie-Antoinette's. Only the most senior officers of the Garde impériale were paid by the civil list. The ministry of war paid all the rest.[2] There were few pensions to pay since the Emperor personally ensured that the pensions of former employees of the *maison du Roi* continued to be paid by the *trésor public* rather than the *trésor de la couronne*.[3]

Indeed the Emperor had an eye for financial detail and checked the expenditure of his court himself. In 1807 he drew up the budget. He also attended meetings of the Conseil d'administration de la maison, which went through the accounts, and fixed the expenditure of each department.[4] If the Kings of France had devoted the same degree of attention to the expenditure of their court, they would have saved a fortune.

The annual surplus in the civil list was so large that the Emperor created a special fund, the *domaine privé*, to administer the money he saved. By 1814 it is said to have contained 150 million francs and was stored in the cellars of the Tuileries. Some of it was used to fund the last war effort; the rest was taken over by the *trésor public* in 1814.

In addition the Emperor controlled the *domaine extraordinaire*, the lands and revenues he confiscated from governments and individuals in the countries he conquered (Italy, Germany and Poland). It probably amounted to the largest single accumulation of property in European history, and was used to reward the Emperor's followers. One of the distinguishing features of the French monarchy, since Henri IV had won the throne of France by buying over the leaders of the Catholic League in the 1590s (or before), had been its pension-list. More than other monarchs, the King of France felt the need to give the leading figures of the monarchy pensions (as well as honours, jobs and presents),

[2] Comte d'Hérisson, *Un Secrétaire de Napoléon Premier*, 1894, pp. 233–43.
[3] AN o2 151, *Note écrite sous la dictée de Sa Majesté*, by Daru, 24 April 1806.
[4] For example AN AF IV 1231, meeting of *conseil d'administration de la maison*, 8 February 1806.

just as he also thought it necessary to maintain the largest royal guard
in Europe. Insecurity was the reason: few other monarchs faced such
repeated attacks on their authority, from nobles, *parlements* and the
city of Paris. Louis XVI had greatly diminished the size and number
of the royal pensions. During his reign they went mainly to his brothers,
a few ladies-in-waiting (including the Comtesse de Brionne, whose
salon was a centre for gossip against the royal family) and the Young
Pretender.

However, Napoleon renewed the tradition. Despite his mastery of
the army and the government, Napoleon was as insecure as previous
French monarchs. He was the first of his dynasty, and had come to
power after a revolution and repeated royalist attempts to assassinate
him. It is not surprising that he created an enormous guard and a massive
pension-list.

By 1810 lands and annuities worth 18 million francs a year were
being distributed to 4,035 individuals from the *domaine extraordinaire*.
They ranged from his most generously rewarded courtier Maréchal
Berthier, who received over 1.2 million, to invalided officers with a
few hundred francs a year.[5] Innumerable court officials benefited from
the *domaine extraordinaire* as well as from the civil list and frequent
presents of cash from the Emperor. For example to mark the birth
of the King of Rome the *gouvernante des enfants de France*, Madame
de Montesquiou, received 50,000 francs a year on the *domaine extraordinaire*. Constant, Napoleon's *premier valet de chambre* and Roustam
his *mamelouke*, both of whom were to desert him in 1814, received
regular and generous presents of cash paid by his *cassette*, the private
income he drew from the civil list. After Narbonne died in 1813, his
aged mother, former *dame d'honneur* of Madame Adélaïde, received
a present of 18,000 francs, although she was still a royalist.[6]

The Napoleonic court was shielded from the need for economy by
other sources in addition to the *domaine extraordinaire*, the *domaine
privé* and the civil list. Napoleon was in complete control of the government; the Senate and the Legislative Body were too servile to ask awkward questions about the budget. He was therefore able to use money

[5] Monika Senkowska-Gluck, 'Les Donataires de Napoléon Premier', *Revue d'histoire moderne
et contemporaine*, 1969, p. 683.
[6] Jean Savant, *Les Fonds Secrets de Napoléon*, 1952, pp. 93, 105.

from other ministries for his court and personal expenditure. This practice had begun under the consulate. In 1802 the First Consul had received money from the ministries of police and foreign affairs, the Portuguese government, the city of Hamburg and the *trésor public*, as well as his official salary as First Consul.

In 1807 the minister of the interior wrote to Fontaine, the Emperor's architect, that 3 million francs were available to be spent on orders to crown factories for refurnishing the palaces, especially Compiègne and Versailles.[7] Until 1808 the Ministry of Finance contributed 600,000 francs a year to the upkeep of the Louvre, which was in reality the responsibility of the civil list. The Emperor was so rich that in 1811 two million francs were spent by the civil list and one million by the *caisse d'amortissement* on orders to the factories of Lyons for textiles (silk, satin, damask) for refurnishing and redecorating Versailles.[8] In 1813 he spent the astonishing total of 7,015,000 francs on his palaces in the French Empire, from the Quirinal in Rome to Versailles. Such expenditure was partly designed to encourage French industry. However, the result was to increase the splendour of his court. Although their fabric had still not entirely recovered from the revolution, Napoleon I left the French palaces more lavishly furnished than at any time in their history, as the returning Bourbons noted with delight. In the history of the French monarchy only Louis XIV had spent as much on palaces as Napoleon I.

In 1814–15 the finances of the two civil lists and of the *domaines privé* and *extraordinaire* are so complicated, and so involved with those of the imperial and royal governments, that they are difficult to unravel. Both the Emperor and the King benefited financially from being on the throne. Both took cash from the *trésor de la couronne* and the *trésor public* with them into exile. Napoleon left for Elba with 3,966,915 francs in April 1814, Louis XVIII took 8 million francs and the crown jewels to Ghent a year later. Some of this money was left with a London bank and provided a financial basis for the royal family when it was once again in exile after 1830. In a similar way, before he left Malmaison for exile in June 1815, Napoleon transferred about 6 million francs

[7] Frédéric Masson, *Napoléon et sa famille*, I, 171n.; Jean Tulard, 'La Cour de Napoléon Ier', in Karl Werner (ed.), *Hof, Kultur und Politik im 19. Jahrhundert*, Bonn, 1985, pp. 57–8.
[8] *Fontaine*, I, 210, entry for 25 May 1808, 295, entry for 28 May 1811; Jean Coural, *Mobilier national, Soieries empire*, 1980, p. 467.

from his civil list to a private account with the banker Laffitte. He used it to live on St Helena and to reward the courtiers, Bertrand, Montholon and Marchand, who followed him there. In his will he left most of his money to these courtiers, and to his servants; he still considered the *domaine privé* his private property and hoped it could be divided between veterans of the army and the towns devastated in the invasions of 1814 and 1815.[9]

In 1814 after the return of Louis XVIII the funds of the *domaine extraordinaire* were devoted to the restoration of Versailles. In 1818 the *domaine extraordinaire* was finally dissolved and its remaining funds transferred to the *trésor public*. There were bitter attacks in the Chamber of Deputies on the grants which Napoleon's followers had received. However, an alliance between Bonapartists and liberals had been formed and a prominent liberal, General Foy, defended the grants. He claimed that they were 'far from being in proportion with the immensity of the services rendered'.

Since he made no conquests, the King did not have as much money as the Emperor with which to reward his followers (although through his personal influence he was able to have some *hôtels* and forests returned to former royalist owners like the Ducs de Castries, d'Havré and d'Uzès in 1814). However he did have the civil list. Again it was in a stronger position than under Louis XVI, despite the rise in prices. Louis XVIII had no subordinate royal households to pay for. Artois, his sons and their wives were voted a separate income of 8 million francs a year in 1814, as they were regarded as a separate family and not the King's responsibility.

Furthermore, in the fervent royalist atmosphere of the beginning of the reign, the cost of the *maison militaire* was attributed to the ministry of war not the civil list. Therefore the King was sitting on a cash mountain. 'He has become so rich since the budget', wrote Chateaubriand to the Duchesse de Duras a few weeks after it was voted, with a longing shared by every royalist; and he asked her to obtain him a grant of 100,000 francs. Ten years later in one of his frank evening conversations with the Dauphin, Lévis pointed out that the royal family had 34 million

[9] Hérisson, *Secrétaire*, p. 243; Mansel, *Louis XVIII*, pp. 220, 226–7; Montholon, *La Captivité*, II, 511–15.

francs a year (another million was added after the marriage of the Duc
de Berri in 1816), while the emigrés had received nothing.[10] A year
later a law was passed giving the emigrés compensation for their confiscated estates.

However extravagant the court was, the civil list could pay. Moreover,
once it had been voted at the beginning of each reign, the civil list
was fixed until the King's death. It did not have to be approved with
the rest of the budget by the chambers. The cost of the court was therefore rarely a matter for potentially embarrassing discussions in the
chambers (except when La Fayette, a personal enemy of Louis XVIII,
brought it up). The advantage of this veil of obscurity was shown by
the recurrent criticism of the size, and even the existence, of the *maison
militaire* when the budget of the ministry of war was discussed.[11] Such
attacks would have been far worse if they could have been levelled
against the *maison civile* in a debate on the budget of the *ministère
de la maison*.

The generosity of the civil list was shown by its ability to absorb
extra charges after the Hundred Days. France had to pay a massive
war indemnity, and the civil list contributed 12,309,000 francs until
the withdrawal of allied troops in 1818. After 1819 it contributed
approximately 3,900,000 francs a year to the cost of the *maison militaire*.[12]

In comparison with the court of Louis XVI, far less was spent on
pleasure. Pradel calculated that 5,699,500 francs less was spent in 1817
on the stables, the hunt and the *menus-plaisirs* than in 1789. Service
became as important in the expenditure as it was in the social life and
composition of the court. Pensions to senior court officials were now
paid by the Chamber of Peers rather than the King. Instead he paid
in 1819 pensions worth 2,080,326 francs to 3,327 people 'ruined as
a result of political events'; similar pensions to ruined royalists were
also paid by the ministries of war and the interior and other members
of the royal family. In addition 1,361,000 francs a year were paid in
pensions to 1,813 former servants and court officials of the royal family.
Former ladies-in-waiting of Queens Marie-Antoinette and Marie-

---

[10] Gautier, *Etudes*, p. 38; Chateaubriand, *Correspondance générale*, 5 vols., 1912–24, I, 383;
       BAVP Lévis, entry for 15 October 1824.
[11] *Moniteur*, 5 June 1821, p. 810, 23 June 1829, pp. 1119, 1121, 1128.
[12] AN o3 2682, *Dépenses de la maison du roi, depenses extraordinaires*.

Josephine received 6,000 francs a year; a servant such as the former *garçon à l'office du petit commun de la Reine* a few hundred.[13]

The restoration monarchy was a cause as well as a government: it was determined to take care of former servants and of those who had suffered for its sake. (Inevitably, however, they never considered themselves well enough rewarded.) These people were the equivalent, for the restoration, of the soldiers and officials rewarded out of the *domaine extraordinaire* under the Empire. In addition, the civil list paid pensions to bishops who had not recovered their sees, and emigrés formerly supported by the British government.

The King also rewarded certain prominent individuals with large sums of money: he was more generous, or extravagant, than Louis XVI had been (see appendices, p. 207). Again service to the royal cause was more important than class. Pasquier, *l'inévitable*, wrote in his memoirs that the Bourbons considered as 'more important than the rest the services and attentions paid to their persons'. But this is not confirmed by a study of the recipients of the King's bounty. Of the 19 people awarded 100,000 francs or more, 4 were court officials: the Ducs d'Aumont, de La Chatre and de Duras and Mesnard de Chouzy, a *chambellan de l'hôtel*. The others were royalists, ministers or marshals, whose political or military services to his government the King wished to reward. Among them were Pozzo di Borgo, a personal enemy of Napoleon who was Russian ambassador to Paris, the family of another enemy of Napoleon, General Moreau, the family of the hero of the Vendée La Rochejaquelein, and Pasquier's colleagues in the government, or their relations, such as Richelieu, de Serre and Lainé.

Like the Empire, the restoration also believed in what Pradel called the *luxe bienfaisant du souverain*. Some of the largest items of expenditure were the crown factories, orders to the factories of Lyons, the purchase of buildings between the Tuileries and the Louvre, and charities in and around Paris (on which about one-tenth of the civil list was spent). Thus, as ministers constantly pointed out, although it was the largest single item of expenditure, the court proper absorbed only about one-third of the civil list.[14]

[13] AAE 347 f. 68, Pradel to Louis XVIII, 13 October 1817; AN 03 539 ff. 68–71, *Rapport au roi*, 18 February 1819.

[14] *Pasquier*, v, 101; AN 03 537 f. 505, *Rapport au roi*, 10 October 1817; BVC FR 96 ff. 107–9, Lauriston to Richelieu, March 1821.

Nevertheless the court became increasingly expensive. It is difficult to compare the cost of the Empire and restoration courts, since the same items of expenditure were often assigned to different departments. This explains the difference in the cost of the *menus-plaisirs* under the two regimes. It was 120,000 in 1813 and 760,000 in 1817, although the Empire certainly spent large sums on court entertainments and gave more of them (see appendices, pp. 205 and 206). In many departments such as the *cérémonies* and the *vénerie* expenditure was roughly similar. *Ecuries* cost more before 1814 because the Emperor travelled further.[15]

But in most other departments the restoration court was more expensive. It revived the extravagant traditions of Versailles. The court officials felt they were part of the monarchy and took for granted privileges which those of the Empire regarded as unobtainable. Even before the return of the King, Compiègne was full of people 'who are having themselves heated, lit and nourished at the King's expense', in the words of the Duchesse de Duras.[16] Such habits were hard to change. It was a fact of life at the restoration court that 'the *bouche du roy* pays for some commodities far more than ordinary people'. The man in charge, the Duc d'Escars, was notoriously profligate: his wife wrote darkly that he was 'completely in the hands of all the worst elements in his office'.[17] Although the *bouche* decreased in cost after his death, expenditure in every other department increased between 1817 and 1827: the *gouvernments*, the *chambre* and the *faculté* more than doubled (see appendix, p. 206).

The households of the Duchesse de Berri and her children were even more extravagant; the cost of the *bouche* of the Duchesse de Berri rose from 185,194 francs in 1823 to 263,928 in 1825. In January 1827 her household bought 237 copies of the *Calendrier de la cour*, and her son's 65.[18] It was a useful book, listing information which every

---

[15] AAE 347 ff. 63–70, Pradel to Richelieu, 13 October 1817; AN 03 2729, *Budget général de 1827*.

[16] Bardoux, *La Duchesse de Duras*, p. 157, letter to Claire de Duras, 28 April 1814.

[17] AN 03 73, 17, Forestier, *intendant des dépenses* to Pradel, 21 March 1818; Archives x, Duchesse d'Escars to Marquise de Podenas, 22 August 1821, 27 July 1822.

[18] AN 337 AP 14 f. 50, *Projet de budget pour l'année 1823*; AN 371 AP 2, *Maison de SAR. Madame, Duchesse de Berri, état des dépenses de la bouche 1825; bordereau des dépenses de l'administration générale janvier 1827*; AN 03 3009 f. 16, *Trésor de S.A. R. Monseigneur le Duc de Bordeaux, exercice de 1827*, purchase on 12 January.

courtier needed to know such as the names of people in office and the dates of religious festivals. But there was no need for so many copies.

Another reason for the extravagance of the restoration court was the fact that the senior court officials, the *chefs de service*, could initiate expenditure, although it needed the approval of the minister. They had to inform him by the October preceding the year in which it would take place.[19] Their primary concerns were the splendour of their department and the welfare of their subordinates, not economy. Inevitably there were rows between the court officials and the minister, as there had been under Louis XVI. A bound volume of letters commemorates Polignac's triumph in keeping a large number of *chevaux de manège*, although the minister thought them unnecessary. Pleasure came before profit in the *domaine de la couronne*. Girardin ensured that the crown forests were devoted to providing good hunting rather than a rising income from the sale of trees. Under the Empire it had been the other way round.[20]

In financial disputes between the court officials and the minister the King often took the side of his court officials. Like them he wanted the court to be splendid and his servants happy and well rewarded. The contrast with the careful watch Napoleon kept on economy could not have been greater. However, after 1827 the rate of increase in the cost of the court slowed down. In January 1827 Charles X expressed his dismay at the contrast between the 'remarkable order' in the state's finances with the disorders and delays of the court's. The *maison du Roi* was still dealing with 1824's accounts when the state had finished 1825's.[21]

The new *intendant-général* La Bouillerie was dedicated to economy and had greater experience of handling money than predecessors such as Lauriston and Doudeauville: he had been *trésorier-général de la couronne* and of the *domaine extraordinaire* under the Empire and *intendant du trésor de la couronne* since 1814. He abolished the separate household hospital in 1829 and began to tackle the problem of the court's expensive journeys to Saint-Cloud.[22] In the interests of economy he

[19] AN o3 531 OD, *Ordonnance* of 21 December 1814.
[20] AN o3 387; AN o3 539 f. 427 vo., *Rapport au roi*, 26 December 1819.
[21] AN o3 531 OD, *Circulaire du ministre de la maison*, 24 January 1827.
[22] AN o3 227, *Circulaire* of 20 November 1827 to the *Chefs de service*; La Bouillerie to d'Aumont, 14 December 1829.

was prepared to be firm, to the point of rudeness, to the King himself. He was furious when Charles X allowed a hunt official's salary to be increased. When positions at court fell vacant he insisted that Charles X appoint 'the former employees who, by the organisation of 1820, have been suspended', and were still drawing their salaries, rather than newcomers, in order to save money.[23] Thus desire for economy as well as its own instincts encouraged the court to remain a self-perpetuating body.

[23] AN o3 557 f. 184, *Note pour le roi*, 6 November 1829.

Epilogue The Citizen King

J'allais dire la cour, si je ne me fûsse souvenu que le roi Louis-Philippe avait
proscrit ce mot.

Auguste Trognon, Vie de Marie-Amélie, 1872

In the eighteenth century the Ducs d'Orléans, First Princes of the Blood
and the largest landowners in France after their cousin the king, lived
in splendour in the Palais-Royal in Paris and Saint-Cloud in the country.
They hated the court and felt, as Louis-Philippe remembered, that there
were 'continual and systematic encroachments of court etiquette on
the prerogatives of the Princes of the Blood'.[1] They were in reality a
sign of the increasing pretensions of the nobility, but the Orléans blamed
the King. Like many other cadet branches of royal dynasties, they turned
to liberalism out of jealousy.

Driven by a mixture of ambition and idealism, Philippe Egalité, who
became Duc d'Orléans in 1785, was an early enthusiast for the revolution. How far his enthusiasm extended has never been fully established.
But the demonstrations which led to the crowd marching on Versailles
on 5 October 1789 began in the section of the Palais-Royal open to
the public. Orléans was seen by several witnesses in Versailles, in the
early morning of 6 October, wearing a grey *frac* and talking to the
people who were surrounding the palace. Many were crying *Vive M.
le duc d'Orléans!*[2] There was a lull in his political ambitions when
Louis XVI sent him to England later that month. But in 1792 he became
a deputy in the Convention and in 1793 voted for the death of the
King.

---

[1] Louis-Philippe, *Mémoires*, 2 vols., 1973–4, I, 322.
[2] *Procédure criminelle instruite au Châtelet de Paris*, 3 vols., 1790, II, 15, 71, 125, *Dépositions*
of Frondeville, Brayer, Jobert.

In 1800 his son Louis-Philippe, a stronger and more intelligent character, was reconciled to Louis XVIII. He was a moderate liberal who had inherited the family love of palaces and splendour. He wrote with pride in 1814, when he saw the King's mass and reception in the Tuileries, 'nowhere are pomp and ceremony better understood than in France'.[3] During the restoration Louis-Philippe entertained on an impressive scale and, with Fontaine's help, made the Palais-Royal more magnificent than ever. After 1830 restoring royal palaces was his favourite occupation. Between 1833 and 1847 he paid 398 visits to Versailles which he transformed from a palace into a historical museum dedicated to 'all the glories of France'.[4]

During the Hundred Days, however, his intrigues with Fouché and refusal to go to Ghent revealed that he had also inherited the family tradition of conspiratorial hostility to the King. Louis XVIII reacted by maintaining the traditional differences in status between the royal family and the princes of the blood, after Louis-Philippe finally returned to France in 1817. At the baptism of the daughter of the Duc de Berri, when the *grand aumônier* was about to present the pen to the Duc d'Orléans to sign the register, the King said in his loud, clear voice 'Put the pen down and let a clerk of the chapel present it.' There were similar humiliations over whether Louis-Philippe had the right to use the royal box in theatres or to kneel on two cassocks at religious services. Despite his liberal principles, Louis-Philippe felt very strongly about court etiquette and was devoured with resentment. His wife Marie-Amélie, born a Bourbon of Naples, wrote in 1819: 'For my part I dread court *fêtes* and functions more than anything else.'[5]

Such humiliations, in front of scornful court officials who remembered his revolutionary past, were hard to forgive or forget. They were particularly difficult to accept since they came at a time when, as a result of the transformation by Napoleon and the congress of Vienna of the rulers of Bavaria, Württemberg, Saxony, Hanover and The Netherlands into Kings, there was a general inflation of honours in Europe. Princes who would have made little mark at Versailles before 1789 were now

[3] AN 300 AP III 16, Orléans to Madame de Saint-Laurent, 12 June 1814.
[4] *Louis-Philippe, l'homme et le roi*, Archives Nationales, 1974–5, p. 127.
[5] AN 03 526, *Relation du Service Anniversaire du 16 octobre 1819*, ff. 4, 6 by Marquis de Rochemore; *Marie-Amélie, journal*, ed. Suzanne D'Huart, 1981, pp. 255, 271, entries for 28 October 1818, 16 December 1819.

Royal, whereas the Orléans remained Most Serene, Highnesses. The Bourbons, who considered themselves the oldest and grandest dynasty in Europe, felt such distinctions were inappropriate. Even distant cousins of the King of France should take precedence of a Wittelsbach or a Wettin.

The moment Charles X ascended the throne, in order to redress the balance, and perhaps to please his cousins, he made all princes of the blood Royal Highnesses. Relations between the two branches of the dynasty improved and Charles X invited the Orléans to dine more often than had Louis XVIII. Nevertheless in 1829 Orléans complained to his youngest son's tutor of 'this hostility of the Court which has always been shown to the younger branches'.[6]

There was little sign of hostility, however, at the ball which Orléans gave, on 31 May 1830, in honour of the visit of his brother-in-law, the King of the Two Sicilies. The Palais-Royal blazed with lights (gas-as well as candlelight). Three thousand guests, including the cream of the Faubourg Saint-Germain, danced until morning. As an unprecedented honour the royal family came too, surrounded by what Cuvillier-Fleury called 'a crowd of courtiers, of gentlemen in gold, of embroidered uniforms, of sparkling swords, their faces glowing with aristocratic vanity'. Charles X was impressed by the Palais-Royal and joked to Fontaine, who was responsible for the decoration, 'You have never done anything so fine for me.' However, the Polignac ministry was extremely unpopular. In the garden below a crowd started to riot and there were cries of 'Down with the braid coats! Down with the aristocrats!' A celebrated liberal writer, Narcisse de Salvandy, said to Orléans: 'A very Neapolitan fête, Monseigneur, for we are dancing on a volcano.'[7]

Two months later the folly of Charles X in signing the ordonnances reawakened ambitions which Louis-Philippe had probably put aside in the 1820s. Louis-Philippe's well-advertised liberalism enabled him to emerge as the only solution, the saviour of law and order, the most suitable monarch for France. He was proclaimed King of the French (a more 'democratic' style than King of France) by the chambers on 7 August. Louis-Philippe then began to destroy the court.

The personality of the monarch had always determined the character

[6] A. Cuvillier-Fleury, *Journal*, 2 vols., 1900–3, I, 114, entry for 11 July 1829.
[7] *Ibid.*, I, 187, diary for 31 May 1830; *Apponyi*, I, 260–1, diary for 2 June 1830.

of the court. Louis XVI had been the antithesis of a court-bound monarch. He had not been sufficiently royal for contemporary taste and his court was a factor in his downfall. Composed of members of the *noblesse présentée*, it emphasised divisions within the elite before the outbreak of the revolution and repelled supporters of the new constitution after it. For until 1792 the leaders of the revolution had wanted to reform, and in some cases join, the court, not to abolish it. If Louis XVI had had a larger and more accessible court, he might have had more supporters.

After Bonaparte seized power France possessed the vital ingredients of court life – vanity, desire for splendour, ambition, plenty of money and a rich and deferential elite. The events of the revolution had been so alarming that most members of the elite, non-noble and noble alike, wanted to associate themselves with the throne even more closely than before. There was an increased appetite for court life at the same time as a breakdown of barriers and a spread of court manners within the elite. After 1804, out of the new elite produced by the revolution, Napoleon I was able to create a new court at least as aristocratic and monarchical as the old.

His court was a triumph for the lower ranks, the outer fringes and the younger sons of Versailles as well as for the new elite. Even on St Helena there were links with Versailles. The Emperor maintained court etiquette: and of his remaining courtiers, Las Cases was cousin of a lady-in-waiting of the Princesse de Lamballe; Montholon was son of the *premier veneur* of the Comte de Provence; and Gourgaud was the son of a violinist in the orchestra of the King's chapel and of a nurse of the Duc de Berri.

Napoleon's court also revealed his ultra-monarchical instincts. As well as increasing the size, he exaggered the etiquette, splendour, aloofness and elitism of his court. When he went to the Hôtel de Ville in Paris, etiquette was more monarchical, and municipal officials played a smaller role, than at similar occasions under Louis XVI. By 1814, with 2,752 officials in France, and over 100 chamberlains, he had a larger court, and more court officials from the elite, than Louis XVI. Napoleon I made his court the centre of his Empire and, for a time, for much of Europe. It became so powerful that in 1814–15 it played as large a part in the history of France as the Senate and the Legislative Body.

Whereas Louis XVI failed to use his court as a weapon, and Napoleon I overused it, Louis XVIII and Charles X achieved a synthesis. Particularly after the only complete reorganisation of the *maison du Roi* in its history took place in 1820, their court was neither social and domestic like the court of Versailles, nor aloof and autocratic like that of Napoleon I. It was a mixture of both, accessible as well as splendid, official as well as aristocratic.

The restoration court shows the continuity which underlay the different courts after 1789. They were trying to do the same things in different ways. They used the same palaces, the same furniture and some of the same staff and they appealed to the same emotions. Just as Napoleon I was influenced by Versailles, so Louis XVIII and Charles X borrowed from 'Bonaparte'. The position of *gentilhomme de la chambre*, created in 1820, was modelled on the chamberlains of Napoleon and gave Louis XVIII and Charles X a larger and more elitist court than Louis XVI. Whereas Louis XVI had 27 senior court officials, all from the *noblesse présentée*, by 1830 Charles X had 496 (12 per cent non-noble, 45 per cent from the old *noblesse présentée* and 43 per cent from the *noblesse non-présentée*).

Service had replaced class as the principle dominating the court. The Bourbon monarchy was finally surrounded by a hierarchy of officers and officials devoted to its service, recruited from all sections of the elite. The constitutional and military character of the court, and the regime, is shown by the primacy given by its *entrées* to official positions and institutions, such as the two chambers, the law courts and the army. Peers, Deputies and officers took precedence over the old nobility. The Protestant and Jewish consistories paid court to the Most Christian King at the same time as the Archbishop of Paris and his clergy. The people who felt excluded from the court, both by the simplicity of their manners and the purity of their politics, were provincial ultra-royalists.

Despite its size and splendour, the court was no more incompatible with parliamentary government, after 1814, than it had been with the revolution in 1789–92. The court had little political influence and acted as a machine for satisfying the vanity of the elite and the monarchy's desire for splendour, rather than as a centre of power and source of employment. Before 1814 ambitious young men like Talleyrand, Narbonne, Stendhal and Decazes had used the court as a springboard for their careers. It had been a means to obtain jobs in the army and the church under Louis XVI and in the army and the administration under the Empire.

Under the restoration the court was used to reward royalists and to link the nobility with the constitutional order. It symbolised, and helped to provoke, the nobility's evolution into a modern ruling class. Individuals like the Comte de Narbonne, Mathieu de Montmorency and the Duc de Richelieu, families like the Noailles, the Talleyrand and the Montesquiou, show how well some of the court nobility survived the revolution. They not only adapted to, but flourished under, subsequent regimes. The Marquis de Dreux-Brézé who had ordered the Third Estate to disperse on 23 June 1789 continued to exercise his *charge* of *grand maître des cérémonies* and to manage his estates until 1825. His son, who combined the *charge* of *grand maître des cérémonies* with a career as a speaker in the *chambre des pairs*, was more representative of the court than Jules de Polignac. Particularly after 1820 most court officials were relatively moderate and, like the rest of France, wanted neither the *charte* nor the dynasty to change. In 1829–30 most court officials were opposed to the fatal Polignac ministry. They felt that, as Lévis wrote, 'there had to be resistance somewhere and after all the chambers were better for the King and the people than the *parlements*'.

If the court had had political influence, Charles X would not have signed the ordonnances which provoked the July revolution. A sign of the court's moderating role is that the last *président du conseil* of the restoration was the Duc de Mortemart, captain of the Gardes à pied ordinaires du Roi, a hereditary court official who had served the Empire and was briefly acceptable to both revolutionaries and the King in the middle of the July revolution. It was no fault of the court that France did not remain a constitutional monarchy with a partly aristocratic ruling class, like other European countries in the nineteenth century.

Thus the revolution of liberty, equality and fraternity had resulted in a larger, more splendid and more elitist court in France – as many supporters of the revolution may always have intended. The period 1804–30 was one of the great ages of the court of France, in literature, music and the arts as well as society and politics. The court was frequented or described by writers of genius such as Chateaubriand, Balzac and Stendhal. The court had its own moralist in the Duc de Lévis,

heir to the tradition of La Rochefoucauld and Chamfort and author
of such aristocratic maxims as 'A king without a nobility is a general
without an army' and 'I have known dedicated advocates of equality
who only needed a genealogy to be the most vain of all nobles.'[8]

Although relatively little was built, the court reached new levels of
beauty and luxury in the decorative arts, china, textiles and furniture.
The throne-room in the Tuileries was grander and more luxurious than
the king's bedroom in Versailles. Artists such as Gérard and Isabey
were primarily court artists who excelled at producing flattering images
of the monarchy and the elite. The court was so popular that by 1830
both the public and the state apartments of the Tuileries were literally
too small to contain all those who wanted to attend it. It was so impressive that it resumed its role as the model for the other courts of Europe.

Louis-Philippe, however, who owed his throne to a revolution, was
determined to break with his predecessors' style of monarchy. He did
not want a court. Just as Louis-Philippe exaggerated the danger of a
republic in order to frighten the elite into supporting his seizure of
the throne, so he assumed his personal resentment of the court was
shared by the rest of France. In fact such hostility was restricted to
certain sections of the extreme left and the ultra-royalists, people like
La Fayette and Villèle. But La Fayette and another enemy of the court
the liberal banker Laffitte were especially influential in 1830.

Rivalries within the Bourbon dynasty proved more fatal to the court
than the outbreak of the revolution or the proclamation of the Empire.
Louis-Philippe's acts show the hatred he had been nourishing during
the restoration. Within a few months of his accession he abolished every
branch of the *maison du Roi* (except the department which looked
after the palaces), even the royal music and the royal hunt. Rossini,
premier compositeur du Roi, left Paris in disgust. Hunting rights in
the royal forests were leased to private hunts. The pensions paid on
the civil list to 11,953 people ceased unless their holder could produce
a certificate of poverty (*certificat d'indigence*). Louis-Philippe accepted
a civil list of 12 million francs a year instead of Charles X's 32 million.[9]

Louis-Philippe was the first monarch in Europe to reign without a

---

[8] Lévis, *Pensées et maximes*, p. 88.
[9] AN 03 880, *Contrôle du Personnel*, decisions of 29 July 1830, 1 November 1830; Gautier,
Etudes, pp. 123, 150.

court. Even Frederick the Great had maintained one in Berlin, although he did not see much of it. As Fontaine wrote with disapproval, Louis-Philippe was determined 'to live quite differently from the two Kings his predecessors'. Although he followed his ministers' advice and moved from the Palais-Royal into the Tuileries in 1831, he transformed the palace into a family house and maintained as little etiquette as possible. His household was only a little larger than the household he had employed as Duc d'Orléans. The King and Queen walked in the streets of Paris like ordinary citizens. When he wanted to talk undisturbed in the Tuileries he had to lock his study doors himself. Ministers and diplomats and their families could drop in after dinner and chat or sew around the Queen's table. There were no formal court receptions except at the New Year.[10]

The changing character of the French monarchy can be judged from the clothes worn by the monarchs. Louis XVI, simple, civilian but committed to the *noblesse présentée*, wore a *frac* in the week and the *habit habillé* on Sunday. Napoleon I, military and ultra-monarchical, wore the uniform of the Chasseurs à cheval or grenadiers of the Garde impériale and, on special occasions, his own imperial *petit costume*. Louis XVIII, a genuinely parliamentary monarch, compromised between military and civilian costume by wearing a *frac* with epaulettes. Charles X, more military and autocratic than his brothers, wore the uniform of colonel-general of the Garde royale and occasionally other uniforms. Louis-Philippe, the citizen King, although he sometimes wore uniform, was generally in the *frac*.

Queen Victoria's royal eye noticed Louis-Philippe's unusual way of life. In 1855, visiting Napoleon III, she wrote: 'Everything is beautifully *monté* at Court – *very* quiet and in excellent order; I must say we are both much struck with the difference between this and the poor King's time, when the noise, confusion and bustle were great'... 'and there was *no* court'.[11]

However, even under Louis-Philippe some traditions of French royal splendour were maintained. He gave balls and banquets at the Tuileries and Fontainebleau to help the shopkeepers of Paris. The wife of the

---

[10] *Fontaine*, II, 910, diary for 26 September 1831; *Sainte-Aulaire*, p. 132.
[11] Queen Victoria, *Letters*, III, 136, 139, Queen Victoria to Leopold I 23 August, to Baron Stockmar 1 September, 1855.

American ambassador in London wrote of one dinner at the Tuileries that it was 'the finest entertainment I ever saw, the *salle à manger* is more magnificent than the [one at] Buckingham Palace and the whole effect is more striking'. Comte Rodolphe Apponyi was equally impressed by a ball: 'The entertainment was really superb, the *salle des maréchaux* decorated marvellously.' But he added that 'except for the corps diplomatique there were few members of high society'.[12]

Most nobles refused to serve the citizen King and his bourgeois monarchy and stayed away from his court. Instead of providing a ruling class, as they had under the restoration, they devoted themselves to their fortunes and their pleasures. Their loyalty to the King in exile was increased by the fact that Louis-Philippe did not offer a real monarchical alternative. The Faubourg Saint-Germain again became an aristocratic citadel opposed to the government. Their unremitting, contemptuous hostility was one of the weaknesses of the regime. The principal exception was provided by former courtiers of Napoleon I, who returned to office after a gap of 16 years. Louis-Philippe's household was full of them. Gourgaud was an aide-de-camp. Flahault and Anatole de Montesquiou served in the households of other members of the royal family, Bondy was *chevalier d'honneur* of the Queen, and the King had the same secretary, Baron Fain, as the Emperor.

Paris lost the drama and colour associated with the court. The social life of the elite contracted. The Faubourg Saint-Germain, the Napoleonic nobility and the bourgeoisie, which had been temporarily brought into contact with each other by the restoration court, retreated into isolation for the rest of the century. After 1830 there were few equivalents of the salon of the Duchesse de Duras, open to aristocrats, writers and ministers. Private salons, shops and businesses in Paris gradually assumed the role of the court as centres of power, jobs, fashion, news and entertainment.

The three generations of the Girardin family (originally tax-farmers from Lorraine) show the changing importance of the court. The Marquis de Girardin was a typical late eighteenth-century *littérateur* and *philosophe*. His friend Rousseau is buried on an island in a lake in his park

[12] Edward Boykin, *Victoria, Albert and Mrs Stevenson*, 1957, p. 125, letter from Mrs Stevenson, February 1838; *Apponyi*, II, 104, diary for 12 January 1832.

at Ermenonville north of Paris. Girardin had little to do with the court of Versailles.

His sons Stanislas and Alexandre, however, used the Napoleonic courts as a means to further their careers. Stanislas became *premier écuyer* of Prince Joseph the Emperor's elder brother and later Prefect of Rouen. Alexandre, through his prowess at hunting, became an indispensable part of court life, managing the dynastic changes of 1814–15 with skill. Alexandre's son Numance, a *page de la vénerie*, was being groomed to succeed him when the revolution of 1830 destroyed the court. Both Girardins had lived for and by the court (although after 1815 Stanislas was a liberal deputy often attacking the restoration government).

After 1830 Alexandre's illegitimate son Emile de Girardin became one of the most powerful men in France, through the press rather than the court. He was a leading journalist and owned the newspaper *La Presse*. His wife Delphine held a famous literary salon. They had little to do with the court and later became semi-republican.

The July monarchy was in nature a supremely rational regime. Unlike the restoration, the Empire and the Third Republic, which derived strength from love of peace or glory, dynastic loyalty and revolutionary pride, the July monarchy had no charisma. The only desire it fulfilled was for a liberal constitution. Even this was not entirely satisfied as it became clear that the King left his ministers less initiative, and intervened more frequently in the day-to-day running of the government, than Louis XVIII or Charles X.

Its rational character and lack of splendour meant that the July monarchy was one of the weakest and least respected regimes in France in the nineteenth century. As Louis XVIII had written to the Duc d'Angoulême during the emigration, to be able to live like Frederick the Great, a monarch first had to be Frederick the Great. A monarch had to have a splendid court since, if he did not show himself in public 'with an imposing entourage, people will respect him less'.[13] One of the triumphs of the restoration court was that it surrounded Louis XVIII and Charles X with splendour and deference. They may have been hated or rejected but they did not arouse the same degree of contempt as that King without a court, Louis-Philippe. Charles X was better received

---

[13] Louis XVIII, 'Les Devoirs d'un Roi', *Feuilles d'histoire*, 1 September 1909, p. 277.

in liberal, nationalist Alsace in 1828 than Louis-Philippe in 1834. Riots, coups and attempted assassinations succeeded each other. Louis-Philippe was forced to abdicate in 1848 by a revolution. His flight to England disguised as 'Mr Smith' was quite different from Charles X's dignified withdrawal in 1830, surrounded by his guard and his court.

The nineteenth century could have remained a golden age for the court of France after 1830, as it did for the other courts of Europe. After the relative simplicity of the late eighteenth and early nineteenth centuries, they all experienced a return to grandeur. Her aunts told Queen Victoria that she must always be surrounded by her court, and it was grander and more ceremonious than those of George IV and William IV. In Russia the court remained a centre of power until the revolution. There was a renaissance of court life in Berlin under Wilhelm II. He had a larger, more splendid and more influential court than his predecessors: it helped push him towards war in 1912–14.

In Austria under Franz Joseph there was what his latest biographer calls a 'reinforcement of the court system'. The splendour and etiquette of the court were increased and, as in restoration France, played an indispensable part in raising the prestige and popularity of the monarch, without which the empire could not have survived.[14] Napoleon III also maintained a splendid court during the Second Empire. It was a simplified, relatively relaxed version of his uncle's, staffed by people with names like Bassano, Montebello and La Bédoyère: its ceaseless round of entertainments added glamour to his regime. The resumption of the revolutionary and later republican traditions in France was caused by the mistakes of Charles X, Louis-Philippe, Napoleon III and the Comte de Chambord, rather than by pressure from their subjects.

One of Louis-Philippe's most outspoken enemies was Monsieur de Cormenin. He was a famous deputy and pamphleteer, so famous that in 1848 he was appointed president of the commission that drafted the constitution of the Second Republic. His attacks on Louis-Philippe were based not on dislike of monarchy and the court – he had advised Richelieu on the reorganisation of 1820 – but on the feeling that Louis-Philippe was not a genuine monarch, that he had a mock court instead

[14] Karl Ferdinand Werner (ed.), *Hof, Kultur und Politik im 19. Jahrhundert*, Bonn, 1985, pp. 234, 289; Jean-Paul Bled, *François-Joseph*, 1987, p. 488.

of a real one.[15] He ended one pamphlet with a cry from the heart typical of early nineteenth-century France: 'It is absolutely essential that we have a court, pomp, splendour, *fêtes*, luxury, sumptuous palaces, a whirl of royal display.'[16]

[15] AN BB30 257 f. 65, note by Cormenin, August 1820; Charles Ledré, *La Presse à l'Assaut de la Monarchie*, 1960, pp. 171–2; Paul Bastid, *Un Juriste pamphlétaire, Cormenin précurseur et constituant de 1848*, 1948, pp. 117–19.
[16] Cormenin, *Libelles politiques*, 4 vols., Brussels, 1836–7, III, 176 (1833), III, 10–11 (1832).

Appendices

The court in 1789

Grand Aumônier Mgr de Montmorency-Laval and 86 officials and servants
Premier Maître d'Hôtel Baron d'Escars and 119
Grand Chambellan Duc de Bouillon, four Premiers Gentilshommes de la Chambre
  the Ducs de Richelieu, d'Aumont de Fleury and de Duras and 127
Grand Maître de la Garde-Robe Duc de Liancourt and 31
Premier Médecin Monsieur de Lassonne and 59
Cabinet du Roi 13
Grand Maître des Cérémonies Marquis de Dreux-Brézé and 12
Grand Maréchal des Logis Marquis de La Suze and 74
Cassette and Petits Appartements 44
Inspector du Garde-Meuble Thierry de Ville d'Avray and 28
Intendant des Menus-Plaisirs Papillon de La Ferté and 199
Grand Ecuyer Prince de Lambesc and 942
Grand Veneur Duc de Penthièvre and 108

TOTAL 1,860

This excludes the staff attached to each royal residence, for which figures have not
been found. In addition there were the lesser royal households:

Maison de la Reine 369
Service de Mgr le Dauphin 44
Service des Enfants de France 77
Maison de Monsieur 524 and seven more royal households

Sources: Almanach de Versailles, 1789 (the most complete list); but cf. AN C 184,
Dépenses de la Maison du Roi et de la Maison de la Reine au premier janvier 1789;
Henri Lemoine, 'Les Ecuries du roi sous l'ancien régime', *Revue de l'histoire de Versailles*,
October 1933, p. 216; AN R5 42, *Sommier de la maison* [de Monsieur], 1778–91.

The court of Napoleon I

	1804	1814
Senior court officials in the households of the Emperor, the Empress and the King of Rome	83	217
	Per cent	
Noblesse présentée	22.5	32
Noblesse non-présentée	33.5	23.5
Non-nobles	35.5	18.5
Foreign nobles	8.5	26

Sources: Almanach Impérial, 1805 and 1814; François Bluche, Les Honneurs de la cour, 2 vols., 1957.

Maison de S.M. l'Empereur et Roi, 1813

Grand Aumônier Cardinal Fesch and 29
Grand Maréchal du Palais Duc de Frioul and 223 (cuisines), and 474 (palaces)
Grand Chambellan Comte de Montesquiou and 317
Grand Ecuyer Duc de Vicence and 726
Grand Veneur Prince de Neufchâtel and 92
Grand Maître des Cérémonies Comte de Ségur and 17
Intendant Général Duc de Cadore and 42
Maison Militaire 39
Santé 37
Forêts de la Couronne 311
Parcs 66
Bâtiments 83
Musées 58
Manufactures 224
Eaux et Jardins 36
Mobilier 33
Trésorerie Générale 63
Secrétairerie d'Etat 70
Gouvernement des Départements au-delà des Alpes 174
Gouvernement des Départements de l'Arno, de la Méditerannée et de l'Ombrone 353
Département de Rome 117
Hollande 131

TOTAL 3,722

This figure is inflated, in comparison with the figure of the *maison du Roi* in 1789 by the inclusion of the technical (forests, museums and so on) and foreign sections of the court. However, it was thought preferable to stick to the definitions of the monarch's household used at the time.
Source: FM 106, Maison de S.M. l'Empereur et Roi, 1813.

Qualifications mentioned for court office under the Empire and the restoration

	Empire	Restoration
Current official position	47	282
Recommendations	–	224
Previous official position	–	136
Wealth	142	79
Ancestry	37	43
Emigration	–	46
Royalism in 1814 or 1815	–	36
Age	108	–
Family position	40	–
Personal reputation	29	–

Sources: AN 349 AP 1, *Liste des personnes qui sollicitent l'honneur d'être chambellans de Sa Majesté l'Empereur et Roy*, 1809–15, AN 03 369, *Demandes de places de gentils-hommes de la chambre*, 1828–30.

Presentation at court, 1783–1822

	1783–8[a]	12 February 1809– 4 June 1815	1 January 1816– 2 February 1822
Total	571	560	748+[b]
% foreign	2	34	45+[b]
Total French	558	371	421
% noblesse présentée	70	39	37
% noblesse non-présentée	30[c]	38	45
% non-noble	–	23	18

[a] These years have been chosen to provide a figure comparable to the six years from 1816 to 1822, but unaffected by the disruptions of 1789 and 1790.

[b] These figures are imprecise owing to frequent presentations of unspecified numbers of English *Mlles*.

[c] This figure is not strictly comparable to the others in the same line since genealogical *preuves* were necessary in the 1780s, but not later, and it consists of families not presented before 1783, rather than 1790.

Sources: François Bluche, *Les Honneurs de la cour*, 2 vols., 1957; AN 349 AP 1 Papiers Montesquiou, *Liste des personnes présentées à S.M. l'Empereur et Roi depuis le 12 fevrier 1809 jusqu'au* ... (4 June 1815); AN 03 199, *Registre des présentations*.

Horses at court, 1784–1820

1784	2,215
1787	1,195
April 1814	1,113
March 1815	885
1820	604

These figures are for the horses in the *écuries* of the King or the Emperor. They exclude horses in other departments of his household, such as the *vénerie*, and in other royal households. In comparison the Emperor Joseph II reduced the number of horses in his stables from 1,250 to 750 in 1766.

Sources: Henri Lemoine, 'La Fin des écuries royales', *Revue de l'histoire de Versailles*, 1933, pp. 182, 205; AN 95 AP 11/20, *Situation comparée de l'écurie au 20 mars 1815*; AN 03 529, *Rapport à son excellence sur les services de la maison du Roi*, December 1820; F. Fejtö, *Un Habsbourg Révolutionaire*, 1953, p. 95.

The Maison du Roi, 1830

Grand Aumônier Prince de Croÿ and 89
Grand Maître Duc de Bourbon and 173 (Hôtel)
                        548 (Gouvernements)
Grand Chambellan Prince de Talleyrand and 414
Chapelle-Musique 154
Garde-robe 22
Faculté 60
Premier Ecuyer Duc de Polignac and 533
Maison des Pages 149
Premier Veneur Comte de Girardin and 113
Grand Maître des Cérémonies Marquis de Dreux-Brézé and 29
Mobilier de la Couronne 137
Bibliothèques 14
Administration des Beaux-Arts 30
Musées 68
Monnaie des Médailles 34
Manufacture des Gobelins 165
Manufacture de Sèvres 123
Manufacture de Beauvais 60

TOTAL 2,921

Source: AN 03 880, *Maison du Roi, Contrôle du personnel.* This figure omits the staff of the *ministère de la maison.*

The cost of the court, 1789

	Livres
Aumônerie	84,960
Chambre	501,322
Garde-robe	248,475
Bouche	1,479,807
Faculté	134,622
Ecuries	3,514,327
Vénerie	517,000
Cérémonies	114,509
Logements	88,804
Menus-plaisirs (including music)	1,376,480
Garde-meuble	1,178,763
Bâtiments	3,305,000
Prévôte	210,210
Education et service de Mgr le Dauphin	736,855
Service des Enfants de France	606,161
Households of Madame Adélaïde and Madame Victoire	2,327,163
Household of Madame Elizabeth	489,615
Household of the Queen	4,660,296
Miscellaneous	2,739,026
TOTAL	24,313,395
Households of Monsieur, the Comte d'Artois and their families	8,240,000

Source: AN c184, *Dépenses de la maison du Roi et de la maison de la Reine au premier janvier 1789*; Marcel Marion, *Histoire financière de la France*, 1, 469.

The cost of the Maison de l'Empereur (francs)

	An XIII	1813
Aumônerie	197,000	241,000
Service du grand maréchal du palais (the equivalent of the *bouche* and the *gouvernements*)	2,248,000	3,090,000
Chambre (including the Empress's household)	1,995,000	3,474,000
Santé	219,000	332,000
Ecuries	3,101,000	3,632,000
Vénerie	370,000	445,000
Cérémonies	113,000	140,000
Cabinet	766,000	809,000
Parcs	322,000	596,000
Bâtiments	2,378,000	2,050,000
Musée	228,000	596,000
Mobilier	113,000	773,000
Menus-Plaisirs	200,000	120,000
Cassette	1,848,000	1,384,000
Intendance	141,000	397,000
Maison militaire	615,000	1,000,000
Secrétairerie d'état	294,000	417,000
Empress Josephine	–	1,000,000
King of Rome	–	261,000
Gouvernement au-delà des Alpes	–	1,400,000
Toscane		1,700,000
Rome		1,500,000
Hollande		650,908
TOTAL	15,148,000	26,007,908

Source: Comte de Montholon, *Récits de la capivité de l'Empereur Napoléon à Sainte Hélène*, 2 vols., 1847, I, 22. Some figures differ from those given in Baron d'Hérisson, *Un Secrétaire de Napoléon Premier*, 1894, pp. 233–43. It has been impossible to ascertain which are correct.

The cost of the restoration court

	1817	1827
Aumônerie	318,000	439,600
Bouche	2,324,500	1,704,100
Gouvernements	655,531	1,812,620
Chambre	506,770	1,206,800
Faculté	97,800	170,000
Garde-robe	281,300	221,400
Ecuries	1,800,000	2,359,246
Vénerie	450,000	665,000
Cérémonies	74,000	113,400
Miscellaneous	1,641,000	4,236,126
Bâtiments et jardins	4,936,978	1,773,870
Musée	501,900	583,010
Garde-meuble	1,508,700	743,000
Forêts et domaines	1,127,053	1,213,000
Menus-plaisirs (including music)*	760,000	–
Administration	686,900	790,400
Monnaie	229,420	287,350
Manufactures	749,665	675,878
Pensions and charities	5,497,000	6,735,200
Monsieur	4,420,000	2,000,000
Duchesse d'Angoulême	1,500,000	1,500,000
Duc d'Angoulême	1,000,000	1,000,000
Duc de Berri (later Bordeaux)	1,500,000	1,000,000
Duchesse de Berri	1,000,000	1,500,000
Maison militaire	–	3,000,000
TOTAL	33,598,317	35,730,000

* The *menus-plaisirs* were absorbed into the *garde-meuble* in 1824.
Source: AAE 347 ff. 63–70 Pradel to Richelieu, 13 October 1817; AN 03 2729, *Budget général de 1827*; AN 03 2678, *Dotation des princes*.

Individuals who received 100,000 francs or more from the civil list

Year	Sum	Recipient	Qualifications
1815	1,500,000	Pozzo di Borgo	Russian ambassador
1827	1,130,000	Maréchal Marmont	royalist marshal
1817–29	438,525	Abbé Louis Leduc	natural son of Louis XV
1816–28	411,000	Duc d'Aumont	*premier gentilhomme*
1817	300,000	Moreau family	posthumous royalist marshal
1820–28	300,000	Mlles de La Rochejaquelein	royalists
1819–24	240,000	Maréchal Oudinot	royalist marshal
1819–24	230,000	Comte and Comtesse de Serre	minister
1819	210,000	Comte de Jumilhac	heir to the Duc de Richelieu
1821–24	173,837	Duc de La Châtre	*premier gentilhomme*
1820	150,000	Mesnard de Chouzy	*chambellan de l'hôtel*
1817–28	148,000	Comte d'Ambrugeac	general, loyal in 1815
1819–28	140,000	M. and Mlle Lainé	minister's brother and sister
1823–24	115,000	Duc de Duras	*premier gentilhomme*
1819–24	107,000	Comte and Comtesse de Vennevelles	favourites
1828	100,000	Comte de La Ferronays	minister
1828	100,000	Comte Portalis	minister
1824	100,000	Comte de Peyronnet	minister
1819	100,000	Comte Charles de Polignac	sheep-breeder

Sources: AN 03 533–58, *Rapports au Roi* and *Ordonnances*, 1814–30; Daudet, *Louis XVIII et le duc Decazes*, p. 53n., Louis XVIII to Decazes, 7 September 1818. This is not a complete list of royal liberalities: it does not take into account the large sums of cash received by the King from the civil list, much of which, in the last years of Louis XVIII, went to Madame du Cayla. It also excludes sums received from other sources, such as the Chamber of Peers and Ministry of War and Louis XVIII's arrangements for the return of government or crown-owned properties to former owners in 1814. Many grants, for example those to Maréchal Marmont and the Duc d'Aumont, were signs of the recipient's indebtedness as well as of royal favour.

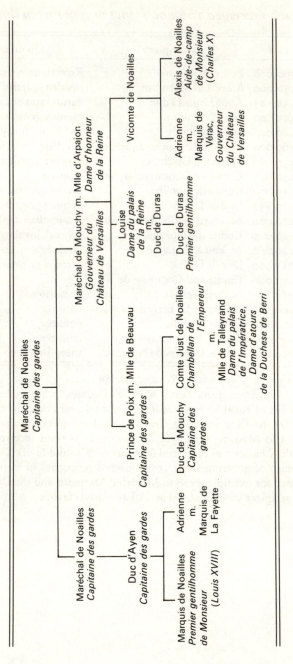

The Noailles

Maréchal de Noailles
Capitaine des gardes

├─ Maréchal de Noailles
│   *Capitaine des gardes*
│
│   └─ Duc d'Ayen
│   *Capitaine des gardes*
│
│   ├─ Adrienne m. Marquis de La Fayette
│
│   └─ Marquis de Noailles
│   *Premier gentilhomme de Monsieur (Louis XVIII)*
│
└─ Maréchal de Mouchy m. Mlle d'Arpajon
    Gouverneur du Château de Versailles / *Dame d'honneur de la Reine*

    ├─ Prince de Poix m. Mlle de Beauvau
    │   *Capitaine des gardes*
    │
    │   ├─ Duc de Mouchy
    │   │   *Capitaine des gardes*
    │   │
    │   └─ Comte Just de Noailles
    │   *Chambellan de l'Empereur*
    │   m. Mlle de Talleyrand
    │   *Dame du palais de l'Impératrice,*
    │   *Dame d'atours de la Duchesse de Berri*
    │
    ├─ Louise
    │   *Dame du palais de la Reine*
    │   m. Duc de Duras
    │
    │   └─ Duc de Duras
    │   *Premier gentilhomme*
    │
    └─ Vicomte de Noailles

        ├─ Adrienne m. Marquis de Vérac,
        │   *Gouverneur du Château de Versailles*
        │
        └─ Alexis de Noailles
            Aide-de-camp de Monsieur (Charles X)

The Montesquiou

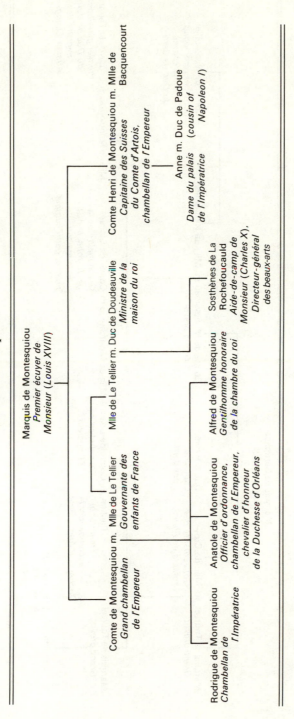

Marquis de Montesquiou
*Premier écuyer de
Monsieur (Louis XVIII)*

Comte de Montesquiou m. Mlle de Le Tellier
*Grand chambellan   Gouvernante des
de l'Empereur   enfants de France*

Mlle de Le Tellier m. Duc de Doudeauville
                      *Ministre de la
                      maison du roi*

Comte Henri de Montesquiou m. Mlle de
*Capitaine des Suisses   Bacquencourt
du Comte d'Artois,
chambellan de l'Empereur*

Rodrigue de Montesquiou
*Chambellan de
l'Impératrice*

Anatole de Montesquiou
*Officier d'ordonnance,
chambellan de l'Empereur,
chevalier d'honneur
de la Duchesse d'Orléans*

Alfred de Montesquiou
*Gentilhomme honoraire
de la chambre du roi*

Sosthènes de La
Rochefoucauld
*Aide-de-camp de
Monsieur (Charles X),
Directeur-général
des beaux-arts*

Anne m. Duc de Padoue
          *(cousin of
          Napoleon I)*
*Dame du palais
de l'Impératrice*

Tourzel and Montsoreau

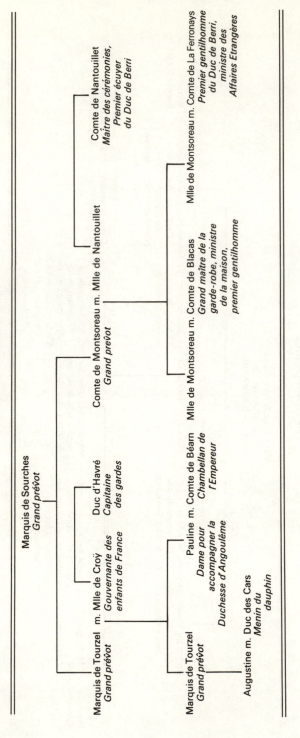

Bibliography

I. MANUSCRIPTS

A. Archives X (descendants of the Duchesse d'Escars, name withheld at request)
Letters of the Duchesse d'Escars to and from her children the Marquise de Podenas and the Comte de Nadaillac

B. Archives Historiques du Ministère de la Guerre (AHMG)
XAD 1–15, 24 Maison Militaire du Roi, 1814–30
XAE 1–11 Garde Royale, 1815–30
XEM 52 Aides-de-Camp de l'Empereur, du Roi, des Princes

C. Archives Nationales (AN)
AF IV 332, 1221, 1231, 1311, 1726, 3177 Papers of the Secrétairerie d'état

BB30 257 60–5 Papiers saisis chez le Duc de Richelieu

C 183–92, 218–23 Papers of Louis XVI and his civil list

O1 201, 262, 747, 1682, 3798 Papers of the Maison du Roi before 1789

O2 1, 5, 6, 8, 28, 41, 56, 79, 83, 87, 108, 150, 156–9, 160, 200, 217, 347, 948, 1040, 1066, 1073, 1083, 1218, 1219 Papers of the Maison de l'Empereur, 1804–15

O3, 1, 8, 9, 11, 12, 18, 19, 55–8, 65, 72–82, 85–6, 90, 116–22, 126–9, 131–8, 139, 142–50, 153–4, 157–160, 164–5, 170, 185–212, 219, 221–34, 239–44, 248–9, 260, 270, 279, 289, 290, 349–75, 386–91, 396–8, 414–17, 421–6, 450–3, 458–60, 463–6, 468–96, 501–2, 504–9, 516–60, 564–6, 569, 579, 587, 603–6, 608–610, 612, 614, 628–32, 651, 652, 663, 691, 706, 724, 801–5, 810–2, 816, 821, 842, 871, 874, 880–93, 1069, 1125, 1192, 1197, 1204, 1205, 1216, 1219, 1222, 1248, 1393, 1398, 1418, 1423, 1499, 1872, 1876–8, 1887, 1896, 1902, 1904, 1911, 1927, 1983–5, 2007–15, 2115, 2096, 2200, 2213, 2487, 2520, 2577, 2681, 2698, 2717–19, 2887–8, 2962, 2929, 2944, 2949 Papers of the Maison du Roi, 1814–30

Maisons des Princes
2678, 2681, 2912, 2942, 2999–3022

R5 26–8, 56, 144, 147, 459, 478, 523 Papers of the Maison of the Comte de Provence, 1771–91

W242, 249, 252, 255 Papers dealing with 10 August 1792

Archives Privées
36 AP Ségur papers
37 AP 1, 2 Papers of the Marquis de Bonnay
40 AP 8–17, 21, 27–9 Letters, police reports to Louis XVIII, by Beugnot
93 AP 3, 13 Papiers Saint-Salvi, écuries du Roi
95 AP 11, 12, 14, 15, 22, 25 Caulaincourt papers
101 AP C2, D2, E2 35 Letters of the Duc de Gramont, Journal du Duc de Guiche
177 AP 3 Letters of the Comte to Comtesse de Bondy, 1805–9
182 AP Duroc papers
197 AP Letters of Louis XVIII to Duc de La Chatre
198 AP 2–7 Papers of Cardinal de La Fare
291 AP Papers of the Président d'Aire
300 AP III 1, 8, 16, 20, 21, 22, 83, 123 Orléans papers
349 AP 1, 2, 19 Papers of the Comte de Montesquiou
359 AP 58, 61–3, 82, 84, 88, 99, 100 Papers of the Marquis de Clermont-Tonnerre
400 AP 4 Archives Napoléon, Registre de Correspondance du Grand Maréchal du Palais
439 AP 1, 3, 4 Papers of Fontaine
286 Mi 2 Rohan papers

D. Archives du Ministère des Affaires Etrangères (AAE)
Fonds Bourbon 630 Papers of the royal government in exile
Mémoires et Documents France 347, Pradel to Richelieu 1817

E. Archives of Scholoss Brunnsee, Austria (ABR)
Letters to the Duchesse de Berri
Diaries of the Duchesse de Berri, 1820–30

F. Archivio di Stato Torino
Mazzo 240–2, 246–8, vols. 38–9, Lettere Ministri Francia, 1814, 1820–1, 1827–1830 (AST LMF)

G. Bibliothèque Administrative de la Ville de Paris, Manuscrits 387
Duc de Lévis, *Souvenirs de cour* (BAVP Lévis)

H. Bibliothèque de l'Ecole des Beaux-Arts
Pierre Fontaine, *Notes relatives aux fonctions que j'ai remplies dupuis le 3 novembre 1799*

I. Bibliothèque Nationale (BN)
Mss Français 32773, J. F. d'Hozier, *Liste des gentilshommes de la chambre*
Nouvelles Acquisitions Françaises (NAF)
4760 Registre de Correspondance de Madame du Cayla
6549–6550 Archives de la Famille de Narbonne-Lara

11771–2, 25123 Journal de Madame de Chastenay, 1815, 1825
11399 Registre de Correspondance du Comte de Ségur
14071–2 Papers of Mathieu de Montmorency
14098–9 Letters to Madame Récamier
14356 Letters of the Comtesse de Montesquiou to the Emperor
24062 Procès-verbaux des séances du conseil du roi

J. Bibliothèque de l'Institut
Mss 3295 Fonds Cuvier, *Mémoire secret sur la politique intérieure de l'état*, January
1820

K. Bibliothèque Thiers, Place Saint-Georges, Fonds Frédéric Masson (FM)
100–07 Household of the Emperor
116 *Registre de correspondance du grand maître des cérémonies*

L. Bibliothèque Victor Cousin, Fonds Richelieu (BVC FR)
70–112 Correspondence to and from the Duc de Richelieu

M. Haus- Hof- und Staatsarchiv Vienna, Nachlass Montenuovo (HHSA)
Letters of the Duchesse de Montebello, Comtesse de Brignole and Marquis de Bausset
to Marie-Louise

N. Musée International de la Chasse, Gien. *Livret des Chasses du Roi* 1829

O. National Library of Scotland, Edinburgh, Mss 6202, Stuart de Rothesay Papers,
despatches from Paris, 1820

P. Papiers de la Famille de Thierry de Ville d'Avray (TVA)

Q. Letters of Monsieur to the Duc de Lévis, consulted by kind permission of M. Alain
de Grolée-Virville

R. McClintock Papers Letter of John Leslie Foster to Harriet Countess de Salis, 6
April 1802

S. Archives du Comte de Saint-Priest d'Urgel, Avignon, Mémoires du Comte d'Agoult

T. Archives du Comte Charles de Nicolay Letters of the Duc to the Duchesse de Lévis

II. PUBLISHED WORKS

Unless otherwise stated, works in English are published in London and works in French
in Paris.
Almanach de Versailles. 1789.
Almanach impérial. 1805–14.
Almanach royal. 1815–30.
Angoulême, Duchesse d'. 'Souvenirs de 1815'. *Le Correspondant.* CCXXX, 25 August
    1913. pp. 650–83.
Anne, Théodore. *Mémoires, souvenirs et anecdotes sur l'intérieur du palais de Charles*
    X. 2 vols., 1831.
Antioche, Comte d'. 'Le Dernier Hiver d'un Règne'. *Revue d'histoire diplomatique.*
    1903.
Apponyi, Comte Rodolphe. *Journal.* 3 vols., 1913–14.

Archives parlementaires, 1st series, rep. Liechtenstein, 1969. 2nd series 1862–82.

Aspinall, A. *The Letters of George IV.* 3 vols., Cambridge, 1938.

Aubier, Baron d'. *Observations sur les mémoires de Madame Campan.* 1823.

Balzac, Honoré de. *Le Cabinet des antiques.* 2 vols., 1839
    César Birotteau. Gallimard, 1966.
    La Duchesse de Langeais Gallimard, 1958.
    Le Lys dans la vallée. Gallimard, 1965.
    La Rabouilleuse. Société d'Éditions Littéraires et Artistiques. 1901.
    Splendeurs et misères des Courtisanes. Garnier-Flammarion. 1968.

Barante, Baron de. *Souvenirs.* 8 vols., 1890–1907.

Bardoux, A. *La Duchesse de Duras.* 1898.

Barrière, F. *Tableaux de genre et d'histoire.* 1828.

Basily-Callimaki, Madame. *Jean-Baptiste Isabey.* 1883.

Bastid, Paul. *Un Juriste pamphlétaire. Cormenin, précurseur et constituant de 1848.* 1948.

Bausset, L. F. J. de. *Mémoires anecdotiques sur l'intérieur du palais.* 2 vols., Brussels, 1827.

Beauchesne, M. A. de. *Louis XVII.* 2 vols., 1853.
    Madame Elizabeth. 2 vols., 1869.

Bernardy, Françoise de. *Son of Talleyrand.* 1956.

Berry, Mary. *Extracts from the Journals and Correspondence*, 3 vols., 1865.

Bertier de Sauvigny, G. de. *Le Comte Ferdinand de Bertier et l'enigme de la congrégation.* 1948.
    La Restauration. 1955.
    Metternich. 1986
    Nouvelle histoire de paris. La Restauration. 1980.

Bertrand, General *Cahiers de Sainte-Hélène.* 3 vols., 1949–59.

Bézard, Yvonne. 'Les Porte-Arquebuse du Roi'. *Revue de l'histoire de Versailles.* April 1924.

Biver, Marie-Louise. *Pierre Fontaine.* 1964.

Blake, Mrs Warenne. *An Irish Beauty of the Regency.* 1911.

Bled, Jean-Paul. *François-Joseph.* 1987.

Bluche, François, *Les Honneurs de la cour*, 2 vols., 1957.

Boigne, Madame de. *Mémoires.* 2 vols., 1986.

Bombelles, Marquis de. *Journal.* Geneva, 1977– .

Bonnechose, Emile de. *Christophe Sauval ou la société sous la restauration.* 2 vols., 1845.

Bonnechose, Louis-Charles de. *Dernière Légende de la Vendée. Louis de Bonnechose, page de Charles X.* 1860.

Boykin, Edward. *Victoria, Albert and Mrs Stevenson.* 1957.

Burney, Fanny. *Diary and Letters.* 2nd edn. 7 vols., 1854.

Butler, Rohan. *Choiseul.* Oxford, 1980.

Caillot, A. *Mémoires pour servir à l'histoire des moeurs et usages des français.* 2 vols., 1827.

Campan, Madame, *Correspondance avec la Reine Hortense.* 2 vols., 1835.

Castellane, Maréchal de. *Journal.* 5 vols., 1895–6.

Castelot, André. *Le Secret de Madame Royale.* 1949.

Caulaincourt, Comte de. *Mémoires*. 3 vols., 1933.

Chapus, E. *Les Chasses de Charles X. Souvenirs de l'ancienne cour*. 1837.

Chastenay, Madame de. *Mémoires*. 2 vols., 1896–7.

Chateaubriand, *Correspondance générale*. 5 vols., 1912–24.

  Mémoires d'outre-tombe, 3 vols., Librairie Générale Française 1973.

  Réflexions politiques. 1814.

Chaussinand-Nogaret, Guy. *La Noblesse française au XVIIIe siècle*. 1975.

Church, Clive H. *Revolution and Red Tape*. 1982.

Clary et Aldringen. Prince. *Trois mois à Paris*. 1914.

Cochelet, Mlle. *Mémoires sur la Reine Hortense*. 1907.

Coigny, Aimée de. *Journal*. 1981.

Colvin, Christine. *Maria Edgeworth in France and Switzerland*. Oxford, 1979.

Constant. *Mémoires*, 1967 edn.

Corbière, Comte de. 'Souvenirs d'un ministre de Louis XVIII'. *Revue des deux mondes*.
    April 1966. pp. 364–80.

Cormenin, M. de. *Libelles politiques*. 4 vols., Brussels, 1836–7.

Coural, Jean. *Mobilier national. Soieries empire*. 1980.

Courier, Paul-Louis. *Oeuvres complètes*. 2 vols., 1828.

  Simple Discours. 1821.

Croÿ, Duc de. *Journal inédit*. 4 vols., 1906–7.

Cuvillier-Fleury, A. *Journal*. 2 vols., 1900–3.

Damas, Baron de. *Mémoires*. 2 vols., 1923.

Damas, Roger de. *Memoirs*. 1907.

Dard, Emile. *Le Comte de Narbonne*. 1943.

Daudet, Ernest. *Louis XVIII et le Duc Decazes*. 1899.

  Madame Royale. 1912.

  Un Drame d'amour à la cour de Suède. 1913.

Du Montet, Baronne. *Souvenirs*. 1914.

Dupanloup, Abbé. *Vie de Monseigneur Borderies*. 1905.

Duras, Duchesse de. *Ourika*. 1824.

  Edouard. 1826.

Elizabeth, Madame. *Correspondance*. 1868.

Ferrand, Comte. *Mémoires*. 1896.

Ferrières, Marquis de. *Correspondance inédite*. 1932.

Fontaine, P. L. F. *Journal*. 2 vols., 1987.

Gachot, Edouard. *Marie-Louise intime*. 2 vols. 1911.

Ganière, Paul. *Corvisart médecin de Napoléon*, 2nd edn., 1965.

Gautier, Alphonse. *Etudes sur la Liste Civile en France*. 1883.

Genty, M. *Discours sur le Luxe*. 1783.

Geffroy, A. *Gustave III et la cour de France*, 2nd edn. 2 vols., 1867.

Girardin, Stanislas de. *Journal et Souvenirs, Discours et Opinions*. 4 vols., 1828.

Girault de Coursac, P. *L'Education d'un Roi*. 1972.

  Découverte, Bulletin Trimestriel du Comité pour l'Etude de Louis XVI et de son
      Procès. 1973–86. I–LII.

  Enquête sur le procès du Roi Louis XVI. 1982.

Godechot, Jacques. *Le Comte d'Antraigues*. 1986.

Gourgaud, Baron. *Journal*, 2 vols., 1896–7.

Gronow, Captain. *Reminiscences and Recollections.* 3 vols., 1900.

Guibert, Comte de. *Oeuvres militaires.* 5 vols., 1803.

Guizot, François. *Du Gouvernement de la France depuis la restauration et du ministère actuel.* 1820.

Hanoteau, Jean. *Le Ménage Beauharnais.* 1935.

Hapdé, J. B. A. *Relation historique, heure par heure, des evènements funèbres ... du 13 fevrier 1820,* 4th edn. 1820.

Haussez, Baron d'. *Mémoires.* 2 vols., 1896.

Haussonville, Comte d'. *Femmes d'autrefois, hommes d'aujourd'hui.* 1912.

Hérisson, Comte d'. *Un Secrétaire de Napoléon Premier.* 1894.

Higgs, David. *Nobles in Nineteenth-Century France.* Baltimore, 1987.

Hobhouse J. C. *The Substance of Some Letters ... during the Last Reign of the Emperor Napoleon,* 2nd edn. 1817.

Hortense, Queen. *Mémoires.* 3 vols., 1927.

Hue, Baron. *Souvenirs.* 1903.

Huisman, Philippe and Jallut, Marguerite. *Marie-Antoinette.* 1971.

Jal, A. *Le Peuple au sacre.* 1829.

James, Surgeon. *Journal.* 1964.

Jaucourt, Comte de. *Correspondance ... avec le Prince de Talleyrand pendant le Congrès de Vienne.* 1905.

Journal des débats. 1810, 1814–15.

Kaunitz, Prince de. 'Mémoire sur la Cour de France', *Revue de Paris,* August 1904, pp. 827–48.

Kerry, Earl of. *The First Napoleon.* 1925.

Laage, Madame de. *Souvenirs.* Evreux, 1869.

La Boulaye, Vicomte de. *Mémoires.* 1975.

Lachouque, Henry. *The Last Days of Napoleon's Empire.* 1966.

Lacour-Gayet, G. *Talleyrand.* 4 vols., 1928–34.

La Fayette, Marquis de. *Mémoires, correspondance et manuscrits.* 6 vols., 1837–8.

La Ferronays, Comte A. de. *Souvenirs.* 1900.

Lamarque, Général. *Mémoires et souvenirs.* 3 vols., 1835–6.

Lamartine, Alphonse de. *Histoire de la Restauration.* 8 vols., 1851–2.

Lambruschini, Cardinal. *La Mia Nunziatura di Francia.* Bologna, 1934.

Lanfranchi, Louis. *Voyage à Paris.* 1830.

Langeron, Roger. *Decazes ministre du Roi.* 1960.

La Rochefoucauld, François de. *Souvenirs du 10 aout 1792 et de l'armée de Bourbon.* 1929.

La Rochefoucauld, G. de. *Vie du Duc de Liancourt.* 1827.

La Rochefoucauld, S. de. *Mémoires.* 15 vols., 1861–4.

   Pélérinage à Goritz. 1839.

Las Cases, Comte de. *Mémorial de Sainte-Hélène.* 2 vols., 1961.

Las Cases, Comte Emmanuel de. *Las Cases mémorialiste de Sainte-Hélène.* 1959.

La Tour, Jean de. *Duroc grand maréchal du palais.* 1908.

Ledré, Charles. *La Presse à l'assaut de la monarchie.* 1960.

Lefebvre, Georges (ed.) *Recueil de documents relatifs aux séances des Etats Généraux.* 4 vols., 1953–70.

Lemaistre, J. G. *A Rough Sketch of Modern Paris,* 2nd edn. 1803.

   Travels ... through parts of France, Switzerland and Germany. 3 vols., 1806.

Lemoine, Henri. 'Les Ecuries du Roi sous l'ancien regime', *Revue de l'Histoire de Versailles,* October 1933, pp. 152–83.

'La Fin des écuries royales', *Revue de l'histoire de Versailles,* December 1933, pp. 201–28.

Lenôtre, G. *Martin le Visionnaire.* 1924.

The Tuileries. 1934.

Lescure, M. A. de. *Correspondance secrète inédite sur Louis XVI, Marie-Antoinette, la cour et la ville.* 2 vols., 1866.

Lévis, Duc de. *Pensées et maximes.* 1825.

Résponse . . . à M. Roger successeur de M. Suard. 1817.

Souvenirs et portraits. 1882.

Lévis-Mirepoix, Duc de. *Aventures d'une famille française.* 1949.

Lhôte de Selancey, A. *Des Charges de la maison civile des rois de France.* 1847.

Limouzin-Lamothe, R. *Monseigneur de Quelen, archevêque de Paris.* 2 vols., 1955–7.

Louis XVI. *Journal.* 1873.

Réflexions sur Mes Entretiens avec M. le Duc de La Vauguyon. 1851.

Louis XVIII. *Correspondance privée.* 1836.

'Les Devoirs d'un Roi'. *Feuilles d'histoire,* 1 September 1909, pp. 221–34.

Louis-Philippe. *Mémoires.* 2 vols., 1973–4.

Louis-Philippe, l'homme et le Roi. Archives Nationales, exhibition catalogue 1974–5.

Lucas-Dubreton, J. *Louvel le régicide,* 2nd edn. 1923.

Maillé, Duchesse de. *Souvenirs.* 1984.

Maine de Biran, M. F. P. G. *Journal.* 3 vols., Neuchâtel, 1954–7.

Maistre, Comte Joseph de. *Lettres et opuscules inédites.* 2 vols., 1851.

Mallat, A. *Histoire contemporaine de Vichy.* Vichy, 1921.

Manno, Antonio (ed.) *Lettere inedite di Carlo-Alberto Principe di Carignano, al suo Scudiere Carlo di Robilant.* Turin, 1883.

Mansel, Philip. 'The Court of France 1814–1830'. Unpublished Ph.D thesis. London, 1978.

Louis XVIII. 1981.

'Monarchy, Uniform and the Rise of the Frac'. *Past and Present.* XCVI. August 1982.

Pillars of Monarchy: Royal Guards in History. 1984.

The Eagle in Splendour: Napoleon I and his Court. 1987.

Marc, Edmond. *Mes Journées de Juillet.* 1930.

Marchand, L. N. *Mémoires.* 2 vols., 1952.

Marie-Amélie, *Journal.* 1981.

Marie-Louise, 'Carnets de voyage', *Revue de Paris,* 1, 15 February, 1 March, 1 April 1921, pp. 497–539, 701–41, 28–46, 470–506.

Marion, Marcel. *Histoire financière de la France.* 6 vols., 1927–31.

Masson, Frédéric. *Jadis et aujourd'hui.* 1908.

Napoléon chez lui, 1893.

Napoléon et sa famille. 15 vols., 1908–19.

Revue d'ombres. 1907.

Mauduit, Hippolyte. *Souvenirs d'une garde à Saint-Cloud en 1829.* 1835.

Mazères, E. *Comédies et souvenirs.* 3 vols., 1858.

Maze-Sencier, A. *Les Fournisseurs de Napoléon Premier.* 1893.

Méneval, Baron de. *Mémoires pour servir à l'histoire de Napoléon Premier.* 3 vols., 1894.

Mennechet, E. *Lettres sur la restauration.* 2 vols., 1832.

Mercier, L. S. *Tableau de Paris (nouvelle édition corrigée et augmentée).* 8 vols., Amsterdam, 1782.

Molé, Comte L. M. *Le Comte Molé . . . sa vie, ses mémoires.* 6 vols., 1922–30.

Moniteur, 1789–1830.

Montcalm, Marquise de. *Mon Journal pendant le premier ministère de mon frère.* 1934.

Montépin, Xavier de. *Souvenirs intimes et anecdotiques d'un garde du corps des Rois Louis XVIII et Charles X.* 5 vols., 1857.

Montesquiou, Comtesse de. 'Souvenirs'. *Revue de Paris.* May 1948, pp. 51–80.

Montholon, Comte de. *Récits de la captivité de l'Empereur Napoléon à Sainte-Hélène.* 2 vols., 1847.

Moreau, J. N. *Mes Souvenirs.* 2 vols., 1901.

Morris, Gouverneur. *A Diary of the French Revolution.* 2 vols., 1939.

Mortemart, Duc de. 'Trois journées'. *Le Correspondant.* CCXXI, 10 December 1930, pp. 801–24.

Mouchy, Duchesse de. *Vie de la Vicomtesse de Noailles.* 1852.

Mousset, Albert. *Un Témoin ignoré de la révolution française.* 1921.

Napoléon I. *Correspondance générale.* 32 vols., 1858–70.

Naylies, Vicomte de. *Mémoires du Duc de Rivière.* 1829.

Nettement, Alfred. *Henri de France.* 2 vols., 1846.
  Mémoires de la Duchesse de Berri. 3 vols., 1836–7.

Neuilly, Comte de. *Souvenirs.* 1865.

Oudinot, Maréchale. *Récits de guerre et de foyer.* 1894.

Pailhes, Abbé. *La Duchesse de Duras et Chateaubriand.* 1910.

Palmstierna, C. F. (ed.) *Marie-Louise et Napoléon. Lettres inédites.* 1955.

Paroy, Comte de. *Mémoires.* 1895.

Pasquier, E. D. *Histoire de mon temps.* 6 vols., 1893–5.

Pellissier, Léon (ed.) *Le Portefeuille de la Comtesse d'Albany.* 1902.

Percier, Charles and Fontaine, P. L. F. *Description des cérémonies et fêtes pour le mariage de S. M. l'Empereur Napléon.* 1810.

Polovtsov, A. (ed.) *Correspondance diplomatique des ambassadeurs et ministres de Russie en France et de France en Russie avec leurs gouvernements de 1814 à 1830.* 3 vols., St Petersburg 1904–7.

Poniatowski, Michel. *Talleyrand et le Consulat.* 1986.

Portalis, Baron. *Le Peintre Danloux.* 1909.

Potocka Countess. *Memoirs.* New York, 1900.

Pradt, Abbé de. *Petit Catéchisme constitutionnel à l'usage des français.* 1820.

Procédure criminelle instruite au Châtelet de Paris. 3 vols., 1790.

Proyart, Abbé. *Oeuvres complètes.* 17 vols., 1819.

Raffles, Thomas. *Letters during a Tour through some Parts of France . . . in the Summer of 1817.* Liverpool, 1818.

Rambuteau, Comte de. *Mémoires.* 1905.

Rampelberg, René-Marie. *Le Ministre de la maison du Roi Baron de Breteuil.* 1976.

Reiset, Vicomte de. *La Duchesse de Berri.* 1905.

Remacle, Comte. *Relations secrètes des agents de Louis XVIII à Paris sous le Consulat.* 1899.

Rémusat, Charles de. *Mémoires.* 5 vols., 1958–67.

Rémusat, Comtesse de. *Lettres.* 2 vols., 1881.
  Mémoires. 3 vols., 1880.

Révérend, Vicomte. *Armorial du premier empire.* 4 vols., 1894–7.
  Titres, anoblissements et pairies de la restauration. 6 vols., 1901–6.

Riancey, H. L. de. *Le Comte de Coutard.* 1857.

Richelieu, Duc de. *Lettres . . . au Marquis d'Osmond.* 1939.

Robin-Harmel, J. *Le Prince de Polignac.* 2 vols., Paris and Avignon. 1941–50.

Roots, William. *Paris in 1814.* Newcastle, 1909.

Rutland, Duke and Duchess of. *Journal of a Trip to Paris.* 1814.

Saint-Chamans, Comte de. *Mémoires.* 1896.

Saint-Denis, Louis-Etienne. *Souvenirs du Mameloucke Ali.* 1926.

Sainte-Aulaire, Comte de. *Souvenirs.* 1927.

Saint-Priest, Comte de. *Souvenirs.* 2 vols., 1929.

Salamon, Abbé de. *Correspondance secrète avec le Cardinal de Zelada.* 1898.

Savant Jean. *Les Fonds Secrets de Napléon,* 1952.

Ségur, Comte de. *Etiquette du palais impérial.* An XIII, 1808.

Senfft, Comte de. *Mémoires.* Leipzig, 1863.

Senkowska-Gluck, Monika. 'Les Donataires de Napoléon Premier', *Revue d'histoire moderne et contemporaine,* 1969, pp. 681–93.

Serre, Comte de. *Correspondance.* 6 vols., 1876–7.

Sismondi, Sismonde de. 'Lettres écrites pendant les Cent-Jours', *Revue historique,* IV, May 1877.

Soderhjelm, Alma (ed.) *Marie-Antoinette et Barnave. Correspondance Secrète.* 1934.

Solnon, Jean-François. *La Cour de France.* 1987.

Stael, Madame de. *Considérations sur la révolution française.* 3 vols., London, 1818.
  Lettres, 1962– .

Stendhal, *Armance.* 3 vols., 1827.
  Oeuvres Intimes., 1966.
  Napoléon. 2 vols., 1929.

Stevenson, Seth William. *Journal of a Tour Through Part of France . . . Made in the Summer of 1816.* Norwich, 1817.

Suddaby, Elizabeth and Yarrow (eds.), P. J. *Lady Morgan in France.* Newcastle, 1971.

Talleyrand, Prince de. *Talleyrand intime.* 1891.

Thiard de Bissy, Comte de. *Souvenirs.* 1900.

Thiébault, Baron. *Mémoires.* 5 vols., 1893–5.

Thiry, Baron Jean. *La Première Abdication.* 1939.

Thompson, J. M. *English Witnesses of the French Revolution.* Oxford, 1938.

Tilly, Comte Alexandre de. *Mémoires.* 1965.

Titeux, Eugène. *Le Général Dupont.* 3 vols., Puteaux-sur-Seine, 1903.

Tulard, Jean, 'La Cour de Napoléon I' in Karl Werner (ed.), *Hof, Kultur und Politik im 19. Jahruhundert.* Bonn, 1985, pp. 55–60.
  Napoléon, 1977.
  Napoléon à Sainte-Hélène. 1981.
  Napoléon et la noblesse d'empire. 1979.

Vaissière, P. de. *Lettres d'aristocrates.* 1923.
Verlet, Pierre. *French Royal Furniture.* 1963.
Victoria, Queen. *Letters.* 3 vols., 1907–8.
Viennet, J. P. *Journal.* 1955.
Villèle, Comte de. *Mémoires et correspondance.* 5 vols. 1888–96.
Waquet, Françoise. *Les Fêtes royales sous la restauration.* 1980.
Wilmot, Catherine. *An Irish Peer on the Continent.* 1924.
Young, Arthur. *Travels in France during the years 1787, 1788 and 1789.* 1929.
Yriarte, Charles. *Les Cercles de Paris.* 1875.
Zieseniss, Charles Otto. *Napoléon et la Cour Impériale.* 1980.
Zieseniss, Jérôme. *Berthier frère d'armes de Napoléon.* 1986.

Index